One Fine Summer

By

Kevin Zahn

Note: This is a work of fiction. All the characters are imaginary. Any resemblance to actual persons is coincidental.

Other books by Kevin Zahn:
The Bucko Mate: Twenty Years in the Merchant Marine

Published by Createspace Independent Publishing Platform

Cover design: ebooklaunch.com

Dedication

To all the coaches and volunteers who
provide opportunities for city
kids to play sports.

Table of Contents

Foreword

"Well -- it's our game; that's the
chief fact in connection with it:
America's game . . ." -- Walt Whitman

Many years ago, some guys got together and formed a Boys Club in an inner-city neighborhood in Baltimore to provide an opportunity for the local kids to play baseball. Their club was not part of any national association and their teams did not play in the official Little League. It was an effort that stood alone in an area of the city that needed it badly.

The kids in City Heights play gritty baseball while their parents tough things out in the adult world. Although this is a work of fiction, it is based on my experience living in such a neighborhood and coaching kids from eight to twelve years old, in the early 1980's.

Baseball defines the summers in that neighborhood. There is the pro team, the Orioles, but more importantly to the residents there are the kids' teams. In between crab fests and barbeques the locals want to know how their kids did as well as the "O's."

"We made too many wrong mistakes." -- Yogi Berra

Chapter 1: Tommy

It had happened in his last year of playing baseball when he was thirteen. He was in center field, shading towards left because they had a big, right-handed kid up at the plate, and he often hit the crap out of the ball that way. He had checked the distance behind him to the six-foot chain-link fence that formed the boundary of the park. He knew he could get to it if necessary, and on the second pitch it immediately became necessary. Fatty hit one a mile high and it drifted towards the fence. Tommy drifted back there before the left fielder did and called for it. It wasn't a line shot -- it was a giant fly ball, and Tommy was sure he could catch it. The high trajectory had given him the chance to time his jump.

His heroes could do it -- Mays for sure, or Snider or DiMaggio -- they would get it no problem. Tommy jumped and put out his right hand to brace himself against the fence. It was a perfect jump, and he went up as high as he could, with the old, beaten glove up and over the top rail of the fence. His glove and body hit the fence at the same time, and he crashed back to the ground and rolled over. He heard the crowd yelling and knew it was for him! By God, today he would be the hero of the team! He opened the glove, but . . . it was empty -- no ball, no miraculous catch up against the fence, and no heroism. He looked back and saw the ball on the other side of the fence, not six feet beyond it, in the sand and weeds that made up Florida soil. It just sat there, mocking him. Every time the memory came back the damn ball was still there, always mocking him, while Fatty, Fatty 4x4 jumped around his team's dugout and was congratulated. At the end of the inning, a couple of kids said, "Nice try," or "I thought you had it." The left fielder said that the ball was just too high. "Maybe I'm just too short," Tommy had answered.

* * * * *

"Hey mate, you gettin' off this trip?"

"Yeah, bosun, my time's up. The union has a four-month limit on assignments now, ya know. Shipping in the merchant marine is tough for all of us. Gotta get off this tub and give somebody else a chance." The bosun's question quickly erased Tommy's baseball memory.

Two large tugboats nudged the 800-foot ship towards a pier in Newark, New Jersey. The mate turned aft and saw the deckhand with the heaving line ready to throw it on the dock.

"Anytime you can make it, José. Spring line first, bos'."

"Spring line, then head line, right?"

"Yeah, same way as always." They had been sailing together on the huge container ship back and forth to Australia for almost five months. The deck hands up on the bow knew what was required. A nod of the head or a hand motion and they sprang to work, hauling the mooring lines and heaving on the windlass until the 30,000 ton ship was snug alongside the dock.

"Whaddya goin' to do with all that time off work, mate?" bosun asked, as he took the lever that ran the winch.

"Baseball."

The second mate, a Baltimore guy, put the radio to his ear to hear commands from the bridge. He pointed to the spring line, now leading aft from the bow with a long lead to the bitts on the pier. The big ship had come ahead "dead slow" on the engines, and with his guys holding the line fast on the winch, the stern had swung perfectly to the dock. The ship was in position, held there by the two tugs. Soon, a headline, which led forward from the bow, was on the dock. The bosun ran the winch while two able-bodied seamen led the line to the other capstan. When both lines were tight the mate just pointed to each, in turn, and made a signal with his forearms crossed in front of him. It meant to make them fast. Three more lines went out in similar fashion and about ten minutes later the bridge gave the "Finished With Engines" order that the docking was finished. The mate's command to the forward deck gang was simple.

"Gangway."

They moved aft, down the steel ladder, along the port side of the ship to the gangway. When that was rigged, the mate went down below to the mess room to get coffee. He met the chief mate.

"Second, you ready to go?" the chief mate inquired.

"Yeah, mate, but technically I owe the company another three hours' work to get my eight in for today."

"Screw that. Today's payoff day for you. You're a good mate. See the captain for your payoff and get ashore. Goin' home to Baltimore, right?"

"Yeah. Up to the union hall here to reregister for work and then down there."

"You have some vacation time coming. What are you going to do with it all?"

"Coach baseball, drink beer all summer, and see if I can put a life together."

"Oh yeah, that's right. You're divorced. Your kid plays, right?"

"Yeah, he plays with a neighborhood team. I was an assistant coach the last two seasons, and I liked it. I wasn't there the whole time, you know how that goes, but this year I will be home the entire season. I've got a few buddies who work with the kids too, so, even though I don't have a wife or a girlfriend I have something to do."

"Well, that's good, you know. Stay in touch with your boy through baseball. I've missed so much myself, bein' at sea. Shit, you're gone months at a time -- you can miss an entire season." He stuck out his hand. "You take care and come back here anytime. I'd be happy to sail with you again. Get topside and see the Old Man."

The "second" shook his hand, nodded, and left the mess room. He went up the ladder two decks up to the captain's office. The cap'n was a good guy, but he didn't socialize much. The good part was that he already had the articles to sign him off laid out on his desk and the check written. In five minutes, it was over. He had his last check and discharge papers showing his length of service. He went down to his room.

His room was nine by twelve feet with all the bulkheads made of steel. There was a bunk, a desk, and a shower. He threw off the khakis and stuffed them into his sea bag. After a quick shower and shave he took stock in the mirror. He was 34 years old, still young for the merchant marine. He had graduated from the maritime academy in 1972, already thirteen years ago, and he felt older. His skin was leathery before its time, and he drank too much. He was still muscular for his age, and felt he could still handle any of the crew if it came to that. His moustache was a little bushy and somewhat ragged, but what the hell, so was he. He had once met a woman who said he looked better like that -- the hair a little long, moustache untrimmed, "You know," she had said, "a little rough looking." When he had played baseball as a kid he had been skinny. Four years of military college and thirteen years of shipping out had added pounds and muscle. He thought that if he had been 170 pounds in high school instead of 120 he might have gone further in baseball. His height of 5' 10" wasn't going to change.

His situation wasn't good. He was divorced, had money worries, and lived in Baltimore in a dingy, furnished apartment. The ex had gotten the house, and his 10-year-old son lived there with her. When he was home from the sea the kid spent all the weekends with him. During his baseball season, he would pick him up for practices and games. *Yeah, screw it -- go home, and re-establish relations with the boy and coach baseball all summer. Throw in some crab fest cookouts, Oriole games, and maybe a new romance or two, and it would be a good summer,* he told himself. Then he dressed, threw his sea bag over his shoulder, said goodbye to a few of the officers and crew he liked, and went down the gangway.

He walked across the pier, so careful to avoid the trailer trucks that sped everywhere. By tomorrow, the ship would be gone again and he would be back in Baltimore. He went through the gate and out into the employee parking lot. The Chevy van was still there. It was a good feeling that no one had stolen it. He felt lucky that Farrell Lines allowed the sailors to leave cars on the dock.

He opened the sliding side door, threw in his gear, and climbed up into the driver's seat. It was 84 days between trips, and his next adventure was to see if it would run. It was May, and the long winter in New Jersey could take its toll on a battery. The van was filthy with months of dirt, salt, and other crud. He turned the key and hoped. After a couple of tries, the V-8 sprang to life, and he was off to Journal Square, New Jersey, to the union hall.

He avoided as many potholes as possible on the old roads and turned right in the middle of the Square. He whipped into a parking lot right behind the union hall. He took the ticket, parked, and then hauled all his stuff out. He didn't trust the lot even for just an hour or so. He didn't pack a gun, but had a work knife with a six-inch blade in a side pocket in his coat. He went around the corner, watching the street scum all the time, into the building, then the elevator, up to the 10th floor, and into the hall.

It was almost time for job call, that magical moment when somebody might ship out. His ship was on the board, and they would hire his replacement in a few minutes. It was a good assignment, and many guys had their union cards out to bid on it. In the back, the usual gang of rabble-rousers was shouting and screaming about the pension plan. A couple of retired guys snoozed in chairs in the corner.

He sauntered past the other mates and brushed off their questions about the ship and the captain. He filed his papers in the back office, and then sat down to wait for his vacation check. He mentally calculated the amount, and figured he could barely afford to stay unemployed all summer.

In less than an hour, he was back in his van and driving through city traffic, and onto the New Jersey Turnpike heading south. He liked the van. He had the back modified for camping. The fold-down bed, icebox, sink, and table made trips to the mountains in Virginia fun for him and his boy. The sad part was that it was the only decent thing he owned. The divorce lawyers had hit hard for no good reason except that they could. It always felt good to be off the ship and going home, even if you wanted to stay on to make more money and home was a furnished apartment. He dreaded any more confrontations with his ex-wife, but looked forward to the baseball season. Maybe this time he would meet a terrific woman. After months at sea, he felt he could sure use one.

In less than four hours, he was speeding around the Baltimore Beltway on the west side of the city. He took the Catonsville exit, and headed east towards Baltimore on Frederick Avenue. Just inside the city limits there was a neighborhood known as Paradise, and he took a couple of quick turns and stopped in the driveway of an old house. The owners, an elderly couple, lived downstairs and rented out a couple of small, one-bedroom apartments upstairs. The one on the south side was home for the mate.

The good things about the old couple were that they faithfully collected his mail while he was gone, didn't charge much for rent, and were quiet. The down side was that they were somewhat snoopy, and didn't like him having company over. They kept their lawn looking beautiful. It sloped down the hill behind the house and had lots of trees. Last winter they had complained that the mate and his ten-year-old son were ruining the beauty of the back yard by sledding down the little hill. They were quirky that way, but he put up with it because the place was cheap. It even had a fridge and furniture, and although everything looked like it had come from the Civil War it saved him the bother and expense of having to buy those items.

It was also safe there, as the old couple never went anywhere. True to form, they had piled his mail up neatly inside his door, and nothing had been touched. The mate smiled inwardly at the thought that no one had ripped him off. There was nothing much to take except for an old thirteen-inch TV, a beat-up VCR, and a stereo he had owned for fifteen years. There was an answering machine, and the tape was full. He decided to have a cold beer and check the messages and then call his boy and see about picking him up the next day.

He opened the old fridge, the kind with the horizontal handle that pulled out away from the door, and wondered how old it was. To his delight, there were two bottles of Becks in there. He had no idea if beer left in a fridge for five months was still good, but he didn't care. He didn't always buy Becks, but he had been to Germany several times and thought it was one of the best beers in the world. He found the opener and popped off the cap. All at once he felt hungry, and realized he hadn't eaten since breakfast. With the excitement of getting off the ship and going home he hadn't thought about it. Now it was after 5:00 p.m., and food was a necessity. He took stock and discovered that he had a head of lettuce in the crisper drawer, now turned to a sickly, brown, smelly mess, some catsup, mustard and salad dressing, a box of spaghetti noodles but no sauce, and ice cubes. *Not much of a meal here,* he thought. He would have to go out for food and beer that night. He needed some rest, but knew that if he took a nap two things would happen -- he would feel like an old man, and he would sleep too long and go nowhere that night. He sat down in the small living room, on the over-stuffed chair the old folks had provided, and hit the "play message" button on the answering machine.

There were 23 messages on it, and then the tape ran out. Of these, one was from the ex, one from his good friend, Brian, one from a woman he had met named Maria, five were hang-ups with no message, twelve were from bill collectors, and three were from people who said he was sick and had no respect for the dead. Those three puzzled him until it hit him. He played his own message that had been on the machine all these months, and understood. Right before he went to New York, he had recorded a new message with a Ricky Nelson song in the background. The lyrics were about how "It's too late," and his message implied that the caller was too late also, as he was gone to sea. However, Ricky had died in a plane crash while he was gone, and people figured that he was making fun of that. He had grown up with Ricky and actually liked some of his songs. He erased all the messages, rewound the tape, and resolved to change the message.

He called his boy first. He felt lucky that the kid answered and not his ex. She always hounded him about something, and the last thing he wanted to begin his summer was a hassle with her.

"Alex, it's Dad. How you doin' buddy?"

"Hey, Dad. You need to talk to Mom right away."

"Later, kid, I just got in today. How's school?"

"It's fine. Here's Mom."

"No, wait . . . ah, hell."

"Tommy, you're back."

"Right. I didn't drown again. Is Alex okay?"

"Yeah, he's fine. Listen, I told him that as soon as you were back you'd buy him a new bike, so you need to take care of that right away."

"Well, thanks for deciding what I should do . . . again. Look, can I pick him up tomorrow about ten, for the weekend, return Sunday about six as usual?"

"Sure, I can use a break. It's not easy being the only parent all this time."

"I'm sure it isn't, but I wasn't on a goddam pleasure cruise myself. Look, let's not fight. Put him back on the phone, and remember to pack some pjs for him, he doesn't have any over at my place."

"Whatever."

Alex came back on the phone and they had a good talk, although the conspiracy about a new bike upset Tommy. They knew when he came down the gangway that he was flush with cash, but they refused to see how little it was if you considered how bad shipping out was and how long it had to last. The good news was that Alex had sent in his form to play in the neighborhood Boys Club baseball league again this year. He told the boy that he would volunteer to help coach his team, the Giants, again this year and would be home all summer. He also promised to get some Orioles' tickets for the two of them for a few games. The promise of a lot of summer baseball cheered the kid up, and this time at least there was no crying about anything over the phone. Tommy hoped he was getting used to the idea of split parents, as unfortunate as that was. The season would start in a few weeks.

Arrangements over, Tommy decided he absolutely had to eat before doing anything else his first night home. He walked the two blocks down to Frederick Avenue, the main drag through the neighborhood. The street started in downtown Baltimore and ran west through the Paradise neighborhood. If you stayed on it long enough you went through Catonsville, outside the city, then to Ellicott City, the old mill town, and eventually to Frederick, Maryland, hence, the name.

He turned the corner onto the main street, walked past the local grocery store and the barbershop, and went into Mario's Pizza Palace.

"Hey, Mario. How are things in Puerto Rico?"

"Tommy, Tommy, don't talk like dat in-a dis place. You know I Italian. I make-a da bes' Italian pizza in Bawlamer! You back again, eh? Jus' like a bad penny, you. Where you been dis time?"

"Australia, Mario." Tommy didn't need a menu. He knew everything on it, and ordered a sausage calzone, to go. "Remember our deal, Mario."

"Yeah, yeah, I know. You don't tell anybody about Puerto Rico, and I put a little extra cheese on-a your pizza, and a little extra tomato sauce on-a da calzone, right?"

"That's right." The mate strolled over to the glass case in the back and pulled out a six pack of beer to take with him. "You know, Mario, you're a good guy, but I can't understand why I buy beer from you when the grocery store two doors away sells the same damn thing for less."

"Hey, Tommy, I gotta overhead, what you call that, capice? I gotta family, too, you know? And, you, you son-of-a-bitch, I know you. Every summer you come in here with that big guy, your friend, what's his name and you guys talk me into sponsoring one of the kids' baseball teams, no?"

Tommy laughed, and smiled at the truth of his reply. "Yeah, you bandit, and I pay too much for beer because I love ya. And I do expect you to help the kids again this summer. You know why, Mario? I'll tell you. When we keep those kids down at the ballpark all summer they don't have the time or the energy to sneak in here and rob you." Several minutes passed with similar chatter.

"Never mind, I take care of myself. Take the calzone and go, huh? You nuttin' but trouble." Mario was smiling now too. He loved kids and the neighborhood knew it. It was one of the secrets to his success in that tiny place. Tommy remembered back to when he had first moved to Baltimore, five years ago. One of the first times he had been in Mario's with his son, then five years old, Mario had instantly warmed up to the kid.

While waiting for their order, he had asked the kid if he wanted to learn how to make a pizza. *What five-year old wouldn't?* Tommy had thought. Within minutes, he had Alex behind the counter, in charge of spreading the cheese on all the pizzas ready to go into the oven. By the time they left, cheese and flour covered the boy, and everybody in the place was having a great time. Tommy, from that day on, would go out of his way to buy from Mario. There was some new chain in town, but it wasn't like that. It wasn't local. Not a neighborhood Baltimore place at all.

He paid, took the bag with the calzone and beer, and headed for the door. "Hey, I'll see you, Mario. Say hi to all the folks in San Juan for me!"

"Go back to Australia you no good! Never come back in-a my place again, I got high class customers, you know, not no-goods like-a you!"

Tommy headed back up the street to his place, with the sound of the little bell attached to Mario's door still ringing in his ears. Back in his stuffy apartment, he ate and considered the other messages. The bill collectors could wait. There was no sense ruining his first day back with that crap. Maria was a casual acquaintance he had met at a nightclub nearby. They had only seen each other once. She was interesting in some ways, but they hadn't had a hot date, and he recalled that she had said she was seeing someone else. Whatever attraction there was between them was clearly social and physical. He decided to leave her go for a day or two, and then maybe call her. He was anxious to have a little romance, but figured she didn't want that. She had tried to interest him in coming to Parents Without Partners. *Yeah, that's probably what she wants, not me.* He let it go. That left only Brian.

Chapter 2: The Coaches

Tommy had known Brian for two years. They had met on a baseball field. The first year his son was ready for organized baseball he was eight. Tommy had signed him up and taken him to the tryouts. Everybody was placed on a team in that neighborhood. The tryouts were only so the coaches could draft the new players, and see that every team had an equal number of players. His kid threw the ball back and forth, took batting practice, and played in a practice game. Tommy remembered his own experiences with this when he had been about the same age.

He had lived in a small town in Connecticut. The official Little League had a tryout once a year, and it was a real tryout. They didn't pick everybody for a team. It lasted only a few hours, and he always thought little kids had a poor chance. Some team always drafted his older brother, who was bigger and stronger. Tommy, little and scrawny in those times, was never picked. He spent his summers playing for the playground team right near his house. The difference was not lost on the kids.

The kids on official Little League teams received complete, official-looking uniforms. The kids in the playground league were given plain T-shirts. Each team was a different color -- red, blue, or orange, and they had no nicknames. There was a cap to match, but there were no logos. He remembered that after a few years of it he had a dresser drawer full of various dyed tee shirts.

An 8-year-old level City Heights team called the Yankees took Alex. Tommy took him to practices, and was very excited when the season began. He took a lawn chair to their first game, and settled down by first base to watch his son's first competitive baseball game. This relaxation changed in the third inning. The Yankees' manager, a big guy called Brian, came over to where he had been sitting.

"Hey, how ya doin'? You're Alex's dad, right?"

Tommy shook his outstretched hand. "Yeah, that's right."

"Look, one of my guys couldn't show up today. Can you coach third base for us, help the kids out?"

"Well, I don't know. I haven't ever coached baseball before."

"I bet you played, though. Come on, these kids are only eight years old. You send 'em home when it looks right. We don't use any signs to the batters at this age; it's just to help the kids." Tommy would learn how persuasive Brian could be.

Brian figured that Tommy would be hooked on coaching, and he had been right. As a real estate salesman, Brian had developed a keen eye for judging people -- what they would do and when you couldn't push them. Somehow, he could see which dads and moms who came to the games cared enough to help. He was a great organizer. If you couldn't coach you could help get sponsors. If you couldn't do that, he persuaded you to bring drinks in a cooler to the games.

Brian had a son too, Derek, who was a year younger than Alex was, although he was much bigger. This year both kids would play on the same team, and Brian and Tommy would be assistant coaches again. The manager, Kirk, was coming back again this season. Since the Giants had won their league last year, no one would seriously suggest he shouldn't be the manager, even though he had some trouble with the kids. Brian was married -- barely it seemed, to Suzanne, his college sweetheart. He had been a fullback on a small-college football team, and she had been a cheerleader. Over the years, however, she resented how her husband always seemed to be out. She wanted him home at 5:00 p.m. to spend the evening with her and the kids. She hated how he spent evenings and weekends taking clients to see properties, and then compounded the problem by spending so much time with the Boys Club baseball teams.

Tommy hated to be around them when they didn't get along. They had Derek and a four-year-old daughter. He didn't want to see him go through the pain of a divorce like the one he had experienced. When he visited their townhouse on Chapelgate Road, in the Heights, he always noticed the pictures on the little table in the small living room. The wedding photograph and the ones of them when they were in school were beautiful. *People do change*. The old times eventually evaporated from his mind, and Tommy dialed his number. Suzanne answered it.

"Oh, Tommy, it's you. You're back in town, huh?"

"Yeah, Suzie, how ya doin'?"

"Well, I'm okay. I guess you want Brian. He's been dying for you to get back, and goddam baseball to start again, so he can spend all his time with a bunch of guys and ignore me."

"Ah, Suzie, I don't want to get in the middle of that. You want me to call back tomorrow?"

"No, here he is."

"Tommy, you old son-of-a-bitch, you're back! Hey, you know, I called Alex a couple of days ago and he told me he had gotten a telegram from you from the ship saying you'd be back today. Whaddya doin' right now?"

"Brian, I just drove in and had a couple of cold ones. I think I'm in for the night."

"Bullshit. I told all the guys you'd be back today. It's Friday night, for Pete's sake. Let's go down to Slim's."

"No, forget it, maybe tomorrow. I probably shouldn't drive. It's not far, I know, but I'm tired, and a couple of beers, you know."

"I'll pick you up. No problem. Get you home by midnight. Be right there."

He hung up before Tommy could counter the argument. He had heard Suzie yelling at him in the background that he'd better not go out tonight. He knew Brian would be there in ten minutes anyway. *What the hell, it would be good to see him and some of the guys. It is Friday night, why not go out?* He was single, after all, would spend all weekend with Alex, and he deserved a night out, even if it was just down to a little neighborhood bar in City Heights.

Sure enough, Brian's six-foot two, large frame filled Tommy's doorway in less than ten minutes. In college, he had weighed about 200 pounds but was now much heavier. Mr. Real Estate was clean-shaven, and had closely-cropped black hair. His cheeks were a little pudgy, and sometimes he looked like a giant chipmunk, but a happy one. You couldn't get him mad. Tommy bitched at him because he had a business suit on, while he was in jeans. Brian had a late sales appointment that afternoon, he told him. He was always selling. It was the one thing that bothered him about his friend. No matter where they went, Brian eventually starting asking everybody they met about their real estate plans. It was part of the business. The mate understood that, but hoped he would skip it sometimes.

They got in the car and headed east on Frederick Avenue, towards downtown Baltimore. It was only three miles from Tommy's apartment to Slim's bar, but they passed several different neighborhoods. It seemed that wherever you lived in Baltimore, your area had a name. The names were not official. They weren't legal jurisdictions and had no government or official boundaries. They were all a part of the city, but the locals used the neighborhood names. In the space of their short trip, they went from the neighborhood called Paradise through Ten Hills, Edmundson Village, and Uplands on the left, and Simpson, Norwood Heights, and City Heights on the right. The bar was located between City Avenue and Loudon Avenue, on Frederick Avenue, in a small strip of stores and bars. Tommy always considered it a part of City

Heights, which was the residential area just to the south, but the locals who had grown up there called it Irvington. Nobody seemed to know who or what "Irving" was.

They pulled into the parking lot between Slim's Bar and the Sub Shop. There was the usual litter scattered around, and Brian was careful not to run over any beer bottles. It wasn't the cleanest neighborhood in town, but if you were a local and knew what was up it was safer than it looked. Tommy had been trapped in Slim's during a rare Baltimore snowstorm, and had walked all the way back to Paradise with no problems. Just around the corner from the bar was the post office and across from that, a cemetery.

They weren't inside Slim's for two minutes and Brian was glad-handing everybody in the damn place, much to Tommy's chagrin. He was good at it, but it was embarrassing. He called everybody by name, asked about his or her kids, and gave out some business cards.

"Cut the crap, Brian, let's get a beer."

"Hey, no problem. Just making sure folks know I'm here to help 'em."

"Bullshit. You're off duty. C'mon."

They sat down at the bar, and as his eyes began to adjust to the light, things looked a little different to Tommy. As you walked in the door, the long bar was on the left and the video poker machine to the right. In the back was the restaurant area, with tables. This was a key to Slim's success. The official restaurant license meant the locals could bring in kids to eat there. They couldn't sit at the bar, but it was a strange combination of people -- those who came to get drunk and watch the Oriole games, and families in the back ordering sandwiches and burgers, ignoring the cussing from the bar area. He noticed two new dartboards in the place now, and one was all lit up, with some kind of official-looking scoreboard on the wall next to it. He also noticed four or five young women in there and a couple of them were damn good-looking. He had never seen that before. Slim's was a drinking bar for local guys only it seemed. You hardly ever saw a young woman in there, unless her mother had sent her down to fetch the old man to come home. He sipped his beer and casually picked up a menu from a rack on the bar, something else that was new. There were different sandwiches on it and a couple of salads. *What the hell is going on? Salad in here, for chrissakes? What kind of bar food is that?* Then he checked out the rest of the people.

Slim was sitting at the bar, on the customers' side, not behind it. All 300 pounds of him was just sitting there, watching TV and not working. There were two guys he vaguely knew behind the bar. They were both in their late 20's, and worked for the power company. He asked Brian about all this.

"That's right, you weren't here. Slim sold out."

"No shit, who owns the dump now?"

"The two guys behind the bar and two other meter readers. They pooled their money and made Slim an offer. He was getting tired of being on his feet in here day and night, so he took it. Sweet deal -- those guys are smart. They all keep their day jobs and take turns tending bar at night. They kept Mary on to work the day shift, and their wives or girlfriends wait tables at night. The old guy who cooks is still here, but he bitches all the time about the changes on the menu, such as it is."

"Christ, what's next, Brian? Next thing you know they'll put in fake brick paneling and ferns, you know, like the places down in Fells Point. And what about the dart boards?"

"They have leagues now. Still do a softball team outta here in the league that you subbed on last year, but now a lot of new guys show up for dart matches, couple nights a week, I think."

"Goddam, maybe we need to start hanging out at the Horseshoe, or Max's."

"Hey, give it some time. Look, it's not all bad. They get some babes in here sometimes now. Besides, they're going to sponsor two teams this year. Slim's a good guy, but he was only good for one. They're keeping up with the neighborhood, just more of a mixed crowd than Slim had. He never really wanted the young guys in here unless they came to holler at the O's. Besides, I did some business with one of them, which I never could do with Slim -- he has a buddy in the business."

"Well, I knew you'd find a way to make something positive out it. I'm goin' over to see Slim for a minute." Tommy walked to the end of the bar, gave an eye to one of the twenty-something girls hanging around near the new dart board, and threw his arm around Slim, at least as far as his arm would go around the huge back.

"Slim, you bastard, what'd you do, retire while I was gone?"

"Tommy, hey, good to see ya. Yeah, I'm tired, ya know. Had enough. These guys are okay for young bastards. Times are changing, Tommy. My kind of bar ain't as popular as it used to be. Besides, they gave me a good deal. Thinkin' of buying a boat and goin' crabbing in the summer, sit on my fat ass all winter. That ain't so bad, huh? Could be worse."

"Slim, you're a fixture around here. I hate to see it, but that's good for you. So now you're a customer in your own place."

Slim smiled. "Yeah, but that's the best part. I get my beer for half price for life. Had the lawyer put it right in the damn contract."

"I always said you were a genius, Slim. Remember the Monday Night Football thing? That was your best stunt. Christ that was funny."

Tommy laughed out loud, remembering that. Slim's busiest times were when the Orioles were on TV. Even though guys had it on at home, many would walk down to Slim's to watch the games with other rabid O's fans. Monday Night Football was the only other attraction, and ever since the Colts had slipped out of town, in the middle of the night, in a snowstorm for God sakes, a lot of people had stopped showing up for it. So, to attract his kind of customer, Slim had started an event for football night. He would bring in a cheap black and white TV on Monday nights, and set it up on a table in the back. You bought a raffle ticket for a buck, with half the money going to the City Heights Boys Club. The winner was encouraged to throw a brick through the TV at halftime. Tommy used to wonder if you could start a fire, what with the sparks shooting all over, but it was great. It had been especially popular when the new Indianapolis Colts were on. This was second only to smashing a virtual Howard Cosell -- Baltimore fans hated him, because he had made disparaging remarks about the city.

"Smash John Elway Night" had been good too, because a lot of locals said that his refusal to play for the Colts when they drafted him out of college had led to their demise and their subsequent move out of town. Elway swore he would play baseball before he'd play for the Colts, and not only that, but for the Yankees. Slim hated all of that, and tried to drum up support for those "Smash Elway" games, but it seemed that not everybody hated him as much as he did. The TV smash died out. In remembering those times, Slim lamented that now even damn Yankee fans would probably be welcome in the bar.

"Ah, forget it, Slim. They have rights, too, you know. Whaddya think, any chance for the O's this year?"

"Yeah, maybe. People sayin' Palmer ought to go to the bullpen this year, you know, ain't got the arm to be a starter anymore. If he can go, yeah, maybe we can do it."

Tommy felt a tap on his shoulder.

"Tommy, come on, time for a coaches' meeting." Brian stood there smiling. Behind him were the other guys who had already volunteered to help coach the Giants that summer.

"You son-of-a-bitch. I just pulled in and you're starting this already?" Tommy snarled, but was happy about it. It was difficult to keep friends with his being gone so much, and Brian had cared enough to arrange a meeting.

"Bullshit. The season starts in a few weeks, and if we're going to repeat as champs of the 9-10 league, we need to get started. Besides, I know you have all this free time, and will help me with sponsors, Opening Day, the parade, and the tournament, too."

Brian just flashed that big smile that made him special. He could organize anything, anytime. He had a gift for it, and the Boys Club, its teams, and the neighborhood would be worse without his cajoling and prodding everybody he met about baseball and kids. It was always for the kids, that's what he told 'em all, but Tommy knew it was just as important for the coaches. They would stay connected with their kids and neighborhood, through baseball, all year long, not just during the season.

The group left Slim to his memories, and went to the back of the bar. They grabbed a table and a pitcher of beer and sat down. Besides Brian and Tommy, there were two more men, Kirk and Terry. They all had sheepish grins on their damn faces.

"Okay, what the hell's up?"

Brian pulled out a paper bag from under the table, and handed out new baseball hats to everybody. He had sneaked out to his car while Tommy was talking to Slim. The City Heights official colors were green and white, and the hats reflected this. The brim and back half were green and the front was white with the letters "CH," in script neatly stitched in black. Luckily, the Giants colors were also green and white, so the kids' hats would match. Every team had a different uniform color, orange and white, or blue and white, and so forth, and their hats had those colors. Tommy remembered when he played as a kid, and the embarrassment of having a plain hat with no logo and no name.

"Put it on, and you're committed for the season," Kirk said, smiling, knowing Tommy would do it. That bastard

Brian had it all lined up. They all knew Tommy was off for the whole summer, thanks to his outgoing friend, and could spend inordinate amounts of time with the kids and baseball. They weren't taking any chances. They were going to hook him right then, and reel him in for the duration, on his first night home. They all put the hats on and toasted the Giants, City Heights, Australia, and a few other things Tommy would not remember the next day. Brian looked ridiculous with his gray business suit and baseball cap on.

The hat business had seemed a little silly to Tommy the first year he had coached, but he now knew the importance of it. The coaches and players in City Heights would wear them everywhere, all season. Many a time, Tommy had seen kids in the middle of winter still wearing the cap they were given the previous season. It didn't matter to them if the cap was dirty, faded and worn. They had it on, and were proud of it. They belonged to something, and it was meaningful. It wasn't just the love for the game which drove people in the club. It was the good they all knew they were doing, even if most of the talk was about the kids' chances in their age group, and secondly, the Orioles chances that season. The kids thought it was cool to wear an Orioles cap, but wearing one from a team you were on was better. It was, of course, the only part of their uniform they were allowed to keep. Otherwise the club would spend a fortune it didn't have trying to replace stuff. As it was, they had to replace some pants and shirts every season. If they could give away everything to the kids, Tommy figured that the neighborhood would be full of kids wearing complete baseball uniforms, running around even in the snow.

Tommy also remembered the first year he had a "CH" hat and some of the things that had happened which were associated with it. He had an older car then, and had gone to get the new emissions test. It had failed. He had parked and gone into the building, with his baseball hat on, to get an explanation. The guy behind the counter had greeted him strangely.

"You from City Heights?"

"Yeah, but I need to know . . ."

"Coach there?"

"Yeah, that's right, but what the hell does . . ."

"Lemme see your sheet." The guy looked it over, and then told the other workers he was going on break. He took Tommy outside, and asked him if he had a screwdriver. The baffled Tommy found an old one in the trunk. The guy popped the hood, looked at the inspection report again, and made a couple of minor adjustments to his carburetor.

"Get right back in line. You'll pass this time," the guy had said.

"Hey, thanks, but how come you're my new best friend?"

"I used to live in the Heights. I know what you guys do. Just don't tell anybody. I could get in a lot of trouble for doing this."

The car then passed. He wasn't even in the Heights for the test -- he was miles from it. He also remembered a time that first year going into Max's Place, another neighborhood bar in Irvington, with his new baseball hat on. When the bartender brought him his beer, he had questioned him.

"You coach with the kids?"

"Yeah, my kid's on the Yankees, 8-year-olds team. I help 'em out. Why?"

"Your beer's paid for. Guy down the end. He don't even have any kids, you know, but he likes what you guys are tryin' to do."

Tommy had realized right then that wearing a coach's cap in that neighborhood was, to some people, like wearing some kind of badge of honor. He also learned that first year that there was a negative side to it -- the parents who bitched about their kids not playing enough, or complained about umpires' calls, coaches' decisions, or hell, even the kids' uniforms. Maybe the people who respected the effort understood the down side.

His mind came back to the present, and he knew it was about time to leave. He wasn't driving, so he no longer cared how much he drank, but Brian was driving, and he had kept up with the group, beer for beer. Times were changing. You couldn't blow off a drunken driving charge anymore; you had to be more careful. He proposed to Brian that they leave, as he, Tommy, was tired. It was a lie, but it seemed to work. Just one more they all agreed. It was always one more. That was part of the problem. As they filled the glasses just one more time Tommy studied the faces of the other coaches.

They were all about the same age, mid-thirties. All had kids who would be on the Giants this season, but the differences ended right there. He and Terry were divorced. Brian seemed on the verge of it. Kirk had married his high school sweetheart, and seemed to be okay in that department, although he frequently bitched about marriage. He had been an accountant for the city, but had quit that and gone into business. He now did contract figures for a large bank. He was about six-foot one, still lean, and kept his dark hair short.

Kirk was the manager and no one disagreed with that choice. He was still a terrific athlete, especially in baseball. He had gone to college at the University of Virginia on a baseball scholarship, and still held some records there. Most doubles, Tommy recalled, was one of them. He had been a right fielder. The Dodgers drafted him, and he spent a few years in the minors. He never made it to "The Bigs," and it was no secret that he harbored resentment about the team calling others up and not him. He had one child, a son, Kirk Junior, who, naturally enough, everybody called "Junior." The kid was ten, played on the Giants, and was their best player. Like his dad, Junior was a leftie. He had pitched and played first base last season. Kirk worked with him constantly. Almost all year long, you could see them out on the playgrounds and ball fields of the neighborhood. Kirk pitched batting practice to the kid until the bucket full of baseballs was empty. Then they would pick them all up and start over. He yelled at the kid a lot. That was his only weakness. He was a brilliant coach, but could not handle little kids. He could not understand why they couldn't do some things as well as he had.

Many a time during the last season, Tommy had sat on the bench and listened to Kirk bitch about how a kid wasn't in the right position to take a cut-off throw and a hundred other things. Even though the Giants had won their age division Kirk still complained about mistakes. The only time Tommy had ever won a baseball argument with him was when he couldn't take it anymore and had asked him why, if it should be so easy to teach a ten-year old to play perfectly, did the best baseball players in the world spend weeks in spring training, going over everything? Kirk had no good answer to that one. *His heart is in the right place,* Tommy thought, *but his brain wants to treat kids like adults. And they were not adults.*

Kirk was clearly grooming his boy to make it in the major leagues. Talk around City Heights was that the kid might just make it, if he didn't go bananas first, having such a taskmaster for a father. Kirk always said that the dopes in City Heights had no idea what it took to become that good a player, and he didn't give a damn what anybody said about how hard he drove Junior.

Tommy's divorce had also been something of a problem to Kirk. He used to have Tommy and Brian and their wives over to his house a lot. The couples took turns having each other over for dinner or an informal party, but now they left Tommy out. It seemed that no one would invite Tommy or his ex to the same event, not wanting to appear to take sides. Tommy had heard from other divorced dads that it was typical, and caused by the implied threat a single friend might be to their own shaky marriages. The women simply did not want their husbands hanging out with a bachelor who had every right to check out girls.

The last member of the happy group was Terry. He had, in Tommy's opinion, the best personality of all. He was an easygoing, divorced dad, with two boys on City Heights teams. The older boy played with the 13-14's, and the younger was ten and on the Giants. Terry worked for IBM in a large office building. He did something with computers, a new and growing field that Tommy didn't know much about. He was in his early thirties, had hair a bit on the long side, and grew a blond beard every winter. He loved his boys and the three of them were sports crazy. He never talked about his ex or why they split up, so no one asked. There was a rumor he had another ex, back in Tennessee, a result of a youthful indiscretion, but he never said anything about that, either. There was another rumor that he occasionally smoked dope. Tommy and Brian sometimes thought Terry acted strangely, but he denied using dope, and they left it alone.

Terry sometimes had the Giants coaches' meetings at his row house, and cooked up crabs and corn when they were in season. His boys were fun but mischievous. A large German shepherd completed the chaotic scene in his place, with sports equipment scattered all over the place. It wasn't just baseball equipment, but skates, footballs, basketballs, and equipment for just about any sport. The stuff was always all over the floor, and none of the three males seemed to care. Tommy never could decide if the overdosing on sports in their house was the way he tried to stay connected to his kids, or if Terry was trying to stay a kid himself. The kids never talked about their mom, and nobody questioned why not. Tommy was a bit jealous that Terry never had to fight with his ex. She was out of the picture. Nothing seemed to upset Terry very much. He handled close games the kids lost better than anybody did. On those rare nights when the coaches ended up in a bar where there were available women, he seemed to attract more than his share. Tommy believed that the women could see what a nice guy he was, right through his baseball hat. If anybody married again, it most likely would be Terry, but he seemed in no hurry. Watching an Orioles game with his boys seemed more important than asking women in bars for their phone numbers.

Semi-sober agreement finally prevailed, and the coaches agreed to break up the meeting and go home. Kirk and Brian would return to their wives. Tommy guessed that Kirk would have the easier time of getting home late. His wife, Robin, seemed to have no problems with all the time Kirk spent with baseball. Many times last year, when Tommy and Alex had gone down to the field behind Simpson Elementary School, where the 9-10's played, to practice on their own, Kirk and family were already there. Robin would have a glove on and be running around the outfield, fetching the balls Junior had hit, and throwing them, underhanded, back towards the pitching mound, where Kirk could save time from having to pick them all up. No wonder the kid could hit.

Brian's situation was different, but if he caught hell from Suzanne about it, he always brushed it off. "She'll get over it," was Brian's standard reply. Tommy and Terry had no one to answer to, but they went home to no women -- one to an apartment, the other to a brick row house.

Chapter 3: The City

Tommy slept in on Saturday morning. He called his boy's house before he went to pick Alex up. This was to make sure that Alex was ready to go with Dad, and thereby avoid any waiting around time with the ex. It went smoothly. He avoided the old arguments that had led to the divorce. Tommy still thought his pretty, tall, ex-wife was too Southern for him. *Mississippi girls are different.* They seemed to expect the husband to do and provide everything without any effort in return. If the house or yard needed work, she expected him to do it. When money was tight, she had refused to work, reminding him that her father had always provided for her mom. Tommy's response was usually something like, "I'm not your father. I'm your husband. You have to help."

The two males drove off, took a shortcut through Wickham Road, Athol Lane, and Nottingham Road, through the area known as Ten Hills, to Edmundson Avenue. They were headed to a small racquetball club Tommy had joined.

On the way, they passed a little neighborhood theater on Edmundson. It was the only neighborhood movie house around, the last of its type. Every time Tommy went by it, he always remembered when Alex was little and the first Star Wars movie had come out. He lost count of how many times they had gone up there to see it. Alex, like many of the kids, had become so enamored of the movie that Tommy and his wife took turns taking him there. The manager of the theatre had bought a cool Darth Vader outfit and, for the evening show, would roam the sidewalk in front of his place and scare the little kids. They loved it. In the future, there would no longer be any of these small theaters. Locals would have to drive somewhere to see a show at one of those huge, multi-screened complexes.

The general area around City Heights was typical of most neighborhoods in Baltimore. It was racially diverse, although there weren't many Latinos. It was definitely blue collar. Guys worked the waterfront or at McCormick's spice factory or Bethlehem Steel. It was Orioles Country -- Brooks Robinson was a broadcaster, and you could meet him at one of the many places he showed up to. Tommy had taken Alex to a gas station in Catonsville to meet him. Brooks signed the baseball card they had, but Tommy never mentioned to the boy that, no doubt due to how many places he had been to that day he had signed it with his left hand.

It had been Colts Land, too, and Johnny Unitas, known as "Johnny U," still lived there, still had a restaurant, and, unlike a lot of sports heroes who owned places like that, showed up there and met his fans. Once, when Tommy took Alex to the Maryland State Fair, he noticed the famous quarterback walking ahead of them with his family. Alex didn't believe it was the real Unitas. Tommy walked faster, caught up with the retired star, apologized for bothering him at the fair, but told him the boy wanted to shake his hand. Of course he did it. That memory from the state fair was the only thing that exceeded Alex's other favorite. After a hot dog and a beer, Tommy went on a ride that took you upside down. He had barely stepped out of the damn thing when he lost his lunch, throwing up in a trashcan. Alex thought that was a riot and would retell the story every year at fair time.

Many people who had traditional steps in front of their row houses washed them, as was a city tradition. Steamed crabs were the local specialty, and you could buy them fresh from guys by the side of the road all summer. A boat and a truck put you in business, if you knew what you were doing. The Chesapeake Bay was a fantastic resource for other reasons, including the maritime industry, which drove much of the local economy.

The Rouse Company had built a tourist attraction right in the center of the city, called the Inner Harbor. Tommy thought that the Constellation, the old fighting ship which was the sister ship to the Constitution in Boston, was the main attraction. The tourists thought it was the shops and restaurants. A new National Aquarium was going up too, and the Science Center was gearing up for more visitors. Tommy remembered sailing into the harbor years earlier on merchant ships, when the whole waterfront was a rotten mess. The changes had made the downtown come alive. Some folks were even saying they could build a new baseball stadium downtown, too, on the site of some railroad tracks known as Camden Yards.

The city government had a program that had fueled much of the city's revival. It was becoming a model. They sold old, beat-up row houses right downtown, in areas like Federal Hill, for one dollar. You had to sign a contract to fix the place up and live there for three years. If you were handy with plaster and wiring, and did most of the work yourself, you could do very well. The outsides of these dollar homes had to conform to their original style, some more than 100 years old. These neighborhoods developed character. Young, professional people who worked in the downtown banks and businesses soon moved into the area and walked to work.

Fells Point, on the eastern side of the harbor, began to revive mostly as a place to go at night. Brick and fern bars, people called them, but the young people liked them. It wasn't as touristy as the Inner Harbor and was one of the few places you could park your car and walk several blocks, choosing among the bars, restaurants, and specialty shops, most locally owned. Tugboats still docked at the foot of Fell Street, ignoring the new bars, and the Polish-American Club still catered weddings and dances up the street. Hanging around Fells Point for a Friday night was like going on a British pub-crawl.

There were ethnic areas in Baltimore, too -- Polish, Italian, and Asian. There were Black areas and White areas and gypsy peddlers who drove around in horse-drawn wagons, selling fruits and vegetables. Baltimore didn't seem to have the racial problems other cities had. Tommy wondered if the long history of the city, coupled with the desire of all people to see it revive, drove this. Somehow, the residents knew that they could not make it if they didn't at least tolerate each other. People were beginning to be proud of their city. When relatives from out of town came to visit, there were places to take them.

Fort McHenry still guarded the harbor and was a beautiful park. The view from there was the same as when the British bombarded it in the War of 1812. A Star Spangled Banner still flew, and it was visible from all around downtown. It seemed to remind people of their patriotism. Most locals knew about the land battle that was fought at the same time as the Fort McHenry fight, but which seemed to have been almost forgotten in the history books.

Some knew how close the area, and all of Maryland, had come to joining the South in the Civil War, but they didn't mention it much. Lesser-known historic places existed too. Journalist H. L. Mencken's home was there, if you knew where to look. If you knew where to look in the Green Mount Cemetery you could find the grave of John Wilkes Booth. Another place the tour busses sometimes skipped was the Shot Tower. This place had been around since colonial times. It looked like a giant chimney. Some patriot had figured out that if you dropped a dab of molten lead from a great height into a pool of water, it would form a perfect musket ball.

If you left downtown and went north on Calvert Street, you could make a quick turn and go to the Hotel Belvedere, one of the oldest and finest places in town. They had a fancy bar on the top floor. Tommy had been there a few times when he wanted the fancy treatment, but there was another place he liked better just around the corner. It was Peabody's

Bookstore, but he didn't go there to buy old books. There was a small bar in the back, and a larger one upstairs. For years, there had been an old guy who did magic tricks for tips in the small bar. He had a white beard and wore a shabby coat. He did the usual card tricks, and the rings, things like that. He had died the year before and Tommy just knew it was because of the "New Baltimore" going up all around. He wouldn't have fit in with all the changes.

There was Johns Hopkins University, and its famous hospital and medical school, contrasted with a place like Druid Hill Park, which was dangerous at night, and frequently held lifeless bodies on Saturday mornings. There were housing projects and a few grocery stores where it was common knowledge you could sell food stamps for cash.

There was Towson, an upper class area that was also home to Towson State University. The wealthier folks who didn't want to live in the new townhouses of Federal Hill were moving out to Cockeysville and other suburbs. There were military installations around Maryland, and tons of Civil War History not far away, in Sharpsburg, Antietam, and just across the state line, in Gettysburg, Pennsylvania.

People hung flags out on July 4th. Before his divorce, Tommy used to climb up on the roof of his 90-year-old house and tie a wooden pole to his chimney with a flag nailed to it. That house was on top of a hill, and you could see the flag from all over City Heights. Dundalk, the waterfront town on the eastern edge of the city, docked many container ships. It also had an Independence Day celebration that was pure Americana: a parade, a fair with rides and live music, beer and steamed crabs, or crab cakes. It was no secret it was mostly a white area, but on July 4th no one cared who came to it, only that you behaved yourself. Catonsville, just to the west of Tommy's neighborhood, had a great fireworks show. The town firemen came around the night of the show with empty buckets, working the crowd for donations for the next year's show.

The small, wall-to-wall row houses that Bethlehem Steel had built for factory workers in the Depression were there, and people lived in them. You could still see the reddish hue on the outside of the houses, stained from smokestack pollution years ago. There were numerous piers where the large merchant ships still docked and worked their cargo. An old coal pier was still in business, and you could see the huge piles of coal stacked up on the docks, waiting for trucks to haul coal to the factories. The GM plant was near there too, and many of the City Heights guys worked the shifts in it.

On the right day you could drive through Baltimore, from City Heights on the west side, through to Dundalk on the east, and smell spices from McCormick's, seafood from the fishing boats, bread being cooked from the bakery, and pollution from the steel mill. You would pass through rough neighborhoods, both White and Black. You would pass near the house where Edgar Allan Poe had lived, with his child bride, and if you turned down a narrow street near downtown, you could see the row house where Babe Ruth grew up. His father's bar had been nearby. Poe's grave was in a churchyard right in the center of the city. Locals repeated the story of Poe passed out in a gutter, literally dead drunk, but recent research was saying he died of rabies. It seemed to ruin the story, as Baltimore was a drinking town.

Interstate 95, the main north-south highway from New York to Florida, went right through the middle of the city, and under the Bay through an old tunnel. Only double, yellow lines separated the northbound and southbound lanes, so it was dangerous to drive through if you had a few. There were plans to build a new, larger tunnel, under the Bay. Tommy sometimes wondered if the new tunnel would shoot people past the city so fast they would never stop and see any of it or learn to appreciate the local color of the place he loved so much. It seemed that Baltimore had a bad reputation up north, and folks would gas up before they drove near it and not stop until they were past Washington, about 40 miles to the south.

There were art schools and museums in Baltimore, but they weren't as famous as the ones in New York or Washington. Washington, about an hour's drive if you timed the traffic right, wasn't a big attraction to "Bawlamer" residents. They didn't like it. Maybe it was the politics of the nation's capital, or the sports, or the lifestyle of places like Georgetown. If you rooted for Baltimore teams, you hated Washington teams, including the Bullets, who had moved from downtown Baltimore to suburban D.C. However, the locals had the Orioles, while the richer folks in D.C. had lost the Senators to Texas, and had no baseball. That made the old-time sports fans feel a little better. Even the University of Maryland was nearer Washington than Baltimore, and the college teams there did not attract Baltimore support as much as they might have because of it. Memorial Stadium, where the Orioles played, was in the northern part of the city, just beyond Johns Hopkins University. It was almost in the inner city, and narrow streets surrounded the stadium. The locals lived in brick row houses in the racially mixed neighborhood. The team belonged to them. As the Orioles went, so went the city.

The coaches from City Heights went to a few Orioles games a year, depending on their financial situations. When Tommy had just come home from sea, he would buy some tickets for future games, and he and Alex would go. Orioles games sold well, but you didn't need to be a season ticket holder to get in. It just wasn't necessary. You bought tickets for the games you liked. It was tradition to holler "O!" during the National Anthem, when it was at the part which went: "Oh, say does that Star Spangled Banner yet wave." Tommy had been to some Yankee and Red Sox games, while working on the ships in those ports, and had heard a handful of the Baltimore faithful doing that. No one else understood it. Locals remembered a Colts game when a small plane had crashed into the upper deck of Memorial Stadium, right after the game had ended. No fan was hurt and, amazingly, the pilot walked away down the steps.

A Memorial Stadium tradition was the parking situation. As you approached the stadium on one of the local streets, the kids who lived there would hang out on the corners, offering to find you a parking spot for a tip. If you called the kid over, he hopped right in your car, and directed you. Turn right here and go down that alley, like that, until he found you a spot on a narrow street, or behind an apartment. The kid would then run back up to the main street to get another customer. The problem you had was finding your way out of the maze of narrow streets after the game.

Women in Baltimore called you "Hon'." Kids used a peculiar combination of salutation, calling you "Mr." or "Ms." with your first name, like "Mr. Tommy." It seemed to be a compromise between paying proper respect to elders and being friendly. The kids who played on the City Heights teams called you "Coach Brian," or "Mr. Brian." They didn't use last names, and probably didn't know most of them. They did the same things with their neighbors. Your neighbor might be "the old crazy bitch next door" to your friends, but you addressed her as "Ms. Sally." There was an old woman who hung around the downtown area that Tommy was sure was crazy. When he took Alex downtown, they frequently passed her corner on the way back to City Heights. She was old, shabbily dressed, and had long hair that was matted and filthy. She would be leaning against the wall, sometimes talking to herself, usually sleeping. Alex always asked about her, if she was a bag lady, and how she ended up like that. Dad had no answer, and eventually, they noticed that she no longer lived on that corner. They never saw her again. She was one of the street bums, it seemed, and easy to dismiss. Whether she lived or died didn't seem to matter much to most people. It was a part of the city life of Baltimore as much as other cities, yet Tommy felt bad that he had never done a damn thing to find out about her, or help her. Somehow, it was easier to forget about the male bums he saw.

On their trip, they passed an apartment complex that was on the downhill side of Frederick Avenue. Every time there was a bad rainstorm, the apartments on the lower level would flood. These places were half below ground level and half above. Some of the City Heights players lived there. Every time it flooded, some folks would say that the city should not allow the landlord to rent them out at all. But they were cheap, and there were always people who would take a chance. Brian tried desperately to interest the tenants in some renters' insurance. He knew a guy who could write up the policies so no evidence of prior flooding would show up and it was cheap, but few did it. There was even a side to the insurance business in Baltimore where folks paid weekly, in cash, for life insurance. Brian had tried to get Tommy to work it when he needed money, but he wanted no part of it. You had a "book" they called it, like a newspaper route. It took you into some of the roughest neighborhoods around, and you had to knock on doors and collect cash from the people. It was mostly term insurance, and they wrote policies so that they never seemed to pay off. If you missed some weeks here and there, which was typical, you might never see a dime, even when you had a death in the family. Brian never worked that business, and Tommy said he would never get that desperate to do it. Others did. When the apartments flooded out, many of the coaches and parents in City Heights knew that the people would lose almost everything, and they would come down and donate bedding and clothes, even a little cash. The flooding would make the local news, and then everyone forgot about it until it happened to someone else the next time.

Tommy drove down Edmundson, past the Beltway, made a couple of quick turns, and was at the racquet club. It wasn't fancy like the big ones around town. It only had six racquetball courts, and two tennis courts, all indoors. There was a small bar where you could get sandwiches, a locker room, and a couple of workout machines. Dues were $40 a month, much less than the big clubs, and you paid a reasonable fee for court time. Because it was small, and out-of-the-way, they never seemed to have enough members. Tommy would join when he was home, and let it go when he was at sea. They always had coupons in the local paper which offered no initiation fee and no contract. You could pay month by month, and that is what he did. It was something he started after the divorce, so he and Alex would have something to do in the winter, when they couldn't practice baseball. Tommy hoped that racquetball, with its need for quick reflexes, was good for Alex's hand-eye coordination, and would improve his hitting. When he had still lived in the same house as Alex, he had put a ping pong table in the basement for the same reason. When Alex was only four, the two of them would bat the ball around for hours. In the good weather, they had practiced baseball outside.

After an hour of playing racquetball, during which Alex almost beat him, they had a soda and beer and left. Alex was a strong player and didn't like it if he caught Dad letting up so he could win a game. He was getting to the age where he would start beating his father at sports and wanted to do it honestly.

Their routine after that was simple -- a stop at the Giant Food Store for groceries for two days and then home to Tommy's apartment. They bought the fixings for manicotti. It was one of the few hot meals Tommy knew how to cook. He always bought some salad and fresh bread to go with it. Like most kids, Alex would try to coax Dad into buying a bunch of junk food, too, but Tommy didn't allow much of it. He could ruin his own body with crappy food, but felt obliged to actually have representatives from all the major food groups in his apartment when Alex stayed over, and for the boy's sake he did not count beer as a food group.

This time the ex had remembered to pack Alex's pajamas. They stayed up late watching meaningless junk on television. On Sunday morning, they had visits from the unofficial pets at Tommy's apartment. He had nailed a plastic tray to the outside of the window in the living room, and they put bird food in it. One huge cardinal chased all the other birds away, and ate most of it. They had tried to give him a name, but "The Big, Fat Cardinal" was the only one that stuck. They sat out on the back stoop, and the local squirrel climbed up the stairs when he saw them. They had trained him to climb all the way up the stairs and take a peanut out of their hands. The last animal visitor was a stray black cat. Tommy never let him in the apartment, as he knew he would be gone a lot, but when he was home he allowed Alex to give him a treat down at the bottom of the steps. They never were sure if he had a home or not. There was one other favorite animal but he was not local. Ever since his split, Tommy had taken the boy on occasional camping trips into Virginia. Their favorite place was Mt. Rogers. It was a treat that they always went on a horseback ride, sometimes for an hour, sometimes for a half-day. The stables they liked had a horse named Apache and he was Alex's favorite. Tommy would make reservations ahead of time, and he always asked for Apache. Those camping trips didn't happen often, but they were special.

They followed a normal pattern for the rest of the day. They drove to nearby Patapsco State Park and went for a hike. Sometimes Tommy would load up Alex's bike in the van when he picked him up on Saturdays and they would ride together. Tommy's bike was an old Raleigh 3-speed he had bought at a yard sale. Naturally, the subject of a new bike for Alex came up again. Tommy told him that if his end-of-the-year grades in school were good he would get him one. In the afternoon, they practiced throwing and catching in the yard behind the house, and watched sports on TV. The baseball season had started for the major leagues, and that was the prime interest. The kids' season would start in three weeks.

As usual, he dropped the boy off at his house about 6:00 p.m. The ex insisted on this, so she would have enough time to get him to do a little homework and go to bed at a reasonable hour. She suspected, correctly, that this did not always happen at Tommy's place. Tommy realized that this was reasonable. It was one of the few things they agreed on.

Back at the little apartment, he went through the rest of the mail that had piled up in the months he had been gone, and wondered about calling Maria. Having the boy every Saturday night put a cramp in his potential for a new social life, but he did not dwell on it. There was Friday night, after all, probably the best night for catting around, and hell, it seemed that all the women he met were also divorced with kids, and they understood. There was no reason you couldn't have a date on a Sunday or a Tuesday, anyway. He knew that if he ever met the right woman, they would do things together with the kids on Saturdays. That had not been the case yet, however, and he was in no hurry. With all that had happened in the first marriage he was in no hurry to start anything like a serious relationship. He and his boy would relate with baseball all summer, and, sooner or later, Tommy would work in a date or two. He felt he was getting older, as he just didn't care about it as much as he used to. He also knew how precious the summer would be, having those months off and helping with the team. No dad he had ever known, his own, or those with bucks, ever had that luxury.

He stayed home Sunday night, struggling with the pile of mail. He paid some bills and threw others away. Only Brian, who called to remind him that the next meeting of the City Heights Boys Club was Tuesday night, interrupted this. He also told him that on Thursday, he wanted Tommy to dress up a little and go out during the day with him, to work on sponsors for the teams. Tommy didn't like that routine, but he knew that Mr. Brian was the only one who could get it done in time for Opening Day, and he deserved what help he could give him. He went into the little kitchen, flipped five monthly pages off the calendar on the wall, and wrote down the Tuesday meeting on it.

Chapter 4: The Club

On Tuesday night, Tommy drove his van down Frederick to City Heights Rd. and turned right, and right again on Chapelgate. He went around the curves and down the hill, and parked in the street across from a three-story brick apartment building. It was just before 7:00 p.m., the time of the Boys Club meeting, and several other cars and pickups were already there. As he walked up the sidewalk, he could hear the chatter from inside.

The clubroom was in the basement. The guy who managed the building had a boy who had played for City Heights, and years ago he had talked the owner into giving them a room for meetings. In the off-season they met once a month. Now it would be every week. Even though some guys had been planning things all winter, there were many details to work on for Opening Day. There was the parade through the neighborhood, ceremonies and games, sponsors, record keeping, parental consent and birth certificates, equipment problems, umpires to hire, and on and on. Sometimes it seemed that there would be no season, there being too much to do, but they always managed.

Tommy shook a few hands and heard the usual jokes about the places he had been, and "how the girls were," things like that. He didn't know everybody there. Out of 20 or so guys, he knew maybe ten of them. He recognized most of the others as coaches of teams on various levels. City Heights sponsored teams in 8-year old, 9-10, 11-12, 13-14, and the big kids, 15-16. Traditionally, the oldest kids did the best. Many said it was because if you survived in that rough neighborhood until you were that old, you were one tough player. To Tommy, it was the coaching, as most of the good coaches liked the older levels. He wondered if the kids from City Heights would do better against other neighborhoods and towns if their best coaches had the younger kids, and taught them the basics early on. It seemed that the younger age groups were always desperate for coaches. Almost anybody who volunteered ended up as a manager or coach.

The president of the club, a guy they called Big John, called the meeting to order. John was about five-foot six. He drove trucks down on the waterfront. Tommy had never run into him when his ships docked in town, but they had a common bond because they both knew the Baltimore waterfront. John lived just up the street from Slim's Bar, and had no kids. His hair was receding, to be kind, and he was physically very strong. Emotionally, he was a softie. He loved kids, the whole neighborhood, and baseball. He owned a complete set of umpire gear, and would do a game if the hired guy didn't show. He managed one of the teams, too. Tommy knew he also liked to gamble on sports, and there were a couple of bookies around who would take his bets.

With the beginning of the season so close, there were a number of issues to discuss. After the usual reading of the minutes of the last meeting, and the treasurer's report, they got down to it. The club secretary was in charge of paperwork. He reported on how many kids had sent in consent forms to play, how many had to go back because of no parental signature, and so on. The goal was to have eight teams at each level. Sometimes they made it, sometimes they didn't. Copies of birth certificates had to be furnished. There were cut-off days, but the club was more lenient with that than the official Little League. If your birthday hit right, you could turn eleven years old, and still be playing in the 9-10 league. Tommy knew that was tough on the younger kids. A kid who had just turned nine might go up to bat against a kid who was already eleven. They traditionally didn't do well in those at bats.

Opening Day, now about two weeks away on a Saturday, was a huge deal. Several guys and their wives had been working on it all winter. There would be a parade through the neighborhood, with every team marching in uniform. The parade ended at the main fields, behind Simpson Elementary. It seemed the whole neighborhood would turn out. They had a ceremony with the National Anthem. The club always had food and snack booths set up, and parents and kids bought hot dogs and drinks all day. It was the second biggest money raiser of the year. Only the August crab fest was better.

Every team played on the first day although some of them played on other fields. It lasted all day until dark. It took a hell of a lot of work to organize the teams, food, umpires, and schedule all the games. Big John knew everybody and was terrific with the food booths. Brian had the parade, and he wasn't finished planning it. He was always trying to add things right up to the last minute. The club had firemen and policemen members, so cop cars and fire trucks were not a problem. Brian had hired a high school band to march, but was still working on some clowns and costumes. Naturally, he wanted to rope Tommy into helping him.

The equipment manager gave his report. This was serious business. It cost a lot to replace uniforms and bats. Their basement clubhouse had been broken into so many times they had stopped storing anything there. Each manager of a team took the balls, bats, and catcher's gear home with him, and was responsible for it. When a guy dropped out, or moved away, the equipment guy had to get the stuff from him. How many bats a team received per year was decided on a vote, and depended on how much money the club had. There was a discussion about supplying better catcher's gear, or a first baseman's mitt to each team. It didn't seem fair to change a kid to first base or catcher and then expect his parents to go buy the kid a new glove. The number of baseballs they used was standard, but there was always a demand for more for practice. Every year guys donated baseballs and equipment they had at home. When a kid outgrew a glove or bat, many times his dad would bring it down to the club. They had used wooden bats years after every other program had gone to aluminum. The aluminum ones didn't seem like real bats to the guys in City Heights, with that horrible "ping" sound instead of a solid whack! They had reluctantly switched to save money, and because they weren't allowed to use wooden bats in tournaments.

A key item was the sponsorship of teams. Brian was in charge of this, too. He always volunteered, and no one fought him for the privilege of begging money from every business in the neighborhood. He was a good salesman and everybody knew it. Still, Tommy knew that it was Brian's taking on more responsibility with the club that drove his wife nuts. The Opening Day parade, sponsors, helping coach, on and on it went and he would do anything to make it all happen, "for the kids."

One of the tricks was to get repeat sponsors. The business name went on the back of the kids' uniform shirts, so, if the same business had a team, you could use most of the same uniforms over again, only replacing those totally worn out, or stolen. The businesses were given a plaque with their business name and a picture of its team on it. Big John called on Brian. He stood up and said about half the sponsors had paid up and volunteered Tommy to go out with him, starting this Thursday, to get the rest. He worked so goddamn hard at all this that Tommy could not refuse. Everybody laughed, knowing how persuasive Brian was.

The subject of the annual City Heights Crab Fest came up. This annual event was the biggest fundraiser the club had, and some people who couldn't coach worked on it year round. They had it in August each year, and the idea was to raise enough to pay off any debts the club had, and leave enough in the kitty to start the next season. Some hands went up to volunteer for different assignments. Before August, every guy in the club, and most of their wives, would be involved. Big John put Tommy on the crew that handled the steamed crabs, and Tommy also signed up to run the Big Six Wheel for an hour. They would work on the details of this party all summer.

The meeting was dragging on. It had been over an hour, and they were still talking about umpires and coaching assignments. Each team had an assigned manager, and as many assistants as he could find or wanted. As expected, Kirk officially was named manager of the Giants again, and he listed Tommy, Brian and Terry as his coaches. There were still two more items to discuss.

The first was painful for many guys. Big John reported that they had a girl sign up to play this year -- a first. He knew the family. They had no sons, and the girl had been playing ball with her dad for years. She could throw and catch okay but not much else. There was no girls' softball league around, so the parents wanted her to play. This set off a huge argument. It was a Boys Club for good reason, many said. She could get hurt, others said. A few said it was okay. One guy said this was okay because she would fail, and then they wouldn't have any more crap about girls playing hardball. Guys asked about Title IX, and whether that applied to the club. Could they lose their non-profit status if they didn't allow girls to play? John agreed to check with the lawyer who gave them free advice, but in a heated debate, they voted to put her on a team. She would play in the 9-10 age division. One guy made a sarcastic remark that maybe they should actually change the name of the club to the "City Heights Boys and Girls Club."

The last item was the usual "50-50" raffle. The club treasurer went around with little red movie-style tickets and sold them for a buck. They drew a number, and the winner was paid 50% of the pot and the club kept the other half. They did it every meeting. It cost you money to go to the meetings, and would cost you a lot more to coach a team. Everybody knew it but did it anyway.

John officially ended the meeting. Groups of guys gathered to decide where to go next. The Giants coaches headed for Slim's, as usual. Others went to the Horseshoe, or Max's, and a few good souls even went straight home.

Tommy drove the van down to Slim's, and parked in the side lot. The new owners had opted to keep the name of the bar the same, but the crowd was a little different. There was a dart-league game going on and there were some younger people there he had never seen. Brian had gotten there first, and had a table in the back. Terry was there, but no Kirk. He didn't always make the Giants' coaches' meetings. Some thought he had a stronger marriage, and liked to go home. Others thought that he felt superior to them, at least in baseball knowledge, and he didn't want to hang out with them.

By the time Tommy went up to the bar for refills, he saw President John in the corner, working the video poker machine. He knew that Big John had a weakness for gambling, as well as a heart of gold for the community. Everybody had a weakness and this was his. A little sport bet here, a day at Pimlico Racetrack there. Hell, you never knew about people. Maybe it explained why Big John still lived in the little row house just up the street, instead of a nice, big house.

He remembered the first time he had been in Slim's with Brian, when he had helped with the 8-year-old team. After a beer or two, Tommy had gravitated over to the video poker machine, and put in some quarters. "For Amusement Only," the large letters had said, and he believed it. He had good luck, and worked it up to more than 100 points. Brian watched, and was excited about the point total.

"Hey, Tommy, why don't you take that, and we'll go get something to eat, or go down to the Horseshoe?"

"What are you talking about?" he had responded.

"Oh, that's right. You're new here. Lemme check."

Brian had looked around, seemingly checking out who was in the bar, and then walked over to talk to Slim. He came back to the game.

"Okay, work it down to a hundred even, and stop. Slim will be right over."

"I still don't get it, but I smell a rat," Tommy said.

"I had to convince him you weren't a cop. You know, vouch for you."

Slim had come over to the poker machine with a key. He inserted it in a notch in the side, and the next thing Tommy knew, the point total was zero. Brian then took him over to the bar, and Slim slid $25 cash across the bar to him. He got it.

Now, Tommy could see that Big John was pumping quarters in the machine all the time. It didn't take a genius to figure out what was going on when the bartender would give you rolls of quarters, like in a casino. All the people who worked there, Slim, Mary, and now the new owners, knew everybody in the neighborhood. If they had any doubt about somebody, they would ask around, or wait until the stranger left, before paying off. It seemed harmless, but was, of course, illegal.

"C'mon, John, let it go. You're not having any luck tonight."

"Ah, screw it, I took over a hundred bucks outta here last week, but maybe you're right."

"Bail out and come to the back with us. We'll buy your dumb ass a beer, even though you should buy for us, with your new-found wealth."

They left the poker business to others, and went to the back. John brought up all the same issues they had discussed at the meeting, and they went over them, now unofficially. The girl who has signed up to play was a hot topic, but John was adamant. He didn't have any kids, and could understand what might happen to someone who loved baseball, but only had girls. "Girls can get in trouble too," he argued. "We need, as a club, to provide for them, too." It seemed the right thing to do, but Terry was uneasy with it. He said that if the female faction of City Heights wanted to do something for the girls, they could start a separate league for them, maybe softball. They all knew that there wasn't enough money in the neighborhood to support a new, girls' league, though, whether it was baseball or softball.

Eventually, sitting at the table in the back, trying to ignore the dart league, and forgetting about the poker machine, Tommy became aware of a new interest. Maybe it was because of his wide travel but he always knew who was sitting or standing near him in a bar or if anyone was staring at him. He had a few bar fights to his credit, or discredit, and he had a good sense for trouble or opportunity. Like most sailors with several years of travel experience, he had an ability to get out of a bar thirty seconds before the fight started. He referred to it as a sailor's sense of timing, as all sailors knew what a night or two in a Turkish jail could mean.

What was different in Slim's that night included the table in the back, next to the one full of coaches arguing about baseball. There were three young women there, all about 25 years old, and two of them were gorgeous. The third one would do as well, after a few drinks. The sailor was interested, but assumed they were too young for him, or that he was too old for them. It was a new thing to see in the little neighborhood bar, but a welcome sight, nonetheless. Then, one of the babes came right over to him.

"Hey, you or your friends want to play darts?" One of the better-looking girls was speaking to him, but looking at them all. She was tall, blonde, and shapely.

"Well, yeah, maybe. Hey, any of you guys up for some darts with these ladies?"

Terry stood up right away. Big John and Brian declined, although you could see the interest on their faces. They were, after all, the married two of the group, but Tommy wasn't sure that always mattered, not for a little flirtation, anyway. Tommy paired up with the blonde girl, as his partner, for a doubles game of darts' baseball, and Terry got the short brunette with the bigger boobs. The third female stayed seated. They set up to play at the second dartboard, which was in the back, in the restaurant portion of Slim's.

Baseball was the only dart game they all knew. You chalked up the nine innings on a blackboard with your names. On your first turn, you had to throw a dart into the "1" sector, and if you stuck it in the "1" section you scored a run, and if you hit the small sections within the same sector, you scored two or three runs. Your second turn you shot for the "2" section, and so on. You combined scores for partners. The girls suggested they play for a drink, and the guys agreed. After a while, it became evident they had done this before. The guys were going to have to concentrate to do well. That was difficult, as both of them were concentrating on the curves of the other contestants. The blonde didn't seem to be wearing a bra. She was showing off little points on the front of her blouse that drew a lot of attention. Tommy began to think that the new look and attitude in Slim's might be a change for the better.

He kept checking for signs of interest, but wasn't sure. She didn't brush up against him, or talk dirty, or even suggestively, none of that. She and the other girl sat down at their table between turns, and had animated conversation. The only thing that changed, as the game progressed, was that a third guy, a young guy, had come over to the third girl, perhaps seeing the opportunity. If these two were paired up the other would be available. Before long, the young guy was buying drinks for all the girls. They weren't drinking cheap beer, either, but mixed drinks. Slim's, like most Baltimore neighborhood bars, was mostly a beer joint, or, for those who wanted to get a buzz faster, a shot and a beer. Fancy mixed drinks were new to Slim's, and mostly ordered by women. You almost never heard anybody ask for a glass of wine.

By the sixth inning, Tommy was getting a strange feeling about the group. At times, he sat down with John and Brian, and stole some looks around the bar. The young guy, who John said was a friend of the guys who now owned the place, was still fetching drinks for all the girls. Neither Terry nor Tommy had been able to hit on their partners, or, as sometimes might happen, switch allegiances to better their chances. Then, he saw a confirmation that things weren't "Jake."

As he looked back over his shoulder, he saw his blonde partner sitting very close to girl number three, who was actively engaged in running her hand up the blonde's skirt. Similar events happened with Terry's partner, and he noticed that the three girls were drunk, and had eyes only for each other. He took Terry aside in the seventh inning of the dart game.

"You see what I see? I think these girls are right from the Duchess Bar in Greenwich Village."

"Yeah, I was just goin' to talk to you. Looks like a bunch of "lesies," and we got no chance here. Different strokes, ya know? Still, it's too bad, I'd like to give that brunette a little therapy, you know, change her thinking, but I know better. Let's finish the game and forget it."

The game ended with Terry and the brunette barely winning. Tommy's blonde partner actually bought the drinks for the winners, surprisingly to Tommy. It was probably the only booze any of the girls had paid for all night. The Youngblood was still sniffing around, and as Tommy and Terry went back to their own table, he seemed to perk up. Now the field was wide open. Maybe he had some guy fantasy about all three of them, who the hell knew? The four coaches had enough, and left. They walked as far as the little parking lot by the side of the building when Tommy stopped.

"Hey, you guys go ahead. I'm going back in for a second."

"What's up, Tommy?" John said.

"We can't leave that young guy like that. He's going to spend his paycheck with those girls. I'm going to warn him."

Tommy walked back into the bar, and the young guy was at the bar again, ordering another round for the four of them left at the table. Tommy sidled up to him.

"Hey, kid, look, my friends and I are outta here, but I wanted to warn you. You're not going anywhere with those females."

"Hey, how the hell do you know? You guys are too old for them maybe, huh?"

"Well, maybe, but check out the action under the table while you're putting drinks on the table. See ya." Tommy left, feeling better that he had done his duty as a right-thinking guy in a bar. If the kid continued now, it was his lookout. "Too old," he had said. *For chrissakes, too stupid is his problem.*

He had Alex over after school on the next day, Wednesday. It wasn't exciting as he insisted on the kid doing some homework at the little kitchen table in his apartment, and going to bed early. He took him to school the next morning, and was reasonably happy that he was part of this routine, too, not just the weekend stuff and the baseball. He promised the boy that he would barbecue that coming Saturday. Then he went home, cleaned up and put on some good duds for the sponsor-getting trip that day. Brian showed up about 11:00 a.m., in his gray business suit, as usual.

Brian had a bag of new hats in the car and a file of contracts in his briefcase. He had oral commitments from several places already, and had called them and told them he would be by today to pick up their checks. The others he would try to sell. They could sign a contract, and he would hound them for the money until they paid up. He did it every year, and he was terrific at it. Tommy was just there for back up. Brian would talk about the kids, the coaches who donated so much time, the other businesses that helped, the health of the community, the moral obligations, the good advertising, and back to the kids again. He would tell them how many coaches, wives, and parents went into their place of business, how much that was worth, and how negative it would be if their company names weren't on the shirts this year. He would smile all the while. He was the kind of guy who could do motivational lectures and succeed at it. But, Tommy noted, there was a down side to it -- his wife resented all the time he spent with it. She would complain about their daughter, who did not play -- what about her? On and on it would go. Tommy always tried to back out when caught between them. They could be so wonderful as a couple that it seemed a shame.

The first stop was Mario's Pizza Palace. This was the one sponsor Tommy had gotten on his own, the year Alex played in the 8-year-old league, and he was expected to close the deal, keeping Mario part of the mix every year. It wasn't a hard sell once you knew Mario. They went into the little restaurant, not much more than a large kitchen.

"Mario, how ya doin'? You know my friend, Brian. We brought you a little present."

"Yeah, I know you-a guys. You want money for the kids. For baseball. Then you probably want a free sub, huh? You guys a-gonna bankrupt me."

"No, no, Mario. No sandwich. The other part is right, though. Brian, what do we have for our friend today?" Brian pulled out a new, standard issue, green and white, official City Heights baseball cap and a contract. He told Mario how he would get a plaque with a color picture of the team he sponsored, and how his business name would stay on the kids' uniform shirts for another year.

"I don't need a contract. You wait right here." Mario disappeared into the small, back storeroom, and came out with $200 cash. He handed it to Tommy. There was no one else in the place, and Mario knew he could count on the guys not to spread the word that he kept cash hidden in the back.

Like most small businessmen in the neighborhood who dealt in cash it was never all in the cash register. Tommy knew that when Mario left at night, he checked things out carefully, and carried a pistol, going out the back door some nights, the front others. It was an unfortunate sign of the times.

Tommy shook his hand, as did Brian. They handed him a receipt.

"It's for the taxes, Mario. We are a non-profit group, you know. And the kids who play, they love ya and we're going to tell everybody to come down here for pizza and subs."

Tommy was glad he had delivered. It was the only place he felt responsible for signing. If Mario backed out it would make him look bad, not to mention the cost of reprinting shirts for a whole team. The club had some generic shirts for each age level they could use, with no sponsor's name, but within a year, you needed to get another sponsor and reprint. There weren't enough blank shirts to go around. It seemed that repeat business was the best kind, just like in Brian's business, or any other. They always had to order a few new uniform pants or shirts each year, but if they lost a team's sponsor, it was tough. Their club wasn't big enough, and the neighborhood wasn't rich enough, to handle very many losses like that.

On the way towards Irvington, Brian went over the sponsors. He already had checks from Slim's, whose new owners took two teams, the law firm that shared his office building, the local community association, the post office, fire station, and the police. The lawyer was the only one who put his phone number in the allowed number of spaces they could print on a shirt. Maybe he was smarter than the others were, or maybe the others believed everybody in City Heights knew of their businesses, and where they were. Ricky's Italian Carry Out would again sponsor Alex's team, the Giants, and they had paid months ago. Brian was on his yearly roll and wanted to finish it. Next, they stopped at the City Heights

Auto Shop. Of course, Brian took his own car there, and sent a lot of business their way. The greasy manager had no chance. They waited around for the check. Brian passed hats around, and showed some pictures of the kids. He could melt the heart of the toughest mechanic.

Back down the street, and a block off the main street of the neighborhood shopping area, right across from the only grocery store in town, was Jimmy's Liquors and Deli. It was a tough little store, and had frequent trouble. Blacks and Whites alike bought liquor there late at night, and the place was frequently checked to see if they sold to minors, or after hours. A handful of parents, mostly the deeply-religious ones, didn't like the advertising of places like that on kids' uniforms, but the club always needed money, and they almost never turned anyone down. The two guys looked a little out of place, dressed up as they were -- one in a suit, the other with a tweed sport coat. A couple of guys were sitting on the sidewalk, early in the afternoon, drinking beer or whiskey out of containers hidden in little paper bags. They eyeballed the two as they went in, but said nothing. *Yeah, that's right, we look like cops.* The owner was in, and, of course, his name was Jimmy. He was a big, tough guy, and rumor was he kept a loaded shotgun right under the counter. You didn't want to be in the cramped store when something went down. Yet, underneath, he was a pushover for baseball. He loved the Orioles and always had their games on the TV.

He knew his customers, which ones had kids on the neighborhood teams, and how they were doing. You could go in there anytime and discuss stats with him. He forked over the check and took the hat, but put in on a shelf, not on his head. There were several others already lined up along the rows of hard liquor bottles on a shelf behind the counter.

By this time it was the middle of the afternoon, and they went a couple of blocks down to Slim's. That sponsorship was secure, but they went to show the flag of appreciation. They ordered sandwiches, but not beer. There was more work to do. They walked two blocks down to the Horseshoe. That bar was a place Tommy didn't go into much. It wasn't as sociable, or as sports-oriented a place as Slim's. It was a hard drinking place. The down and out went in there to get messed up. Sometimes you saw a more regular neighborhood resident, but almost never a single woman, at least not the type Tommy cared to meet. They only served bar food, the kind you didn't need a full kitchen to prepare, just a toaster oven. However, a sponsor was a sponsor, the guys understood. What the hell. It was for the kids that they went into places like this. You couldn't avoid all the bars because there were too many of them. Baltimore was a hardworking, mostly blue-collar town, and the style of the local bars helped define every neighborhood. The upscale suburbs existed, of course, but they were far from City Heights. This time, in spite of his call ahead, the owner wasn't there. The barmaid, who had seen her better days, said that the owner didn't authorize her to sign any damn contract or give out any damn money. She only took money in, she said, not paid it out, and did they want a drink? The boys left.

The next place was Max's Bar. This establishment existed in the basement of a three-story row house. It had been there for years. No one knew how it qualified for a license, as it was right in the middle of a residential street. The guys parked parallel to the curb. There were no parking meters there, as there were on sections of Frederick. It was after working hours now, and some of the locals were stopping in for happy hour. Max wasn't there, but he had left the check with the barmaid. Tommy hoped that would be it, a quick in and out, but Brian thought they should at least have a beer there, to show support. There was no such thing as one beer around there. After a couple, Mr. Real Estate was hustling the barmaid to buy a row house. "It's just business," he would always say. Tommy dragged him out of there and believed the evening was over. Coach Brian said they had one more stop.

A few of the club's players came from a neighborhood to the south called Arbutus. The club had no exact boundary for territory. If a parent from Arbutus wanted to bring the kid to practices and games, and they had room, he was welcome. This, of course, led Brian to the belief that they should start getting sponsors from that area, too. He had a preliminary talk with the owner of a restaurant and bar there, and thought he could close the deal. They had done very well as it was. With a successful Opening Day sale of food and drinks, and the annual crab fest, together with the sponsors, the club would survive another year. They would be able to pay the umpires, replace the worn out uniforms, and have enough bats and balls for all the age levels. Tommy told Brian that he was pushing his luck, but they had shot the evening already, so he agreed.

It started to drizzle by the time they parked in the alley behind the restaurant. They walked around to the front, went in, and checked the place out. It was bigger than most of the bars in City Heights. The bar was to the right, and there were about fifteen tables for dinner to the left, separated by a waist-high wooden wall. They sat at the bar. Brian ordered another beer, but Tommy was getting full, and ordered a glass of white wine. People in Baltimore would sometimes look at you funny if you ordered wine in a neighborhood bar, but this place seemed to be trying to be a little more upscale. He had a sport coat and tie on, anyway, and although you would never describe him with that new term, "yuppie," it might be expected from one dressed like that. As long as you didn't act like a fag, people eventually left you alone. In the Horseshoe, he would never order wine.

They ate snack food at the bar, drank too much, and let it get late. The owner was working the restaurant part, and it was hard to get him aside for very long. Brian worked his magic, but the owner would only give a verbal commitment -- no check and no signed contract. He vowed to come back tomorrow, earlier in the day, before the lunch hour, and close the guy then. Tommy prevailed on him to leave.

As they walked behind the building, down the alley, in the rain, Tommy became aware that someone was following them. A quick sideways glance confirmed it. He was young, tall, alone, and wearing a windbreaker. He had his hands in his pockets. Tommy had not seen him coming out of the bar. He figured that the guy must have been hiding in the shadows, seen the two of them perhaps a bit unsteady on their feet, and was ready to pounce. It was a situation he had been in before in his travels around many waterfronts. He nudged Brian to get him ready, but there was no need.

"You know," Brian said loudly, "I hate it that we have to carry these things even when we're off duty." He was reaching inside his coat, fumbling around. Another step and they both wheeled around at the same time, to face the potential attacker. He was high-tailing it back to the street.

"You dumb bastard, if he had a gun, your faking like a cop might have forced him to use it!"

"Nah, it's two against one, and he won't mess with cops." Brian was laughing, but Tommy was glad when they found the car and drove away.

They drove slower than necessary, as most folks do when they know they've had too much to drink, but they made it. As Tommy got out at his apartment, Brian dropped another baseball chore on him.

"Hey, Saturday morning a bunch of us are meeting down at Simpson School to fix up the fields. Tryouts are only a week away, and Opening Day two. I know you can come down and work with us." The son-of-a-bitch was smiling again.

"I don't even have a lawn mower, for chrissakes, what can I do to fix up the fields?"

"No problem, we'll have plenty of gear. Besides, I bet you can borrow an edger or rake from your landlord. See you there at eight." He drove off, secure in the knowledge that

Tommy would pitch in as usual, and probably bring Alex with him. Tommy and his boy could spend the morning working on the baseball fields, and then play racquetball, rent a movie for Saturday night, and that would be his day. As he quietly let himself into the furnished apartment, he vowed to give Maria a call the next day. Helping the kids was great, but he had no social life. Drinking with Brian was okay for the male ritual, but he needed more than that.

Chapter 5: The Players

Tommy woke up at 6:30 Saturday morning, and, as usual, limited his breakfast to several cups of black coffee and a vitamin pill. He couldn't remember when he had gotten in the habit of not eating breakfast, but he didn't worry about it. The landlords were up early, as was their habit, and he borrowed an edger and a steel rake. He pulled up at Alex's house at 8:00, but the kid wasn't ready and the usual scene of the ex hitting him with all kinds of questions, demands, and requests for more money was repeated. He told Alex to bring his glove, and promised some practice after they finished their work. It took a half hour, but he finally bailed out of there and drove down to the school. Several of the guys and some of their wives had already begun organizing things.

There were three fields behind the school. The 9-10's played on the one closest to the woods, the 11-12's played on the one which bordered it back to back, and the 13-14's used the one farthest from the parking lot. The 8-year-old teams played on two separate fields about a half-mile away. Those fields were smaller but big enough for the balls hit by the youngest kids. Right beyond the Simpson School fields was a Catholic High School, St. Joe's, and they had their own playing fields. Some of the City Heights kids ended up attending St. Joe's, at least some who could afford it and were Catholic. The fathers there were known to be very strict, and the private school seemed to buffer the inner city from the nicer private schools out in the suburbs. The kids wore ties to school, but did not behave as well as one would think. One advantage to having St. Joe's right there was that when they weren't using their ball fields, you could put some kids on it for practice. There was no fence separating the private school grounds from the public ones, and nobody ever kicked kids off the grounds. Sometimes the priests would drift down to the club's fields, to watch or offer encouragement.

Although the city maintained the three kids' fields, they didn't mow them often enough, and rarely did anything else, like laying down chalk lines or reseeding the grass. There were large trees all around the perimeter of the open fields, a playground for little kids, and a flagpole. Tommy did not know who put the stars and stripes up every weekday, but the flag was always there. The club used a flag raising as part of its Opening Day ceremony. Baltimore was proud of its patriotism as well as its baseball.

After some chatter and meeting a few parents he didn't know, Tommy went with the group that was doing the 9-10's field. As usual, it needed work. The field backed up to a small stream that ran through a ravine along the west side of the playing area. There was a climb of about twenty feet up to the street level behind the ravine, and there were row houses all along it. Some of the kids lived right there. There was a decent backstop, the kind that had an angled part at the top extending over the area behind home plate. There were no dugouts, just plain wooden benches with no backs, although chain link fencing protected the benches from foul balls. A cement retaining wall about two feet high ran along behind them. The idea was to keep water off the fields if the creek flooded. Fans brought their own chairs, or sat on the wall. During games, the home team chose which bench to use, and most took the first base side, as that provided a little shade in the late afternoon. You could roast on the third base side if the sun was bright, yet Coach Kirk preferred that one. He liked being able to yell at the kids rounding third.

The Giants were well represented -- coaches Tommy, Brian and Terry, with two complete sets of parents. Brian went with the 11-12 year old group, as they needed help, and he took his boy, Derek, with him. They divided the lawn mowers and rakes, and set to work. Some parent Tommy didn't know named Frank seemed to want to take charge of the 9-10 field. They began by mowing the infield, setting the blades to cut closely. They had two mowers, and Tommy took one and fired it up. There was much discussion about what pattern to use, but in the end they went counter clockwise, from the mound out. One mower followed the other, overlapping, and the little infield didn't take long. The mowers moved to the outfield, going parallel to the infield dirt, back and forth, farther and farther away from home plate.

At the same time, Frank dug around the location of each base, finding the spike used to secure the base. The youngest league didn't tie theirs down, out of concern for injury, but the older leagues did. They were all amazed that home plate was still there, and looked good enough for another season. One mother had a rake and was molding the pitcher's mound into shape. The kids who were there went to get some dirt from the creek bank, and helped her fill it in to a decent height. Nobody measured it. By the time Tommy was taking a break and the outfield was about half mowed, Frank and his wife were working with the edger, cutting a neat line for the inside and outside arcs of the infield.

The mowers cut arcs farther and farther out until they figured they had mowed farther than any kid in that age group would hit the ball. The outfield of the 11-12's backed up to it, and they would meet the cut line. There were no fences on any of the fields. When you hit one out there, it was "all you could get." The richer little leagues would have fences, many adorned with paid advertising, but not in City Heights. After a break, some adults worked on the dirt paths from home to first and from home to third while others raked and packed the infield. They all picked up rocks and pieces of broken glass. The last chore was laying down chalk lines. The city would do some work during the season, but they wanted the fields ready for Opening Day, when each field would be used all day long. It would also be nice for the teams who were already practicing. Most coaches, including Kirk, were already working with the kids from the previous year that they knew would be on their teams.

There wasn't much anybody could do with the teams' benches, but Frank went back to his truck and came back with a hammer and some nails. He drove some long nails into the loose boards. The benches weren't long enough for a whole team, but the club couldn't afford better ones, and they would have to get permission from the city to change anything that was structural, like benches or backstops. Liability issues, the city said. Lawyer bullshit, they thought in City Heights.

It was almost noon, and the 9-10 field crew took stock. It looked damn good, they supposed. One of the women suggested they pick up trash behind the bench and backstop area, and although no one wanted to, they knew it was a good idea. There were bits of broken glass, and pop-top tabs, as well as the paper trash. If you went farther back, into the wooded area, you could find all kinds of other things, some of which the nine and ten year olds would not recognize. The woods behind first was where the kids would go to pee during a game, but most coaches made them go with an older kid, in case there were any of the neighborhood thugs hanging around the wooded area.

By one o' clock, they pronounced it finished. They were, justifiably, proud of their work. A good-looking field helped the kids feel better, just as a clean uniform did. City Heights wasn't among the fancy areas of town, but it didn't have to look like crap unless you let it. As a final touch, Frank brought over a couple bags of grass seed from his truck, and spread it around.

The kids wanted to play on the field, and Tommy, Frank and a couple of others gave them some batting practice. It was the kids' favorite thing to practice. They knew that coaches would not burn 'em in too fast and hitting was always more fun than infield drills or running sprints in the outfield.

The other groups quit too, and everybody packed up their lawn care gear to leave.

"Hey, Tommy, c'mon, let's get a cold one at Slim's. We'll buy the kids a burger or dog, they look hungry. Whaddya say?"

"Brian, I'm game, but it's early in the day, don't you think? And, what about Suzanne, does she expect you to come right home, with no beer breath?"

"She'll be fine. Hell, it's Saturday, she has things around the house to do, you know, let her do the laundry or something."

"You dumb bastard. Okay, let's see if the boys want to go."

They did. In ten minutes, the two dads and their sons sat down at a table in the back of Slim's. During the afternoon it wasn't too bad in here for kids. Late at night was another story. The Orioles were on the TV. They were beating the Red Sox, and all was well in the bar. Tommy noticed the young guy from the dart game. They exchanged glances, but the kid said nothing. If he had heeded the advice, he might have said something, but it appeared he hadn't. If, by some miracle, he had made out with any of the girls, he surely would have bragged about it -- he clearly recognized him. *Ah hell, I have made mistakes myself, wasting time and money on the wrong girls.* The four ordered burgers all around, cokes for the boys, draft for the men, and sat around, talking to the kids about baseball, and feeling good about the morning's work. Tommy didn't want any more sports that day, as he felt old and tired, and his back hurt. He hadn't thought that would happen to him until he was over 40. He canceled the Saturday racquetball with Alex, but Alex didn't mind, because Dad promised to rent a movie and do a barbecue for supper.

After two beers and the food, they all left. Brian would go home, late again, to face the music. Tommy and Alex went to the grocery store and bought steaks and French fries for supper. The weather was getting warmer all the time, and in addition to baseball and crab fest time it was barbecue season.

After watching some baseball on TV, it was almost dark by the time they got the portable barbecue out of the landlord's shed in the back, set it up, and lit the fire. Every time he went to the shed, he couldn't help but notice the tin garage back there amongst the weeds. Inside it was a Hudson automobile, he guessed from the late 30's, just sitting there, rusting away. He had asked Mr. Walker about it, but his landlord would only shake his head and say that he had given it to his son-in-law on the occasion of his marriage to his only daughter. Further, that the son-in-law said he was going to restore the car, but hadn't started yet. The marriage had occurred over twenty years ago. Tommy asked him a couple of times if he could somehow buy it from him, but he always said no, it was not legally his anymore. It made the old man sad to talk about it, so Tommy never mentioned it anymore. Coach Tommy believed it was a damn shame. He lit the coals.

The cookout went well. It was good father and son time. Tommy's secret to cooking outside was to soak hickory wood chips in a bucket of water, and to spread them on the hot coals while he cooked, surrounding the meat in clouds of smoke. They both liked the flavor and Tommy hadn't had too much to drink to burn the steaks. Normally, he let Alex sleep on the couch in the living room, and watch TV as late as he wanted to. Alex was more tired than he realized, and the kid fell asleep about 9:00. Dad carried him into the bedroom and tucked him in. He would sleep on the couch himself. Then he wondered if it was too late to make a call. *Saturday night. What the hell, it's not too late. She's either there or not.* He dialed Maria's number. She answered.

"Hello?"

"Hey, Maria, it's Tommy. Is it too late to call?"

"No, hey, welcome back."

"Thanks. I heard your message. Figured I'd see how things were with you."

"I'm fine, you know -- okay. I left you a message because I wanted to see you again. We only met in that lounge once, and, well, I think you're cute, and I know you're single, unlike some of the married guys who come in there and hit on everybody."

"Well, Maria, those are words that warm my cold heart. What's a good night for you next week?'

"Well, you know I have two kids. Can't get a night off sometimes. How about going to the PWP meeting with me Thursday night?"

Christ, I knew it. She's fishing for another member of Parents Without Partners. "I don't think I can make the meeting. Listen, I'm not much for group therapy sessions."

"Okay, how about meeting at the same lounge we met before. You remember that a few of us girls like to stop by there, about 9:00, after our meeting."

"Thursday, nine o' clock at the Starlight Lounge, off the Beltway. Okay, young lady, you have a date."

That was how they left it. He didn't think it counted as a date since they were meeting somewhere and she would have a couple of girlfriends with her. *Women are getting smarter about that.* Instead of going out with a stranger, they would meet a couple of times first. Each would drive to some public place, and talk, drink, dance, whatever. If you got along, and were convinced the other person wasn't an ax-murderer, then you could make a real date. Still, he was interested. Maria had a terrific figure, for one thing, and seemed like an honest person. He remembered her saying that she was single, but there had been no mention of her ex. She had been married at a young age. She was 33, but had a fourteen-year-old daughter, and a ten-year-old son. Her boy didn't play baseball, she had said. Other than that, and the way her body felt when he had danced with her, she was a mystery -- a possibility, or maybe a potential friend, but maybe not the kissing kind of friend. Her comments, however, induced him to find out more.

The next several days went along easily. Coach Kirk was having kids down to Simpson every day, working drills with all the kids who were, or wanted to be, on the Giants. Tommy went to a couple of the practices, including Wednesday's. By the time Kirk was through with the kids, they were tired. Alex stayed over at the apartment, did a little homework, ate some spaghetti that they cooked together and went to bed. Before he knew it, it was Thursday night, and time to meet up with the PWP ladies at the Starlight. He wore a sport coat with a white shirt, but no tie. He knew it would be an older crowd, and it was a nightclub, but he didn't like ties.

He drove west on Frederick then onto the Baltimore Beltway. About ten minutes later, he took the Liberty Heights exit. The lounge was on the right, and it bordered the freeway. It was just before nine. As he walked in, it looked like an odd place for Maria to want to meet. She lived in Catonsville, and there were decent places right there, which would be convenient for both of them, but he had heard that this particular lounge was, at least on Friday nights, a haven for the divorced and over 30 crowd. He fit that description too, but he was uncomfortable with it. The band they had from Thursdays to Saturdays was a trio, and they played mostly oldies for dancing. It made him feel old to remember all the places he had been to in the world where a band rocked the place, and there were girls in their 20's, without kids, thank you, who would dance with him. He didn't think he looked as old as he was. There had been girls as young as 22 in Australia who danced and drank with him, no problem. Why should he hang out with folks his own age? He knew the answer, as many of the younger ones only wanted him for an evening, to spend his cash on them, like the young guy in Slim's had done. He knew the reality was that he didn't have it all together anymore. He wasn't a great catch for anybody, his age was beginning to show, and he wasn't likely to have any luck with women who weren't divorced with kids. He wondered if there was a column in the new personal ad section of the paper that used "DWK" as designation.

The trio was playing soft stuff, and the bar was about half full. As his eyes adjusted to the dark, he looked around and didn't see Maria. Her meeting started at 7:30, but no one knew exactly when it would be over, she had told him before. Still, he valued punctuality, and made his mind up that if she didn't show by 9:20, he would be free to leave. There was a large, oval-shaped bar on the left, an open area where people could just stand around next to it, then the dance floor. There was a railing that separated the standing area from the dance floor, and it was wide enough to set your drink on. The dance floor was large and he supposed that was one reason the DWK crowd came in there -- it was like high school dances. You could ask a woman to dance right there so you didn't have to come on to her with some stupid one-liner. If there was any spark on the dance floor, then you could ask her if she wanted a drink, like in the old days, then sit with her. There was also a large area of tables behind and around the dance floor, and you could order dinner or drinks there.

He recalled some of the bars he had been to with some younger guys off the ship, in Australia. Nobody asked for a dance. If you wanted to dance to the noise they called music, you just went to the pit and started gyrating. If a girl liked you, next thing you knew, she would be right there with you. The younger guys had been shocked when he had tried the old-fashioned method of going up to a table of girls and asking one of them to dance. Tommy liked the old way better, even if it did make you feel older. His other reservation about places like this was that although he knew many divorced women were desperate, and could be easy pickings, they also needed a new husband to help with the kids and bills. He supposed that was why he had avoided most meat-market bars in the past, yet Maria had seemed different. When he met her, she hadn't immediately whipped out her wallet pictures of her kids.

As was his habit, he rounded the bar completely, checking it out. Then he ordered a glass of white wine, not caring whether it was a macho drink or not. He drifted over to the standing area, and scanned the dance floor for her. She wasn't out there, which was good. It would have been rude for her to arrange a meeting and already be dancing with some other guy. He suddenly became aware of someone to his side.

"Hey, you want to dance?" He turned to his left and saw a slim woman who had to be at least 55. She was petite, and, in her youth, must have been a real looker.

"Thanks, hon', no. You know what? I'm supposed to meet someone here, no kidding. But if she doesn't show, sure, I'll come find you, and we'll tear up the dance floor."

"Well, okay, but maybe you don't know what you're missing."

At least she was smiling as she sauntered away, back to her barstool. It was a refusal without a put-down, or insult. There was no need for that, and he didn't like it when some babe did it to him. *She must be terribly lonely to hit on a strange guy like that.* He also realized that he had better get away from the dance floor, as it was now apparent to him that if you stood near it, by yourself, you were looking for a dance partner, if not more. Before he settled on a barstool choice, however, he saw Maria and a couple other women come in. They headed straight for him. They would now save him from the over-50's.

They exchanged hellos, Tommy thanked her for being on time, and they decided to get a table near the dance floor. On Fridays or Saturdays, the girls said, that was difficult, unless you made a reservation to have dinner. Tommy wondered how often they came in there, but said nothing. Maria was looking fine, and Tommy wondered if any of it was for him. She had on a mid-thigh-length blue skirt, high heels, and a white, frilly blouse with the top two buttons undone. Her cleavage was spectacular. He no longer wondered if women with great boobs did that on purpose -- he knew they did. They rehearsed it in their minds, what effect the show would have on a guy, and what kind of fantasies he might think of, staring at the display. She was about 5′5″ tall, and slightly dark-skinned. He didn't know if she was partly Mexican, Puerto Rican, Italian, or something else, but he didn't care. She didn't overdo her makeup. The lipstick was subtle, not too bright, and she smiled a lot. Her hair was almost black, shoulder length and slightly curly. He remembered his first dance with her, and how clean her hair had smelled. He wondered if women knew that the smell of clean, long hair was more of a turn-on than perfume. They probably did, but he had been to so many foreign countries where it seemed the women overdid the perfume instead of taking more baths. He figured he could find a lot worse than her, as he sat down and chatted with the three of them. One of her friends looked about 29, and was thin and pretty. The other was at least 40, and needed to lose some serious weight. Even so, he wondered if they could imagine how he felt, after months at sea with no women, dreaming of just such a situation, sitting with three available women at a table.

They yakked for a while about jobs, kids, Australia, the music, and a lot of other nonsense. Soon, the other two left for the ladies room, leaving Maria and Tommy alone.

"Look, Tommy, you really ought to go to PWP sometime. We never have enough men."

Oh, Christ, this is it. "Yeah, well, maybe, you know? I think I can handle being a single dad pretty damn good." It was defensive.

"I don't just mean that. I'm trying to tell you something. We don't know each other much, but there are lots of available women in our group. You would make out like a bandit. I mean, I like you, but if you like one of my friends better, that's okay. You like the skinny one, Darlene? Let me tell you, I've seen her naked, and she has the cutest butt you'll ever see. Just be honest, you want to hit on her right now, it's okay, I'll keep looking. That's partly why we need more guys."

Tommy couldn't believe what he was hearing. Here was a woman he hardly knew, but liked, and was physically attracted to, and she was telling him she would help set him up with somebody else.

"No, hey, that's amazing you would tell me that. I liked you the moment I saw you, and I'll tell you this, your figure is better than Darlene's any day from what I've seen, that is." He stared at her cleavage to emphasize the point.

"Okay, then. Want to dance?"

By the time they hit the dance floor, Darlene and the other friend were back at the table, and Tommy caught the smiles between them and Maria. *So, the fix was in.* When he was younger, he didn't realize women planned all these little things out, but he knew better now. Still, it was cool. She wanted him to choose right then. She was willing to let him go after somebody else she knew, but not if she invested time in a relationship. As they danced to the slow tune, he knew she was pressing her body closer to him than when he had met her. She felt warm.

After a couple of drinks and dances, the two friends left. That was probably arranged too, Tommy figured. Maria asked him if he would like to see where she lived. *Whoa, is this "it?"* he wondered. Then she told him that her kids would be there, although it would be eleven by the time they arrived, and they should both be in bed. He didn't figure she was the type to have a guy in her bedroom while a teenaged daughter was in the next room. That was fine with him. He had never yet had a woman at his place when Alex was there.

He followed her down the Beltway to the Catonsville exit. They went west, took a couple of quick turns, and stopped at a small, three-bedroom house. It wasn't palatial, but it was nice enough. It was certainly better than where he lived, and in a better neighborhood, too. He followed her in, and took the glass of cheap wine she offered. She went down the hall, and he could hear her tell a child, probably the daughter, that she was home, had a friend with her, and everything was okay. As Tommy drifted into the small living room and looked at pictures on the shelves, he heard some talk from the back about school the next day. There was a guy in some of the photos, and he wondered if he was the ex. He certainly didn't have a picture of his anywhere. She came in and invited him to sit down on the couch. She sat right next to him, close. Damn, did she want to fool around right here? There wasn't a door to close -- what the hell? She didn't seem that loose. He stayed as calm as he could.

Soon, there was a kiss, and then some roaming hands and his left hand ended up inside the frilly blouse. Her mounds of flesh seemed much firmer than he would have expected. Still, this making out on the couch seemed too reminiscent of kid stuff, and he was almost glad when she stopped it. She explained that she wasn't ready to go further with him, but liked the idea. Not with the kids in the house -- she wasn't that liberal, she said, and he was relieved. As much as he wanted to continue, he would have no idea how to explain himself to a strange kid who might wander into the room. At his age, it was either right to the bedroom, or forget it. It was time to go, and he knew it. She encouraged him by stating that the kids weren't always around, and when would she see him again? They made a date for a week from Friday. It seemed to be the only night that would work. Before he left, he asked her about the guy in the pictures.

"Is that your ex?"

"Well, no, it's the kids' dad, but he's not an ex."

"Oh. Separated then?"

"No, I'm not divorced, I'm a widow. He had cancer real bad, about three years ago, and died about a year and a half ago."

"Oh, man, I'm sorry. You didn't tell me."

"It's okay. It took a while, but I'm getting on with my life now, you know? Don't let it stop you, hon'." She showed him a picture of the four of them, with the guy in a wheelchair, at the Statue of Liberty. He had always wanted to take the kids there, and when the family knew there was no hope for him, people chipped in and they had gone there. It made Tommy feel sad, and she could tell. He almost felt guilty now, fooling around with a widow, but she hugged him hard, pressing her body against his in all the right places, and told him not to worry, she'd see him next Friday. He offered dinner, and told her he knew a nice place not too far away. That was how they left it.

Before Tommy knew it, it was Saturday morning, and time for the annual drafting of new players. The 9-year olds who were new to the 9-10 level, and a handful of 10-year olds who had never played in City Heights before, would all meet behind Simpson School. They would work out until the managers drafted all of them. Unlike Tommy's boyhood experiences of trying out for the official Little League, they would exclude no one. If your kid wanted to play, you just sent in a consent form with a copy of his birth certificate. The club asked for a ten-dollar fee but could waive it for economic hardship, and that part was confidential.

Alex went along, and he and some other kids who were already on a team separated and began working out with Coach Kirk. They went over to a field by St. Joe's and played a pick-up game. Somebody's dad umpired it, from behind the pitcher's mound, since he had no gear. By nine, the new players were ready, and the coaches from all the teams were there, with their clipboards, or scraps of paper, to write names down on. The Giants would pick last, just like in the big leagues, since they had won the championship the year before. The other rule of note was that a manager, like Kirk, could have three official assistants. If those dads had a kid coming up to the league, they could choose to have him on the team they coached. It was easier to get a boy to practices and games, if he and his father were on the same team. Yet, once in a while, a dad decided that it would be better if the kid was on a different team, and he put him into the draft. There was, then, some maneuvering for assistant coaches who had sons who were good players.

On the Giants, Kirk Junior and Alex were holdovers from last year, and, as 10-year olds, and their best pitcher/catcher battery, would be the nucleus of the team. Derek, Brian's boy, was a highly prized 9-year old, mostly because of his size, and he would avoid the draft by being a coach's son. Terry's younger boy, Rick, being ten, would be a Giant again, too. His older boy, Billy, would help coach when he wasn't playing. The more 10-year olds you had, the better off you were, since a year of experience meant a great deal at that young age. The Giants looked like they would be in good shape for returning players. They had a mix of white and black kids, big kids and little kids, and could field a starting nine of almost all 10-year olds. Still, it was important to draft as good a player as you could, and Coach Kirk had a fine eye for it. There was already some banter around the club that the Giants might repeat. That caused some kids to want to be on the team, but Kirk's reputation caused others to feel the opposite way. You could learn baseball from him, but he was tough on little kids. Some kids called him "Kirk the Jerk" behind his back, usually far away from the fields at Simpson.

Throwing and catching was first. The kids lined up in two lines, opposite each other, starting about ten feet apart, and tossed the ball back and forth. Big John, who took charge of the tryouts, would blow a whistle, and the kids would take two steps back. This continued until they couldn't reach anymore. From this, you could get a general idea who had an arm, and who could catch, at least something thrown right at him. Coaches hung around, and asked the names of players. When a coach asked you your name, you figured he saw some talent in you.

Next, they did a similar drill, only you threw the ball on the ground. The kid catching the grounder had to pick it up and fire it back as if he was throwing it to first base. After a while, they switched so the opposite line did this. Coaches wrote down names of kids they hoped could play infield.

Outfield drill followed. Coaches, including Tommy, took a group of ten kids at a time. The kid threw the ball to the coach, then, while he was running, the coach threw a fly ball he had to run to get. Not many kids made clean catches, but it could give you an idea of who could play outfield this way. They ran to their right, then got back in line, and went to their left.

Tommy remembered similar things he had done with Alex from the time he was five years old. They had played in the side yard, next to the 90-year-old house where, in happier times, he, Alex and his mom had lived together. Dad would throw grounders or pop flies, and Alex had to field them cleanly and throw it to him, chest high, and in the air. The older he became, the farther apart they had stood. Alex liked catching the high flies Tommy could throw, up high, over the roof level of the house. If Tommy threw him a ball on the ground, and he fielded it cleanly, moving his body in front of it, and made a good throw, the next ball would be a fly ball, going higher and higher until Tommy could not make it go any higher. Sometimes they hit the house doing this, as the side yard was small.

By the time Alex was eight, they frequently went down to the ball field to get more room, and to practice batting as well. Tommy was so pleased with all this, as when his boy had started playing organized ball, as an 8-year old, he had immediately become a starting shortstop. As he became stronger, he became a catcher, as he was one of the few kids that age that had the arm to throw kids out at second. Tommy knew all that catching and throwing practice had paid off. He remembered his own experiences as a kid, and wished he had had more practice. Maybe then he would have made it on one of the sponsored teams, where he had grown up, and wouldn't have had to play with the playground league. *Who the hell knew?*

Batting was last. The assistant coaches took turns pitching, while the managers kept track of who might do more than just strike out. Trying mightily, some kids just could not hit anything. Some parents cheered when their kids hit a foul ball. Tommy had learned that it was more important to choose a kid who didn't show fear, whether he hit the ball hard or not, or one who had decent form. You could work with kids like that. The players not at bat rotated in defensive positions, so the coaches could get a final look at who could field a grounder, or catch a fly ball. There were "oohs" and "aahs" every time somebody nailed one. Nobody ran to first -- the fielders just threw the ball back in to a kid who stood behind the coach who was pitching, and put the baseballs into a plastic bucket. As soon as a ball came back in, the coach threw another pitch. They didn't use a catcher, and every so often, they stopped so someone could gather up the balls lying all around the backstop area, and throw them back to the pitcher, who refilled the bucket. Each kid had ten pitches to hit.

The girl who had signed up to play was there. She showed decent form in catching, and, as some said, "She didn't throw like a girl." But in her ten pitches, she never hit one, even a foul ball, and seemed to be scared out of her wits, even though Big John himself threw to her, and lobbed them right over the plate. John told Tommy that their free lawyer had said they needed to let her play, as the parents could cause problems if they didn't. Kirk's draft list had her last.

Soon it was over, and the formal drafting process began. With the 10-year olds each team already had, it figured that each of the eight teams in the 9-10 age league would end up with about sixteen players. The bigger programs out in the suburbs had many more. Tryouts there were like what Tommy remembered from his youth with some kids left out. When they formed a tournament team, it was full of legitimate all-stars. City Heights was not that big. You figured a couple of kids would drop out during the season, and you were lucky to finish with thirteen of your original kids. There was a 30-day grace period for kids who moved into the neighborhood to join a team. Whoever was next in the draft order would get the new kid, but then it was "wait until next year." The only benefit from this was that it wasn't difficult to follow the rules and get every kid into every game. Every kid had to play two innings in the field, and bat at least once. Just like the big leagues, pitching was a key. Pitchers at this age level were limited to six innings of work a week. It protected young arms. You needed two very good pitchers, and a couple more "maybes," to make it. Since there was not time to tryout pitching with so many kids, managers drafted kids who had an arm, and hoped to teach them to pitch.

They went in reverse order from the standings in the league the last year. Big John managed a team, the Dodgers, and took the girl with his first pick. Kirk breathed a sigh of relief, as, with last pick, he feared that they would have to take her, and he wanted no part of that. John seemed to be making a statement that the club had to move forward, and accept a girl or two when the situation presented itself. Tommy reasoned that because he never had kids of his own, John was more sympathetic to those parents who only had a girl, but loved baseball. He still preferred that they have a separate girls' league.

When it was over, Tommy checked out Kirk's list, and could not fault it at all. Kirk knew what to look for better than anybody. Tommy was particularly interested in a skinny, short, 9-year-old black kid named Stevie. He had great speed, showed no fear at the plate, even though he didn't hit a fair ball, and came dressed for the tryouts in a complete, matching Orioles uniform, including wristbands. This, together with the fact that he stayed excited during all the drills indicated that he loved the game, and would work hard to make it. Speed was important for the first time in a kid's baseball playing years, as the 9-10 league was the first level you could steal a base. You couldn't lead, but you could steal as soon as the ball crossed the plate. Another kid that caught his eye was a tall black kid named Joe. He was ten and had lived in City Heights for years, but had never come out for baseball before. He had fielded grounders well, and had smacked two hits that might have gone for home runs in a real game. The downside was he didn't seem to throw very well. He was quiet, and seemed to be afraid of Kirk. Tommy figured he would try to make friends with Joe, and see what they could bring out of him. Joe was a lot like a kid they had drafted last season named Fred, except Fred could throw.

A 9-year old named Shawn, who lived a couple of houses down from Alex, ended up on the Giants. He was tall and fearless, but didn't have very good skills. Tommy figured he had potential as a hitter, but would take a full year to work on his defense. The drafting was too serious. They had to do the best they could, for the team, of course, but the kids were so young. No one really knew which of these kids would be a good player in time. It was hard to tell. The Giants drafted a few more players who would probably play outfield, and it was over. Of the last few, Tommy liked a short, skinny, white kid named Joshua. He heard some of the kids call him Josh, and noticed that his dad was there. This was usually, but not always, a good sign. He was new to the neighborhood, so, even being ten, he was in the draft. What he liked about Josh was that, in spite of his small stature, he threw very accurately. Kirk thought outfield, maybe second base, but Tommy wondered about the accuracy and strength of his arm, and whether there was more there than he showed in drills. He also liked the way the kid smiled at everybody, and called all the coaches "Sir." Like Stevie, Josh had come dressed in cool baseball gear, including rubber cleats, which many kids did not have. The poorer kids wore beat-up sneakers, and not everyone had a clean shirt on.

As the group went home, Tommy noticed a few tears from the kids who didn't get picked until the last round.

Some dads or moms had their arms around those kids, telling them that the coaches were crazy, but at least they were on a team. Everybody would get a uniform. The Giants had their usual green and white, with "Ricky's Italian Carry Out" on the back. There was only one week until Opening Day, and Kirk gathered all his new players to inform them they would meet behind Simpson Elementary School Monday to Friday, at 5:00 p.m. for practice. Tommy and Brian convinced him to cancel the Friday practice, since the kids would have to march in the parade Saturday morning, and play that afternoon. He reluctantly gave in to his assistant coaches.

The rest of the weekend went by quickly. From Monday to Thursday, the Giants practiced every day, behind the school. Kirk could get off work early, it seemed, and he always got the field he wanted before any other coaches arrived. Tommy took turns with batting practice, and hit grounders or fly balls, as the manager wanted. Kirk was never satisfied, but, by the end of the week, Tommy and Brian thought they had the makings of a decent team. Only one kid dropped out. No one knew if the practice was too intense for him, or if he just didn't like it. He never came back, and no one returned phone calls.

On Wednesday, Tommy had driven over to Memorial Stadium, and had bought tickets to a handful of Orioles' games spread out during the rest of the season. For the hell of it, he bought two to the last game -- front row, upper deck. He also bought the game in the middle of the summer when the Oriole wives had their annual auction for charity. You bought tickets for the game, and tickets to the cookout and auction behind the left field wall before it, separately. It would be good father/son time, especially now that they were both working on baseball skills themselves.

At the end of practice on Thursday, Kirk went over the schedule for Opening Day. They would meet in the school parking lot at 8:30 a.m. to form up. They had drawn a 4:00 p.m. game, against Coach Arty's team, the Cubs, and Kirk told the kids to go home in between the parade and their game, to rest. Most would hang around the park all day, though, watching other teams, and wheedling money from their parents for hot dogs and drinks. Brian, of course, had a flyer printed up to hand to all the kids. He had spent time during the week also putting posters up on telephone poles in the neighborhood reminding all the residents of the big parade. The new kids had their uniforms, and were told to make sure the shirt, with the logos and number on it, the standard white baseball pants and the baseball socks, color-coded for each team, were clean for tomorrow. A few complained about the parade, asking, "Do we hafta?" The answer was the same from all the coaches – "Yeah, you hafta."

The coaches agreed on wearing blue jeans, the club polo shirts, and sneakers for the parade. They would add cleats, if they had 'em, for games. The Giants' coaches' shirts were short sleeved, white, with a green collar, and, like all the others, had the letters "CHBC" screen-printed above the shirt pocket. When the kids went home, the coaches went down to Slim's for a last coaches' meeting before the season.

They discussed administrative issues first. They had turned in all the paperwork on the kids, so that was no problem. Josh's mom had offered to keep the scorebook for the team for each game. She only worked part-time, in the mornings, and could make every game. She had played softball as a girl and knew how to keep a book. The home team's book was official, but the routine was to check with the opposing team each inning. It was also crucial to keep track of how many innings each pitcher worked, and who was due up at bat. Some managers cheated on these things here and there. Kirk would keep most of the gear, in duffel bags, at his house. This included all the balls for the whole season, bats, a rosin bag, batting helmets, and bases.

Tommy would keep the catcher's gear, since Alex would do most of the catching, and because the mitt he used was a good one Tommy had bought. He kept the chest protector, shin guards, and the batting glove Al wore on his catching hand. Al kept his cup at home, but Tommy would ask before every game that he was wearing it. His helmet was a full one, like a football helmet, and Tommy had bought that the previous season when Alex had begun to catch. Most teams had the kids use a batting helmet turned around, but Tommy had seen catchers injured with a bat when a kid swung and missed, and it came all the way around his back. He had tried to get the club to buy them for all the kids, but the treasurer said they couldn't afford it. The better helmets were required if you caught in the official Little League.

The season had two halves and the winner of the first half played the winner of the second half one game for the championship, unless you won both halves, in which case it was over. That was what had happened last season. You played twice a week, and had a third day as a makeup for a rainout. There was usually a day or two between games, unless you were making one up. Tommy knew they needed to work harder to develop at least one other starting pitcher.

Coaching assignments were next. Kirk liked to stay on the bench, where he could keep track of everything. Brian would coach first, Tommy third, and Terry would be the dugout coach in a league that had no real dugouts. His job was to prep the kids to get ready to bat, use his calm approach to talk to them, and take subs behind the wall to warm up their throwing arms before they went into a game. Terry liked doing that, but Coach Tommy knew he made out the best. He liked coaching third and making crucial decisions to send kids home or not. Kirk did not want to use coaches' signs to the kids. He didn't think they could handle it. Brian would tell a kid to steal verbally, and Tommy would just holler and wave them over to third on the rare occasion they attempted to steal that base. The pitchers and catchers wouldn't use any signs either. Most all the kids at that age just threw fastballs. A few knew how to throw a changeup, but it frequently was just a blooper. Tommy knew that Junior was developing a curve ball. Many coaches would say that his arm was too young for that, but he couldn't say anything.

Then, they went over their starting lineup. It was Kirk's decision, but he was not above asking opinions once in a while. In going over all the kids, he seemed unhappy, mostly about the defense. He just could not understand why some kids could not turn a double play, or get under a fly ball properly. Tommy just injected his opinion that it was early in the summer, and the kids would get better as they went along.

The third beer settled it. On defense, there was no question on pitcher and catcher -- Junior on the mound and Alex behind the plate. They would start with Fred at first, Stevie at second, Josh at shortstop, Joe at third, and Derek, Rick and Shawn, left to right, in the outfield. The subs would be Danny, Henderson and Robert for the infield, and Billy, Jason, Frankie and Lee for the outfield. Brian was pleased that his boy, Derek, would start and knew that he would have to hit better than most nine-year olds to get more than his minimum of two innings. Kirk liked to use right field for three players a game, two innings each. Left field and second base were the other spots he usually rotated the subs in and out of the game, and most managers had a similar strategy. Tommy remarked that they looked strong up the middle -- pitcher, catcher, short, second and center field were all kids who could catch and throw. The corners were a serious concern, infield and out.

Next was the pitching rotation. Each pitcher was limited to six innings a week, the normal length of a game. You had two games a week, so two very good pitchers could carry you, but not all the way. You needed a third kid for long relief, or makeup games, and one or two who could give you an inning or two in relief. You didn't get extra innings for a pitcher if a game was rained out after it started. It was a fair rule to save young arms. Junior was a lock, as he had a terrific fastball, and was their only lefty. Fred was designated number two. He had pitched some games at the end of the last season, and was a big kid who could intimidate some hitters. They settled on Rick, Coach Terry's boy, for long relief, or third starter, as he generally threw strikes, although he didn't have a lot of speed. Terry seemed pleased, and Tommy knew that he had been working with him on it away from team practices. This wasn't the big leagues, but you needed to think about using a bullpen. Tommy nominated Josh for short relief, and the others seemed surprised. He was such a little kid. He won them over by asking, "Who throws the ball around the infield more accurately?" Brian wanted Alex to try it too, as he had a terrific arm, but Kirk said he didn't want to take him away from catching, but maybe he could pitch an inning or two sometime.

Batting order was next. Kirk drew it out on a scrap of paper: Josh, leadoff, then Fred, Alex, Junior, Joe, Rick, Derek, Shawn and Stevie. None of the three assistants had a problem with him batting his own kid cleanup. He was clearly their best player, at least until somebody else developed into the role. He was also a lefty, and frequently smacked line drives out to right field, where most managers put their weakest fielder. There was speed at leadoff and the bottom half of the order. Kirk had his best hitters bunched from the 2-spot to the 5-spot, and hoped to score runs in bunches with those kids, then cross his fingers the last four could get walks, or lucky hits.

Substitution patterns were last, and probably the most difficult. As in all levels of baseball, once you took a kid out, he could not return to the game. Until the new players developed or sorted themselves out as to who had potential, it was a crapshoot. After a game or two, some parents would surely be hounding the coaches about why their boy didn't play more, or why he batted last. Feelings would get hurt, eventually, as the kids knew who was a scrub, and sometimes rubbed it in. Tommy had seen kids older than ten in tears after striking out several times in a game. The nines would have the most trouble hitting. Some of the 10-year-old pitchers would be eleven by the time the season ended, and they were much bigger and stronger than the nines. A smallish 9-year old could be easily intimidated.

Tommy looked over the lineup. They had a decent balance -- six starters were ten and three were nine. Even if you had more 10-year olds, it was good for the kids and the team to develop the nines. They had about 40% black kids, and that was about right for the neighborhood. They did not have a black coach, though. He wondered if that would help, but said nothing. When you played your weakest kids was a decision to ponder. You could start a few of them to get their two innings in, and then finish the last four with your best players. One problem with that was that you could get too far behind early in the game, with the errors and strikeouts the subs made. Was it better to try to get a good lead the first couple of innings, and then hide your subs in the outfield?

They had a "ten-run rule," also known as the "mercy rule," which stated that if a team was ahead by ten runs or more after four complete innings, the umpire declared the game over. This was to prevent teams from losing by huge margins. There was no such rule in the big tournament at the end of the season. Tommy remembered several games when a team fell behind eight or nine runs early and still won the game, but it was tough. One solution for subs was to shuffle them in and out from the 2nd inning to the sixth, trying to leave your core of good players in the whole game, and not getting too far behind early so the kids wouldn't get discouraged.

By the time he got home, it was getting late. He made a quick call to Maria to confirm their date for Friday night. He would pick her up at 7:30. Her sweet voice temporarily took his mind off baseball. He also made an eight o' clock reservation at a little restaurant down the road in Ellicott City.

During the day Friday, he worked on bills, cleaned up his apartment, and checked Alex's catcher's gear. He cleaned off the dusty helmet and then used some press-on letters to spell out "Giants" on the back of it. It would be a nice surprise for their first game. He found a replacement for a worn shin guard strap at a sporting goods store. He used some spot remover on the dirtiest parts of the chest protector. He rubbed a little mink oil into the mitt. He used a little black spray paint on the bars of the facemask, to make it look newer. Alex's batting glove went in the bag, too. He made Alex use a mouthpiece, over his objections, and checked that he had a spare to bring. Alex had conveniently tried to forget it before. It wasn't just basic protection, but Alex had been wearing braces since last winter, and it was best to protect those too.

He put all the catching gear into a gym bag that he would bring to each game. Then he threw in some band aids, a roll of athletic tape, and a tube of antiseptic cream, one of those ice packs that became cold after you broke the inner bag, and, after thinking about the $2,300 he had spent on the braces, he put a wire cutter in the bag. He had seen kids with braces get hit with a baseball. Finally, he remembered he had some leather strings to repair gloves with, and he added those to the collection, along with an old pocketknife to cut them with, and needle-nosed pliers to pull the strings through holes in gloves. It wasn't particularly professional looking, but it was the best he could do. The Giants' third base coach was ready for the season.

He picked up Maria on time and unlike some other women he had known she was ready to go. She looked just fine, and Tommy told her so. She showed a little thigh, a lot of cleavage, and, as he had noticed before, had on just the right amount of perfume.

On the short drive west, through Catonsville to the little town of Ellicott City, she told him how nice it was to go out to dinner. She seemed impressed that he would spend a few bucks on her in a nice place on their first real date. They crossed the bridge over the little stream called the Patapsco River, and pulled into the town parking lot just beyond it. The town had been a mill town in times past, and was making a comeback as a touristy, artsy-craftsy place. Most of the buildings on the town's main street were made of stone. Some were shops, some were bars and restaurants, and a few were regular stores. It was a short walk to Donato's, the Italian restaurant that Tommy liked.

They waited at the bar for their table. Tommy had been there a couple of times before, with the ex, but he didn't mention that to Maria. He figured the last thing a woman wanted to hear about was an ex-wife, or former girlfriend. *Concentrate on her, talk about her, that's the ticket if you want to get anywhere.* They both had white wine, and the table was ready before they finished it. The dining room was small, with only sixteen tables, and that was one reason Tommy liked it. It was intimate, as they say, just like he had in mind for later. Since they had been out twice before, he figured it wasn't a first date. Besides, she had encouraged him the last time.

He also liked the menu. It wasn't a spaghetti house -- it was fancy Italian, and Maria seemed impressed with it. She ordered chicken primavera, and he had Veal Marsala. The waiter was good, and not intrusive. He knew enough to leave people alone, not try to be their friend during dinner. Tommy hated that, especially in a nice place, and when you clearly were on a date, and trying to get to know one another. He didn't go to restaurants to become the waiter's new best friend.

The food was excellent. When the table was clear, Tommy asked her about dessert.

"No thanks, I'm watching my figure."

"I'm watching it, too." It seemed like a stupid line once it was out of his mouth, but she smiled.

"That's good. You keep watching, you never know what might happen."

It seemed like a fastball, right down the middle, to a fastball hitter. He paid up and walked out of there, fast.

Back in the van, she kissed him and thanked him for dinner. He offered to stop somewhere for a drink. There was a nice roadhouse just a little bit down the road, he told her. She said she would just as soon go home.

Another dumb bachelor line popped out. "Your home or mine?"

"Mine, if you don't mind," she said.

Tommy's dreams of being alone with her began to evaporate. Did he misread the signals? She'd have the kids at her place, and that would be that. She knew he didn't have Alex on Friday nights, and what it would mean if she came to his place. He said, "Okay," but his disappointment must have shown, even in the darkened vehicle.

"Tommy, I bought a nice bottle of French wine for tonight. You know, I thought we could just relax at my place after dinner." She punctuated this by reaching across the divide between the seats and placing her left hand gently on his thigh. The hitter who believed he had struck out now had another pitch. Dreams of a home run flashed through his brain, kids or no kids, and he had trouble concentrating on the curvy road. They were at her house in no time.

She opened a bottle of Merlot, and poured two glasses. She had no dining room, and they stood in the kitchen, sipping the drinks. *It isn't the most romantic place*.

"You didn't really see my house last time, did you?" she asked.

"No."

"Well, it's small, but come on the tour." She led him by the hand, down the little hallway. She opened a bedroom door. "What do you see?" she asked him.

"Looks like a boy's room. Model cars and stuff."

"Very good." She opened the door next to it. "What about this one?"

"Girl's room. Stuffed animals, dolls." He began to get it.

"Do you see it yet?" she asked with a wry smile.

"It's what I don't see that you're showing me, Maria. No kids home."

"That's right, hon' -- they're at a friend's house; for the night." She led him back up the hallway to the small living room and gently pushed him down on the couch. "There's one thing I ask you, Tommy, is that you be gentle with me. It's been a long time for me, longer than I care to think about. Now just sip your wine and wait here a minute." She tuned in a radio station on the little stereo, and disappeared down the hall. He tried to concentrate on the music, but couldn't. He didn't have a clue what station was on. Then he became aware that she was standing in the doorway and he turned towards her. She was leaning against the doorframe. She had the glass of wine in her hand, a smile on her face, and wore only a frilly, green, silk slip.

"There's one more bedroom you haven't seen. Want to check it out?" It flashed through his head that she was posing like some dame from a 1940's movie, leaving him to "slip into something more comfortable," the sexy sneaking back into the room, posing at the doorway and all. It was old-fashioned, yet, it was romantic, and it worked.

"Oh, yeah. All of it." He nearly knocked over his glass and the table it was on getting over to her. *Slow down, stupid, she doesn't need some charging beast,* he told himself. He took her glass, put it down, and ran his hands up her back, around her neck to the front, across her chest, then down and up under the slip. Damn, she felt good, and the sexy slip was clearly the only thing she was wearing. She led him by the belt buckle to the third bedroom.

Driving home the next morning, he reviewed the whole night, as he supposed anyone would do when the lovemaking was new. She had been terrific, but seemed sad at times. At one point, during the height of the first time, he had detected a small tear in her eye, and wondered if he was the first since her husband had died. He hadn't asked her. He had suggested, at that point, that he go home, but she preferred him to stay the night, and it wasn't a difficult decision. She offered him a coed shower in the morning, and that had settled that. Soaping up those curves had been incentive enough to stay.

At another point in the night, she confirmed his suspicions about the firmness of her breasts. She caught him examining a small scar underneath one of them, while he assumed she was sleeping.

"What do you see now?" she had said.

"Nothing, I was just enjoying touching you."

"It's okay, Tommy, I know you see a scar. Yes, I have implants. I had some insurance money, and it was something I did for myself when I decided I was ready to date again. You don't think it's selfish, or stupid, do you?"

"Hell, no, I mean, it's great. You're so firm and shapely. I love it."

"I knew you could tell, but I want you to understand. I'm over 30, and have two kids. Guys don't realize how competitive it can be for a woman my age. There are younger women out there who look better, and there are gals my age who don't have kids, you see? I don't want be alone all the time, this gives me a little edge."

"Does it ever."

Back at his own apartment, at 7:30 Saturday morning, Tommy changed to pick up Alex and get down to the parade. He felt happy. It was Opening Day, sunny and bright, baseball season in City Heights was underway, and he had a new romantic interest. Nobody had said anything about love, and maybe it was just two lonely people spending time together, but it sure beat the alternatives. He now had her, baseball, guys to drink with, seafood, and probably enough money to handle all of it until August or later. What could be a better summer for a guy from Baltimore?

He picked up Alex without dealing with the ex, mostly because she was still sleeping. Alex was dressed and ready, and said he had some cereal. He could tell that his dad was pissed that she didn't get up and make a big deal out of this most important day, and the kid told him that Mom was going to be down at the field for their first game. Alex could get defensive about his mother, and Tommy had learned long ago to keep the criticism to himself.

The parking lot behind the school was packed. One driveway was the entrance for units and kids in the parade. Two motorcycle cops blocked the other, and behind them, the parade was forming up. Brian, of course, was in the middle of the confusion, putting everybody in order. Other club members, with lots of help from moms and dads, were busy finishing the food booths they would work in all day. President John took charge of that and did a masterful job. He would be cooking the burgers and dogs on the propane grill by himself. It also raised a good bit of money for the club, and was the only day of the season they had permission to set that up in the public park. The booths would be open until dark. They could make a lot more if they could sell beer, but it was probably better that they couldn't.

The first unit in the parade was Frank's shiny, new pickup truck, with loudspeakers on the roof. He had a microphone in the cab and would announce the event all along the route, telling people it was Opening Day for City Heights baseball, and to come down to the fields to watch the games. He had a tape player rigged up, too, and played Sousa marches. A police car followed and the driver would use flashing lights and sirens off and on during the parade. There would be no sleeping in around City Heights that Saturday. After that was a color guard from the local VFW. Some of those guys were old, but they never complained and would always volunteer for parades.

The teams were next, and marched in order of their ages, with the 8-year-old teams first. Two girls with the club's banner, spelling out "City Heights Boys Club," led them. Then, as per tradition, the team who had won the league the year before was first, in this case, the Yankees. The other teams in the 8-year-old league followed in whatever order they showed up in the parking lot. Between them and the 9-10's was a fire truck. The Giants were first in their league, and it was not lost on the kids that marching first in your league was important. After the 9-10's was the local high school marching band. They were paid for doing the parade, unlike the police and firemen, who donated their time as a community service and for public relations. Brian had paid the band director a little extra to play a lot of marches, not just tramp along. The parade was relatively short, and they had agreed. The older age groups followed in like fashion. A small unit of a dozen cops marched between two of the older age groups. One of the club members had a beautiful '65 Mustang convertible, and this was inserted, too. The only other non-baseball unit was a group of about eight Army Reservists, who marched along with M-16's. The last unit was a bunch of clowns Brian had hired. They would walk along near the sidewalk, and goof around with the spectators. Brian had also rented a Miss Piggy costume, complete with a huge head. He convinced a teenage girl to wear it. The clown unit was there for the little kids who would sit on the sidewalk, watching, but also to generate interest in what the club did. All the coaches were given some flyers to hand out, telling about the club, the teams, and how you could help out, or sign your kid up to play. Another motorcycle cop ended the parade -- his job was to make sure traffic did not creep up behind the kids.

It wasn't an impressive parade. There were no floats or huge balloons, and the whole thing could pass by your house in ten minutes. Still, it was great. How many parades of any kind came right through the little residential streets of any city neighborhood? The teams looked fine, with all the kids in uniform, and every one wearing a brand new, clean cap. The players carried their gloves like trophies. They belonged to something and it was something good. Many moms and dads of team players also walked with their kid's team. Sisters and brothers would race up and down the line on their bicycles. It was City Heights at its best -- clearly the biggest day of the year. Many parents wondered what all these kids would be doing that day, or all summer, without the club. Even if you didn't like baseball, you had to love it.

It was just after nine, and the cop in charge found Brian, told him the parade permit said to begin at nine, and he was ready to go. Brian walked down the line, high-fived some of the kids, and smiled at everybody. *He can really work a crowd,* Tommy said to himself. A brief talk into the radio, and one of the motorcycle cops, with lights flashing, took off, out of the school driveway, and down to the first intersection to block off traffic. Someone blew a whistle, the marching band began to play, and they were off on their annual trek through the neighborhood. As they stepped off, Tommy noticed the Giants players, some of whom had bitched about having to do a "dumb ol' parade," straighten up and stick their little chests out. They were proud of themselves, whether they would admit it or not. Little Josh and Stevie had the biggest smiles. They were in baseball heaven. There was hope in the hearts of the players and coaches. There were no won/loss records now, everybody was even. *Maybe this is our year. Maybe this year I'll really hit the ball, and make the all-star team,* the players dreamed.

The parade turned left from the school, and began its circuitous route through the narrow streets. There were many turns, as the club wanted to show off in as many local streets as possible. Some residents knew about it, others were surprised. The noise drew them out of their row houses. Some sat on their porches. Others, especially the little kids, came down and sat on the curb or stood on the sidewalk. People yelled at the kids they knew, and the players waved back. The people who came up to a coach and asked, "What the hell is this?" were given a flyer.

The band was true to its agreement, and played almost continuously, with intervals punctuated with the thunder from the drum line. Small children sometimes covered their ears from the din, while others marched along with the band. The Army Reservists surprised many when they sometimes stopped, aimed their rifles in the air, and fired blanks. This was very popular. After they passed by, little kids ran into the street to pick up the empty shell casings.

People along the route waved, and white and black parents stood together, pointing out their kids to each other, smiles all around. Tommy wished everybody would get along this well all year, but he knew it would not be. There were tough times in many of the houses in that neighborhood, and it seemed the older kids were getting tougher to handle every year. He wondered if the club would always have enough players, and parents to support it. *Interest the young ones, that's the key*, and it was clearly a big part of the club's efforts every year.

Miss Piggy was a big hit. The costume was very professional, and the kid inside was acting just like the TV version. She even had a purse, and hit some people with it, joking around. The color guard was the only unit who didn't wave or joke around. They were serious about their patriotism, and felt it wasn't proper to clown around. Along the route, many folks stood silently, or took off their caps when they came by, perhaps remembering their own service, or in honor of others.

The cops did a great job with the traffic. Considering it wasn't a very long parade, most of the motorists who had to wait stepped out of their cars and enjoyed it. In just over an hour, they had wound all around City Heights and were marching back into the parking lot behind the school. From there, the police, fire, and army units went home, but everybody else formed up around Field #2, where the flagpole stood. As per tradition, the coaches lined their teams up all around it, in a giant circle. Sweaty and tired veterans then presented the colors. The band played the Star Spangled Banner, just like at the Oriole games, many noted. Some kids took off their hats, but others weren't sure what to do. John had a bullhorn, and thanked everyone for their support and then he reminded them that there would be games all day, and the hot dogs and burgers were already on the grill. That was it, for ceremony. The teams who had the first games of the day split up onto their fields, and began to warm up. Everybody was thirsty, and the lines at the booths were long. Some parents had brought coolers with drinks for the teams, and soon, their thirst slackened, the kids were either getting ready to play their first game, or horsing around all over the park. The 8-year-olds left for their fields, food and drinks in hand. By 10:30, they heard the traditional umpire's call of "Play ball!" on all the fields, and the season was underway.

Tommy wasn't assigned to work the booths that day, but he knew that John would rope him into it. Soon, he was giving the parents their breaks by working the soda machine, or handling the money. John did most of the cooking, and he seemed to relish it, in spite of all the sweaty, greasy work involved. It seemed a shame he had no kids of his own.

Eventually, Alex walked home, to rest up. It wasn't too far, and during the day, Tommy didn't mind if he walked through the neighborhood, but not at night. Tommy hung around all day, as did most of the coaches and some of the players. The kids were wound up, and played catch behind the fields, and over by the playground. Some of them were going to be exhausted by the time their 4:00 p.m. game time. *What the hell. They're having fun, and baseball should be, first of all, fun.* The kids from the other team would be in the same shape.

By 3:30, the Giants had assembled near the parking lot behind field #1, their field, and Kirk was going over the lineup for the game. He hadn't changed it since the coaches' meeting. Brian and Tommy worked with the kids on the grass, throwing and catching, and playing pepper. Terry took Junior and Alex aside, and warmed up the starting battery. Cheers and groans from the field indicated the previous game was over, and they grabbed their gear and moved over to the 3rd base bench. The happy winners and sad-faced losers paraded by. Some parents had arms around kids. Others were lecturing them on what they had done wrong. A few adults made comments about the lousy coaching or umpiring, too. The season was definitely underway.

Soon, Josh's mom exchanged lineups with the Cubs, the umpire dusted off the plate, and, with the brief pre-game warm-ups complete, the game began. The Giants were the home team, and took the field first. The small crowd of parents and siblings on their side cheered and all was ready. It was a mixture of hope and nervousness they saw on the faces of the kids as Junior threw the first pitch. It was high and outside, and sailed over Alex's mitt. The Giants' quest to repeat as champions of the 9-10 league had begun.

Chapter 6: The Season - First Half

The next pitch was also a ball, and two more after that. Kirk started hollering at his kid, for walking the leadoff batter. He walked the next one, too. Alex went to the mound to talk to him about it. He had good instincts for a young catcher. He told him that he was trying to throw too hard, that nobody had gotten a hit, not even a foul ball. "You don't need to throw it so hard, but you need to throw strikes," Alex said.

Junior struck the next kid out on four pitches, and the Giants had their hopes restored. Then there was a hit, an error, another walk and another error, and before the inning was over, the champion Giants were down by four runs.

In their first at bat of the season, strengths and weaknesses became evident. Josh led off with a walk, but Fred grounded out. With Josh at second, Alex hit a single up the middle, but the centerfielder was known to Tommy to have a good arm, so he held up Josh at third. Junior smacked a double, scoring Josh, and Alex advanced to third, barely beating the relay throw from the outfield. The increase in Alex's physical strength, which had helped make him a tough little catcher, had cut down his speed since his days as an 8-year-old shortstop. Joe hit a fly ball to left, and, to the amazement and cheers of the Cubs' parents, the kid caught it. Tommy sent Alex in, though, after tagging up, and they cut the lead in half. Rick struck out, to the dismay of his dad, and the inning was over. Still, scoring some runs gave the little Giants new hope, and they ran out to their positions.

Junior looked a little better, but he walked the leadoff batter again, and Kirk was not happy. The next kid hit an easy grounder to third, but Joe threw it short to first, bouncing it, and it skipped by Fred and rolled out of play. The batter was awarded second base, as a result, and the leadoff kid went to third. Joe didn't seem to have the arm, or maybe he was nervous. This was followed by a grounder to Stevie, at second, and the smallest kid on the team fielded it cleanly and took the out at first, as Kirk had hollered for the kids to do, letting a run score, and sending a runner to third.

Outs seemed harder to come by than runs on that level, and plays at the plate were always an adventure. Tommy and the other assistants usually agreed with this strategy, except when the game was on the line in the late innings. There were times when you just had to make a play at the plate, and Alex was tough. He made good tags, but the ball had to be there. That was usually the problem. The Giants had made a reputation sending runners when coaches at older levels would not, knowing that a relay throw from the outfield was often rushed and off-line. On defense, the Giants would take the easiest out, unless they had to go home. Plays at third base were tough -- the problem was that if the fielder missed the throw, it usually ended up beyond the field of play, and then the umpire granted the runner home. A few kids knew how to back up third. Junior for one did, from the mound -- but the foul ground area was so small that it was difficult to make the back-up play. They usually threw to first, except for a grounder hit to second or short with a runner on, and less than two outs, when they did try to turn two.

Junior struck the next batter out, but something looked different.

"Hey, Kirk, did Junior just throw a curve ball?" Brian asked.

"Yeah, I'm teaching it to him."

"Isn't that tough on his arm, at his age?" Tommy chipped in.

"Nah, he's tough. I've been working on that arm since he was four, when I made him a leftie. I only let him do it once in a while." Kirk was proud of the pitch, but the assistants looked at each other behind his back. Tommy believed that no game is worth a kid's arm.

With two outs, things looked better, but the next batter hit a fly ball to right, their weakest defensive position. Sure enough, Derek didn't get it, and a run scored. The next hitter popped up behind home, and Alex made a diving catch on it, ending the inning. Junior had his head down as he came off the mound, never a good sign. Kirk bitched at him, but Terry, the ever-positive bench coach, took him down to the end of the bench for some water and tried to pump up his confidence. Hell, it was only 6-2 now, and they had limited the Cubs to half as many runs as in the first inning. Besides, they were the home team, and had been at bat only once. All the coaches told the kids they could catch up, and, at this age level, a big inning could happen at any time. It wasn't unusual to score six or seven runs in an inning. However, this did not happen for the Giants in the bottom of the second, or any other inning.

In their at bat, Shawn struck out, taking vicious swings at the ball. He was trying to kill the ball, but he did look fearless.

"Kirk, if he ever gets a hold of one, they're not going to find the ball," Tommy said, trying to be positive.

"Shit, with that swing, he'll never hit anything!"

Stevie struck out also, and looked terrible doing it. He seemed to be trying to use his tiny stature to get a walk. He never even swung the bat, even though the Cubs' starter was throwing easy pitches right down the middle.

With two outs and nobody on, they had the top of the order up again, starting with the second smallest player, Josh. He seemed to have a good eye for the strike zone, and did not swing at anything that wasn't close. He fouled a couple of pitches off, and the count went to three and two. During his at-bat, Tommy noticed his parents, sitting on the wall behind the team bench, with their heads bowed. At first, it seemed that they could not stand to see what might happen, and then he realized that they were praying, praying for their boy to get a hit, no doubt. He pointed this out, subtlety, to Brian.

"Yeah, didn't you know? They're real religious freaks, pray for victory, all that stuff. I've been to their house. Crosses and pictures of Jesus all over the place. You should hear their grace before a meal. It goes on for hours, seems like."

"You don't think it's right to pray for stuff like that, do you, Brian? I mean, it's just a game. Besides, what about the kids on the other team, don't they have just as much right to win? You think God really cares who wins?"

"No, hell, I don't know. But if it improves his hitting, so what?" Brian flashed that smile of his and laughed it off. Tommy watched the parents out the corner of his eye. Josh grounded out, and the inning was over. They hadn't scored any runs, and Kirk was raising his voice to the kids as they picked up their gloves, a bit more slowly this time.

Junior took the mound, down 6-2, and he didn't look happy. To Tommy, it was sad that he wasn't having any fun. *What the hell, it's the first game.* Kirk didn't use signs with his pitcher and catcher, but he called for a changeup or curveball with code words from the bench. Something like "give 'em the hook" would be used for the rare, but physically detrimental curve ball, and "smoke," for the changeup, not the fastball. He walked a couple of batters, gave up a hit, the left fielder made an error, and two more runs scored. The Giants came off the field in the third already looking defeated. Terry did his best to pump up the spirits of the 9-10-year olds, but he was having a tough time.

The Giants did not score in the bottom of the third. Things looked a bit brighter when they held the Cubs scoreless in the top of the fourth. They were down 8-2 and would now have to use some subs in the fifth and sixth, to make sure everyone got into the game. The Cubs had a similar challenge, so things seemed equal, but Kirk didn't feel that way. He groused about everything, out loud, where the players could hear him. Tommy and Brian had their own conversations about what to do, but stepped away from the bench area to do it. It served no purpose for the kids to hear everything, like who not to put in, for what reason, at what position or spot in the batting order. They managed only one run in the bottom of the fourth, on hits by Fred, who showed some power, and Junior, who was hitting well if not pitching up to expectations. Tommy wondered why it was at that age level, and up to about sixteen years old, the best hitters were typically also your pitchers, perhaps simply because they were your best athletes. But, by the time these same kids were in college, or the minor leagues, the pitchers didn't hit worth beans. Maybe it was because they weren't expected to, or asked to, but Kirk was the only one there with professional level experience, and he just said it was "just the way it is."

In the top of the fifth inning, they only gave up one run, and the coaches knew they still had a chance. Nine to three was not an insurmountable lead at that age. However, the players were downcast and it showed. Some parents were trying to be positive, talking to their boys behind the bench area between innings, about how they could still win. Others were bitching at theirs, telling them what they were doing wrong, or quietly telling each other what the coaches were doing wrong. Tommy knew that if all the complainers volunteered to help, they would never have a shortage of coaches.

In the bottom of the fifth, the Giants didn't score, for the third time in an inning. At this level, you would expect to score something in every inning. Nevertheless, the Cubs' pitcher just threw it over, and they didn't do much with it. Brian and Tommy talked and thought their kids were trying too hard, maybe to please Kirk, or their parents, who knew? They went out to the field for the sixth and last inning, down 9-3, and with several subs in the game. It didn't look good. Joe threw another easy grounder low to first, Danny, playing second, had one go right between his legs, and the new left fielder, Jason, missed a fly ball. Still, Junior looked better, getting two Ks, and they only gave up one run.

The top of the order was up again, and some of the 10-year olds were still in the game, including some of their best players. Kirk told the batters that they needed base runners, and the smarter ones took a pitch or two, to try to draw a walk. The Giants did not believe much in taking pitches -- kids should learn how to hit. There were times, like now, when you should take some pitches. Josh went to first base with a ground ball single, but substitute Robert struck out behind him. Alex was up next, and he belted one to left center. Josh scored easily, and, as Alex rounded second, Tommy waved his son over to third. By the time he neared the base, the throw from the outfield was in to the cut-off man, and Tommy knew he should stop him right there. Something from his own childhood must have flashed in his mind. Maybe it was the memory of only hitting a triple in his last year as a player, never a home run, so Tommy waved his son around third. It was not a smart play while being down by a lot of runs. Maybe it would inspire the team if he made it. Maybe he was giving his kid a chance to hit his first home run. It didn't matter, the relay throw was good, and the catcher was holding the ball while Alex was still ten feet from the plate. He slid in, and the ball scooted away. Safe! The Giants high-fived Alex and were rejuvenated, but Tommy knew he had gotten away with one.

The game ended like that, a 10-5 loss for the Giants. After the traditional handshake, where the kids from each team lined up and passed each other, with the usual complaints that some kids spit on their hands and so forth, Tommy asked Alex about the slide.

"How did that ball get away from the catcher, Alex?"

"I kicked it out of his mitt," he replied.

"You should have been out, but I wanted to give you the chance. Why did you kick it?"

"Look, Dad, guys do that to me all the time. That's why I get low when they slide in, and hold the ball with my right hand, inside the glove, like you showed me. We needed that run. It's part of the game, Pops."

Tommy knew some Cubs' folks would think it was a dirty play, but he hadn't taught him to do that. *It's part of the job of a catcher to hold onto the ball.* Even at that level, you teach catchers to block the plate, and the runner has the right to knock you down. Kids had done this to Alex too. Maybe his 10-year old kid was tougher than he knew. Besides, the ump had the call, and said nothing. He might have, in an instructional way, if he thought there was anything improper about the play. Good umps worked with the younger kids that way. They would make the call they were required to make, but would then take a coach aside and tell him how a kid might have done something that he wouldn't tolerate at an older level, or would get him hurt.

Handshakes over, spit or not, the players returned to the bench. The Giants gave a half-hearted effort at the old "2-4-6-8, who do we appreciate?" cheer. Kirk told them they would have practice Monday afternoon, on one of the St. Joe's fields, at 4:00 p.m. Then he became a little excited, telling them that they couldn't hit, field, or throw, and if things didn't change, they would have a rough season. He was hard on his own kid, too, and Junior was hanging his head. He slipped one "goddam" into the lecture, but backed off when Brian gave him a dirty look. You could cuss at kids at the 14-year-old level, or higher, sometimes, but most coaches felt it was inappropriate for these kids, even if they knew the words, and heard them at home all the time.

The post-game meeting broke up. Some parents were there to take their kids home, while other players began the walk home up through the woods or down the streets and alleys, alone. Brian tried to interest everybody in getting some ice cream from the truck that was now in the school lot. The driver was clever. He knew when there were games, and his timing was great. A few kids, maybe the ones who didn't have much to go home to, lined up, while Brian shelled out cash for cones and nutty-buddies. Tommy tried to chip in some cash, but Brian wouldn't take it. Kirk did not participate.

After the long day, none of the coaches even felt like going to Slim's, or anywhere else, so the group broke up. Brian asked Tommy to meet him Monday morning to return some parade costumes, and said he had arranged his business schedule to have the morning free. They arranged to meet about 10:00 a.m., at Brian's house. Alex walked towards the van for the ride home to Tommy's house. His mom was by the truck, waiting, and gave him a hug. That was good. Even though she knew little about baseball, or what he went through as a catcher, she did show affection for him and never bitched if he did poorly. It would be an early night to bed for all the tired Giants, both kids and adults. Tommy drove west, out from Simpson School, and promised his son pizza for dinner, and maybe a Sunday trip out to a park or somewhere. He also wanted to work on Alex's throwing. He always wondered if he could become a pitcher, and they were going to have to find another one to make it through the season, especially if Junior struggled. *Yeah, the season has begun.*

On Monday morning, Tommy drove his van to pick up Brian. They went around returning stuff from the parade. There were costumes to return, checks to deliver that Brian wanted to do in person, and a few more chores. The return of the Miss Piggy costume was the first chore, but Tommy wanted to go to the drive-up window at his bank first. As he waited in line to drive around the building, Brian picked up the giant Piggy head.

"Hey, put this on before you get up to the window, it'll be a riot." Tommy did it. He could barely see well enough out of the eyeholes to drive, but he pulled up to the window. The van window and the teller's window were at the same height. The young gal spoke into the microphone without looking up, as she slid the tray out.

"Can I help you?"

"Why, yes, I'd like to have some money please, hmmmm?" Tommy hollered in his best, high-pitched Miss Piggy voice. The teller looked up. She stared for a second then burst out laughing. Tommy put the bank slip in the drawer, but she ignored it. She called the other bank workers over to the drive-up window. The pointing and jokes went on for a minute, and then she gave him the money.

"Say hi to Kermit for me," the teller told Tommy as he drove away. Tommy pulled up a bit and took the head off. It was getting hot in there, and he had a new appreciation for anybody who would wear something like that in a parade. Still, the bank joke had given the rental of the outfit added value. It had made the day fun for some bank tellers, most of whom didn't make much and put up with rude customers.

The Giants had until Friday for their next game, versus the Red Sox. Then they would maintain a regular schedule of games on Tuesdays and Fridays, with Wednesdays and Saturdays for making up rainouts. Kirk worked the kids every day except Sunday, and he was hard on them. It was clear he knew so much about baseball, but so little about kids that age.

Brian saw the treatment too, and did his best to lighten things up without pissing off Manager Kirk. On Thursday, he jumped into the "end of practice -- we've got a game tomorrow" talk. Far across the fields was the flagpole, and they used it every year as a traditional punishment tool. If you screwed up repeatedly, or talked back, you had to "run around the pole." Once every year Brian used it for a joke. He had previously gathered the kids together and gave them secret instructions. When Kirk finished with his lecture, Brian spoke.

"Okay, guys, now, to end the practice, everybody run around the pole!" With smiling, laughing, huge ol' Brian in the lead, the whole team ran around Tommy. It was clear a few of them didn't know "pole" from "Pole," but they knew it was a joke, and they knew they didn't have to run all the way out past centerfield to the flagpole. Little things like that helped keep the fun in baseball. Tommy vowed to get even.

The Giants' second game was a bit closer, but they still lost, and Kirk was not happy. He took care not to use the very bad cuss words, but he let 'em have it. "We can't pitch and we can't field and we can't hit, and there's not a damn thing left for you guys to screw up!" he hollered. Tommy winced but said nothing. After they broke up to go home, Kirk spoke. He told Tommy that he had to go to New York on a big business contract and wanted him to take over the team.

"How long you gonna be gone?"

"At least two weeks, maybe more. It's with a major bank and a huge deal for us. I have to stay there until all the numbers add up," Kirk told him.

"What do you want me to do with the team, you know, for pitchers, whatever?"

"Do what the hell you want -- you're the manager now. Change something -- we're not winning as it is. If my new job continues like this, you're going to inherit the team for the rest of the season anyway."

Tommy and Brian took their boys and headed for Slim's. Over a beer, the coaches worked out a new strategy for the team, while their kids played darts in the back room. Having Kirk away meant that the mice would play and things would be different. They would start right away the next day, with Saturday morning practice. The talk energized Tommy. Without asking for it, he would have his first chance to manage a team, during a season when he had plenty of time to do it. His relationship with Alex was good, now that he was home all the time. He had every expectation that he would have more hot dates with Maria. *What more could a guy want?*

The next day, Tommy, Brian and Terry gathered the kids together on the practice field. Coach Tommy explained about the temporary change in leadership. A couple of the kids started to cheer, and then realized that Kirk's son was right there, too. He went on, about how they were not playing their best, and how all the coaches, including Kirk, wanted to try a few changes. First, anyone who wanted to try out for pitcher would go with Coach Terry. Everyone else would start practice in the field. Tommy would take the infielders and Brian the outfielders. Then he made a couple of changes. When Junior wasn't pitching, he would play shortstop. Shawn and Henderson would be backup catchers, and work with Coach Terry on that. He moved third baseman Joe to first base. When Fred wasn't pitching, he would move from first to third. Josh would move from second to short when Junior pitched, and to third base when Fred pitched. Terry's boy, Rick, would also get some infield time, in addition to center field.

As they broke up into groups, Tommy took Joe aside. He told him that he was great at catching the ball, but having some trouble making the throw to first. He was as big as Fred was, but Fred threw better because he had been pitching for two years, Tommy lied. "All you gotta do at first is catch it, and sometimes make a throw home," he explained. Joe was happy, and Fred didn't care much as long as he played. In fact, the two kids lived on the same street, and before any coach had a discussion about where Joe would get a first baseman's mitt, the two kids had switched gloves, promising to switch back at the end of the season. That move was going better than they had planned, and looked even more promising when Tommy hit grounders to Fred and he threw effortlessly over to first, where Joe flashed a big grin with every put out.

Eventually they all took a break then switched to batting practice. Tommy and Brian took little Stevie aside. He hadn't hit the ball in two games and didn't look like he ever would. However, they had a new idea for him. "Only as a temporary measure," Brian told him, "until you start smacking the snot out of the ball, we're going to teach you to bunt. You're really fast, and we need you on base. Not only that, but Coach Tommy will teach you the new secret sign for bunting!" Stevie's reaction was very positive, as evidenced by his jumping up and down and hollering about how he could do it.

The rest of the weekend went quickly. Tommy and his son spent Saturday night watching a rented movie at his little apartment, and took a bike ride at Patapsco Park on Sunday. He dropped the boy off Sunday evening before supper, and actually drove off as his ex was coming down the driveway to give him some more demands. He stopped by Maria's house for a bit, to keep things going. *Have to get to know the kids, too,* he knew, but they were polite but distant. There was something with that little group he was not a part of, but he didn't know what. He did arrange to see her on Wednesday night, which was unusual, but Tommy wanted more than one date a week, if they could arrange it. She seemed to want that also. Still, there was a bit of hesitation in her voice.

Tuesday's game was with the Orioles. Many of the little kids wanted to play for them, as they shared their name with the pro team in town, the team that had most of the local kids' sports heroes. The uniforms were very similar to the major league Orioles, and that fact was not lost on them either. Most of the kids in City Heights had orange sweatbands and an Orioles' cap, if not the whole uniform. There was a lot of Colt stuff, too, but it seemed, at least in the blue-collar neighborhood around City Avenue, that baseball was the king of sports.

Being the first game of a new week, anyone could pitch. Kirk Junior was still their best, on paper at least, and Coach Tommy started him. He walked four of the first five batters, and clearly was over pitching. Tommy went out to the mound and switched him with Rick at shortstop. As per the club's casual rules, the coach stayed out there while Rick threw a few pitches. He told him just to throw easy strikes. As he walked back to the bench, the sailor heard from the Orioles' manager.

"Hey, Tommy, you gonna play with a left-handed shortstop? Ha ha!"

"Yeah, just hit the ball to him, see what happens," he answered. Inwardly, he hadn't considered that. It looked funny. He might be the only manager in baseball with a left-handed shortstop. Before going to the bench, he stopped to holler to right-handed Josh at second to take any throws down to second. At least this would prevent the shortstop from having to reach across his body to tag a guy trying to steal second. *Hell, Junior is my best infielder. Let him play short.*

Little Rick threw it over the plate, just like his dad had been teaching him, to "play catch with the catcher." He gave up one hit, and they got out of the first inning with a grounder to third. Fred threw it easily over to Joe, who made the final out and came to the bench all smiles.

It was only two runs, which wasn't much at that age level.

In the bottom of the first they scored three times, with Junior getting a hard double. Brian reminded Tommy that Junior would now be more confident, and maybe they should switch him right back to pitcher. Taking the field for the second, that's what they did. The scorekeeper for the Orioles came over to their side to bitch about how hard it was going to be to keep track of how many innings Junior pitched. Terry explained to her that they would not overuse him no matter what, as they had respect for a kid's arm. He also explained to her that each out the kid pitched was 1/3 of an inning, and to keep track that way.

The game stayed close, with the Giants hanging on to a slim lead. Little Stevie batted ninth, and when he approached the plate for his first at bat, he stopped short of the batters' box to get the new signs from Coach Tommy. Tommy went through a quick series of ear lobe tugs and elbow grabs that meant nothing, then gave the "key," his right hand swiped across his chest. The next thing he did would be the sign. If he pointed at Stevie, it was "hit away." If he touched his nose, the bunt was on. He touched his nose, then added a couple more meaningless maneuvers, then stopped. The whole thing took about seven seconds, but the secret sign lit up Stevie's face. He stepped into the batter's box and waved his bat around like he was going to kill the ball, for added effect. It was hilarious, and it seemed that everybody in the park would know that it was all bullshit and the kid was bunting. But the third and first basemen stayed put, and on the first pitch, the skinny, little kid with the spotless uniform, matching dual arm bands, and polished baseball shoes with the rubber cleats, laid down a great bunt towards third and sped off to first. He was safe by a mile and stood on first with a smile you could see from Catonsville. It was his first hit of the year. He was clearly so happy it brought a tear to the corner of Tommy's eye. Now, Stevie stared at him for more signs, while Coach Brian, at first, talked to him.

The team now had a steal sign and Tommy couldn't resist. He gave the signs to the batter quickly. It was "hit away," as usual. After the batter was ready and everyone in the park concentrated on pitcher and catcher, Tommy gave his little player the secret steal sign. Per rules, Stevie waited until the ball reached the plate, and then took off for second. The Orioles' catcher threw a bit high and little Stevie slid in under the tag. His smile grew and Tommy wondered if he had created a monster, and if there would be any living with him now. The Giants cheered madly, for they understood that now Stevie was not an easy out. He was so small he often drew walks, but now he had added bunting and stealing. He would help the team.

The Giants took the field in the top of the sixth and last inning, up by two runs. The Orioles scored one run, and with one out had the tying run on second. Their cleanup hitter smacked a ground ball up the middle, but little Stevie fielded it, reaching across his body to his right, then spun around and fired a strike to first. Joe made the out, but the runner from second was fast, and by this time, he had rounded third and was part way home. Players on both sides, and their parents and friends started screaming. Alex was ready for a throw and collision at home, but neither happened. Joe panicked, and ran towards the pitcher's mound with his arms raised.

"Time out! Time out!" he hollered. The ump said nothing. The Giants' coaches said nothing. The Orioles' third base coach said and did nothing. The runner, now halfway home, stopped and went back to third. Then, correctly, the umpire granted the time out. The screaming from the Oriole coaches got louder. Their manager was a guy named Russell, who stuttered when he became too excited.

"You c-c-c-can't call t-t-t-time out while the p-p-play is going on!"

Others chipped in.

"Hey Tommy, where'd you learn that trick, from Kirk the Jerk?"

"Cheaters!"

Tommy and Brian went over to the umpire, close enough to let the other side hear them. They wanted the ump to know that they never taught Joe to do that. He was just new at first base and had panicked. Tommy directed some comments to the Orioles' staff.

"Hey, the kid panicked. He's never played first before. And, the ump never granted time out while your kid was running. The ump played it right. Your kid and your coach decided not to go home, that's your mistake. Nobody cheated anybody."

Tommy switched pitchers and brought Rick in again to get the last out. He struck the kid out and the Giants had their first win. The green shirts jumped up and down, and then lined up on their side of home plate for the traditional, required handshake. The Oriole manager, however, was still upset. He started to call his players back, telling them the Giants had cheated, and they should not shake hands. Brian charged over there, and for a second Tommy wondered if he would punch Russell out. After a few words, though, the Orioles lined up, and the ceremony was quickly finished.

"What'd you say to Russell about the shaking hands thing?" Tommy asked his friend.

"Well, I just politely reminded him of the club rule about it, you know, and also how embarrassed he might be if I beat his ass right in front of his whole team, that's all."

As coaches stuffed equipment into duffel bags, and players begged their parents for a drink or ice cream, Tommy noticed the usual phenomenon. It was only the parents who were still upset about the time out call. The players were fine with it. They all lived in City Heights. Some of them lived on the same street. Ten minutes from now, some of the players from the Giants would be over at their neighbors' back yard, playing catch with a kid from the Orioles or some other team. They would do this, replaying the game and practicing, until made to come in the house, or it was too dark to see the ball coming at them. As Tommy cinched up the duffel bag he kept the bats in he was aware of a stranger approaching him. The guy was black, had a mustache, was about 35, and looked very fit. Tommy was sure he had never seen him before.

"Coach Tommy?" The stranger was staring intently right at him.

"Yeah, that's me."

"I'm Stevie's dad. Name's Theo."

He wasn't smiling and this bothered Tommy. He stuck out his hand.

"Great to meet ya. Stevie talks about you all the time."

"You the guy who taught my kid to bunt?"

"Well, yeah, but hey, that's just temporary, you know? I mean, we don't believe in having kids bunt much, we try to teach 'em to hit, but after a while, well hell . . . "

Theo reached out and put his hand on Tommy's shoulder.

"Hey, man, chill. I love it. You're a hero in my house. Stevie is so happy now. He loves baseball so much, and now he can get on base more, you know? You should see it. He has a footlocker at the foot of his bed for all his sports stuff, but his Giants uniform gets laid out on top of it. His mom will have to wash his uniform tonight, and before Stevie goes to bed he will have it all laid out -- shirt, pants, socks, wrist bands, shined shoes -- it's like a damn shrine or an altar in there. You're like a God to him." Theo smiled.

In further conversation, Tommy learned that Theo was an undercover Baltimore City cop who was currently working narcotics. He talked about the job very little, except to say that he worked a lot of nights, because "that's when the bad guys work too," and to say that was why he missed most of the games. Things were a bit better now that he was on the day shift, and he hoped to spend more time with Stevie and baseball. Brian had come up by this time and introduced himself. Tommy hoped his friend wouldn't start asking Theo if he owned his own home. Instead, his large friend talked Theo into going for a beer right then. They agreed to meet at Slim's. Theo seemed to wince at the mention of the bar, but he said nothing. Terry went home.

Down at Slim's, some heads turned when Theo walked in. Baltimore was an integrated city, but at the blue-collar level, there were neighborhood places where "your kind" went, and neighborhood places where "their kind" went. When Theo sat with the coaches, however, the heads turned back around to their own business, be it television, or the attention of the few single women in the place. If you worked with the kids, you were okay. It didn't matter who you were. The two Giants' coaches knew two things - they could use a black coach, and they had a chance to get one right then.

Brian did most of the selling - "It's for the kids," he would say over and over, smiling that infectious grin all the time. Tommy kept the beer coming, in case they needed to loosen Theo's resolve. They couldn't play good cop/bad cop with a real cop. Tommy noticed that Theo sat where he had the whole bar in front of him. He also implied that he knew about the poker machine in the front section of Slim's, but as long as it was penny-ante neighborhood stuff, the cops didn't care very much about it. Finally, Brian excused himself, and Tommy noticed that he went outside, not to the men's room. He was going to get a City Heights hat from the trunk of his car.

Back in the bar, Brian laid the hat on the table right in front of Theo.

"You know we need you with us. You'll have a lot of fun too, and your boy, Stevie, will love having his dad as one of the Giants' coaches. Hey, if work keeps you away now and then, no problem, my buddy Tommy here, is off all summer, he can cover for all of us. Whaddya say?"

"You put the hat on, you're committed for the rest of the season," Tommy added. "It's our tradition. But the good news is that if you do it, we'll get you a coach's shirt, too."

"You bastards are too much, you know," Theo said. Then he put the hat on and smiled. He was in, and the Giants now had a black coach. *It shouldn't matter, but it did.* The black kids now had one of their dads on the team. It just seemed right. Brian went to the bar and brought over three shot glasses of Irish whiskey to seal the deal.

Wednesday's date with Maria was quick, but hot. They just went out for a couple of drinks at a roadhouse near his place. Her kids were home by themselves. She wanted to see his apartment, a clear euphemism for something better. At least she didn't say anything about how poor or cheap the place looked. She just went right to the bedroom. It was over before he could revel in it, or reexamine parts of her like the first time. She wanted to get home before her kids went to bed. It had seemed more like an arrangement for sex than an evening together. A couple of visits a week like that would make him forget about all those months at sea.

On Friday, they played the White Sox, and the new, positive attitude that winning a game brings, carried the Giants. New Coach Theo was there, and although he was reticent to say much about the mechanics of the game, he helped the kids get ready to bat, and his presence was beneficial. Everyone liked having the new coach except Terry.

"Whaddya doin' putting a goddam cop on the team?" he asked Tommy. Tommy was busy, and ignored the remark.

Also helping the Giants was the normal habit of the White Sox manager, Rod, who always told his players to take a strike before swinging. He coached third and didn't use signs, but everyone at the field could hear him holler to his batters, "Make 'em throw you a strike!" In Tommy's opinion, it was stupid. There were times when a young pitcher was wild, so he drew some walks doing that. Rod would say that he was teaching his kids not to swing at bad pitches. However, the feeling on the Giants' bench was that he was helping them, and hurting his own kids by limiting their opportunities to hit. The Giants' pitchers understood that they could lob the first pitch over the plate and no one would swing at it.

The Giants took a slim two-run lead into the sixth. The Sox leadoff batter fouled Fred's first pitch off, and it landed in the creek. Coach Terry had his older boy, Billy, who was watching the game and helping with the little kids, go fetch it. He brought the ball back, and it was wet and heavy. Terry pocketed the ball, and thought about the wet ball trick. The Giants were the home team, and had to supply the baseballs for the game. They would give the umpire one or two to start the game, and toss him others during the game. They used foul balls and hit balls repeatedly. It wasn't a rich league and they could not afford to use up many baseballs. When the leadoff hitter drilled a single, Terry had an idea.

Sure enough, the next batter fouled one off up over the backstop, and the umpire turned to the Giant's bench for another ball. "Here ya go," Terry said, and tossed the wet ball directly to the pitcher. Fred had seen this before, and when he caught the ball he looked over to the bench. He knew it was damp and heavy. No one said anything. It worked beautifully. The hitter hit the ball, but it made a "thud" and went weakly to short. Junior flipped to Stevie, and they turned the rare double play. That took the starch out of the Sox, and they retired the next hitter easily. The Giants' record went to 2-2 and again, they were a force in the 9-10-year-old league. Everybody celebrated, especially Stevie, who now had Dad there, and in a cool coach's shirt.

Tommy packed up the gear, and he and Alex went over to Terry's row house. He had accepted an invitation to hang out on Friday night with Terry, his two boys and their dog, and eat pizza. The golden retriever would have pizza too. It was a bit sad, but Tommy had no better place to go. He parallel parked in the street, as no one on the block had a driveway, and went in. The two-story brick house was its usual mess. Sports equipment, kids' clothes, and dog toys were all over. They stacked their dirty dishes high in the kitchen sink, but no one seemed to mind. It was a macho thing, maybe. Tommy knew they usually cleaned the place up only on weekends. Monday to Friday, the three of them were busy with school, work, and baseball. Not much else mattered. Tommy helped himself to a beer out of the fridge. The downstairs had a small living room, a dining room with a sliding door to the tiny, fenced-in yard, and the messy kitchen. Upstairs there were three small bedrooms and a bath. They didn't have the end house, so they had common walls on both sides with other row houses. It was typical Baltimore, and there were neighborhoods like it all over town.

"Where ya wanna go to pick up pizza? Mario's? Ricky's Carry Out? I'll drive if you want."

"No," Terry said, "there's a new deal around, they bring it to you. Let's do that. Hell with driving."

"What's the deal with that, home delivery, like a newspaper?" Tommy asked.

"Yeah, new company called Domino's. I think they're from Detroit, and expanding. They got a little storefront place near Jimmy's Liquors in Irvington. No tables or seats, you pick it up or they deliver it. And, get this -- if they don't get it to your house in 30 minutes, it's free!"

They ordered a pepperoni and a sausage, and Domino's gave them the exact time of the order, which the younger boys wrote down. As they hoped, the delivery guy was late. He announced his arrival with the squealing of tires as he double-parked in the little street. Rick and Billy were waiting on the sidewalk, already knowing that it was past thirty minutes. "Free pizza, free pizza!" they hollered at the unfortunate teenager who stepped out of the old car. The kids clearly had done this before. The driver had a long face but didn't argue. Domino's put a time on every pizza order, and he knew he hadn't made it. Tommy went out and gave the kid a couple of dollars for his trouble. The amazing thing was that the pizza tasted pretty good.

"This is decent you know, Tommy, but the Domino's people are nuts. They'll never make it like this. Go bankrupt in six months, you watch," Terry advised.

Tommy's weekend went quickly. He had Alex for most of it. He sneaked in another date with Maria, while Alex spent Saturday afternoon at his mom's, but noticed she wasn't as happy as usual. Something was up, he could tell, but she wouldn't say anything. Tommy tried to interest her son in baseball, but he did not care about sports at all. Tommy had wondered if he could begin to combine some Alex outings with Maria's family, but their interests were very different. Tommy and Alex liked to do sports -- baseball, bicycles in the park, or watch a game. The only sport he heard Maria mention was motor racing, something he didn't like. He wondered if she was going to give him the "I need to know if you're serious about me" speech, and, if so, how he would respond. No one was talking about love. He was just trying to have one happy summer.

His baseball world changed drastically Sunday night. After taking Alex home, he was in for the night, just watching television. Brian called him and was most anxious.

"Hey, big guy, I've got some news for you," Brian said.

"Good or bad?"

"Well, that depends on how you look at it."

"Cut out the philosophical crap, you're no good at it. What's up?"

"Kirk just called, he's back in town."

"Okay, good. He can take over again. No problem, he knows more about baseball than the rest of us put together. You and I can keep him in line with how he handles the kids."

"No," Brian said, "that's not all. He's quitting, effective immediately."

"Well, shit, I guess his new job will keep him away. He warned me that could happen. Good thing is I can't ship out all summer, I can put the time in with the team."

"Well, that ain't all, big guy," Brian added. "He's taking Junior out of City Heights. Says he signed him up to play in the suburbs -- Reisterstown Little League, you know, out with the rich kids."

"All the way out there? What the hell for?"

"Tommy, he thinks Junior will make the majors someday and that the kid is wasting his time in our inner-city baseball league -- not learning much, poor equipment, you know. Plus he signed up over there right before the deadline, so Junior can play post-season."

"Fuck him, then! Traitor! He lives right here, for chrissakes. City Heights and the kids in this neighborhood need coaches with knowledge. But he can go to hell if that's the way he feels. The Giants will win their league without him and his superstar kid."

"That's the spirit, coach. Listen, I gotta go, Suzie's yelling at me and we're supposed to go to her mother's. I'll try to make practice tomorrow. You gonna break it to the kids then?"

"Yeah, why not? We'll really need another pitcher now. I'll get one. No leftie and nobody with an arm like Junior, but we have prospects. That'll be our concentration this week – pitching. See ya."

Tommy tossed and turned in bed, thinking about lineup changes. Hell, it was a kids' league, it shouldn't bother him, but somehow he knew how important it was to the kids, their parents, hell, and the whole working-class neighborhood. When he told the Giants about it, their little faces would be full of questions. They won't miss Kirk much, but they will his son. Josh can take over shortstop now. He was looking better and better at almost every position. Maybe even pitcher, he wondered, and maybe Alex should try it too. Al had a strong arm -- who knew? Maybe.

Tommy remembered his own playing days. His last years were in a 13-14 year-old league in Florida, and he had played for the Lions Club, not his school. The coach had him play center field because he had a great arm and ran well. His job was to run down anything in the outfield he could get to and fire it back into second. Tommy had been good at it, and eventually the coach realized that he might use his arm on the pitcher's mound. Tommy remembered having no one to work with in preparation for his big chance. He had a paperback book from the library, and he had studied pitching from that.

He had pitched almost a whole inning. He threw all heat, and no one hit him, but he was wild, and he had walked four batters in between getting two strikeouts. His coach put him back out to pasture and never gave him another chance. Tommy knew that he might have made it as a pitcher had that jerk been willing to work with him, or able to teach him. Speed and arm were two of the main talents in baseball, and they were mostly natural. A kid who had an arm was coachable. Tommy vowed to give his boy a fair chance at it, maybe in the next game.

The memories of childhood baseball would not leave his mind. The humiliation of playing in the playground league, rather than the real, official Little League, in Connecticut, was still strong, all these years later. *Damn those plain, dyed, tee shirts!* He arose out of bed and roamed the apartment clad only in his boxers. He knew one more memory was coming up, and he could not avoid it. He went into the kitchen for a drink and saw on the little stove clock that it was 2:00 a.m. *Christ.* He needed a drink, not stupid beer. All he usually had around was beer, and maybe an emergency bottle of wine, in case he was lucky with a female visitor. Vodka was his drink of choice at sea, and maybe he had some left? He tore through the closet and his old sea bag, still stuffed with work gear from his last trip. *Damn, I need to dump this crap out and clean it up.* There it was -- a pint of vodka, unopened, wrapped up in a discarded nautical chart. He took it back to the kitchen like a trophy, and mixed up some powdered orange juice. He mixed a huge glass of vodka and orange juice, and sat down in the over-stuffed easy chair in his living room. *Now let the damn memories come. I'm ready for you now.* And, yet again, he went back, back, back to that damn chain-link fence and jumped up, just so, with his worn glove, and again, he missed it.

This flashback led to others, and not all baseball ones. The level of negativity of each memory now became worse and worse, with thoughts ever blacker, about divorce, money problems, his industry's lack of work, near collisions at sea, terrible weather, the seeming impossibility of having any investments again, no steady girlfriend, his crappy little apartment – it snowballed until the pint of vodka was empty, and Manager Tommy fell asleep, or perhaps passed out, in the old chair.

He barely arrived at morning practice on time, and was hung over. As usual, he was alone as all the other coaches had day jobs. He worked the Giants hard with fielding for an hour, until the thermos of coffee kicked in and the sweat helped. Then he called the kids together and told them about Kirk and Junior. Some of the little mouths hung open. They could not believe that their best player had defected to an enemy team in the suburbs. There were a few cuss words muttered. The smarter kids knew they could never replace Junior's pitching. Tommy told them that in the next couple of games he would be trying out more kids at pitcher and to be ready. He would give any boy a chance who wanted it, and anyone who showed promise would work with Coach Terry to improve.

Tuesday's game was versus the Dodgers, who had Jimmy's Liquors as a sponsor, and club president John for a manager. John was well-liked and respected in the club, both for his leadership and for baseball knowledge. He would play small ball with his team, bunting kids over, stealing a base here and there, and he taught his kids to hit the ball squarely, and not to try to kill it. Tommy, Brian and Terry knew they would have to play well to win. Brian tried hard to cheer up the little faces, but it was going to be a struggle. Fred would start as pitcher, with Rick taking third, leaving Josh at shortstop and Stevie at second. Alex stayed as catcher, Joe at first, and the outfield was by committee, as that was where they would shuffle in all the substitutes to get their minimum of two innings. The infield was still solid, even without Junior, but the outfield now suffered. Then, uncharacteristically, Fred began to struggle in only the third inning, and Tommy had to do something. He had runners on first and second, and no outs. Worse, the coaches could see the look in Fred's eyes, and knew that he was finished.

As Tommy called time out and walked towards the mound, he hollered at his own boy to go to the bench, take off his catcher's gear, borrow a fielder's glove, and come out to the mound. He told Shawn to come in from right field and put on the catcher's stuff.

"Dad, no, I don't want to pitch."

"Well, the team needs a new pitcher, and I want you to try it. Now hurry up."

Then he put Fred on third base and shifted the third baseman, Rick, to center, where he could control the outfield, and moved the centerfielder to right to replace Shawn, who was now the catcher. It looked confusing to some parents, but not to the coaches. It was common to shift kids around a lot at that age level.

When Alex looked ready as he could be, Tommy told him, "Just throw it right over the plate. No signs, just fastballs. You've got a good arm, they won't hit you."

What happened over the next few minutes made Tommy think of Yogi Berra's comment that, "It was déjà vu all over again." Alex did not give up hits, but he walked the first two batters he faced. *It's like watching a movie of me.* Alex had the power, but not the control. Acting more like a manager than a father, Tommy called time and walked out to the mound. The only girl in the league was up next.

"Look, no one's hitting you, just like I said, but you gotta throw strikes."

"I know, Dad, what do you think I'm trying to do?"

"Don't get smart, mister. You see who's up next? She hardly ever even swings the bat, and I know she hasn't had a hit all year. Ease up and throw it over. Relax. We need an out, and you'll be all right."

However, Alex was not all right. Instead of easing up, he tried to fire one right down the middle, perhaps because he was mad at Tommy, or the macho injustice of having a girl in the league, who knew, but the ball sailed high and inside. The girl never ducked, and the ball nailed her squarely in the helmet. Down to the ground she went, and Manager John ran out to her. Next thing, the girl's mom was out there, "Poor Dearing" her, and staring out at poor Alex, who felt bad enough, and that was about it for Alex. She stood up and went to first. Alex wanted out, but Tommy told him that he had to pitch to one more batter, "To get the bad stuff outta you." "Otherwise," he told him, "you'll always be afraid to pitch, and, even though you might not want to do it, you need to leave the option open."

"Okay, Pops, but after this guy, I go back to catcher, right? Promise?" Pops promised.

Alex held up his end of the bargain, striking out the batter, and Tommy went out to get him. As he watched his son jog off to get the catcher's gear back from Shawn, he hoped that at least the strike out would encourage Alex. He already knew who he would try next. Coach Terry had been working with his son, Rick, for a long time. He called him in to pitch, took Shawn out of the game, and called Jason off the bench and put him out in center.

Ricky, smallish in stature, and a kid his own father often called "Little Ricky," in honor of the television show "I Love Lucy," did fine. The Giants managed a couple of runs, but went into the last inning trailing by four runs. Tommy switched pitchers again, calling for Josh, again on Coach Terry's recommendation. They didn't seem to have any power pitching prospects besides Alex, so they would try to develop some little guys as control pitchers. Josh did fine, giving up no runs, but the Giants only scored one run in their last at bat, and they lost. They were now 2-3 on the season, with three games left in the first half. They would probably have to win out to have a chance. The winner of the first half played the winner of the second half in a one game championship, unless, of course, you won both halves.

Brian wanted a coaches' meeting, but they decided to go to The Horseshoe rather than their usual place. The reason had nothing to do with preference. The Horseshoe was a reluctant sponsor, and Brian wanted to show the City Heights flag a bit. Bring three or four coaches in there for beer and eats and it helped their image with the owners. Still, they sat in the back, with a clear view of the U-shaped bar. It was a rough bar with a reputation. No single woman with a brain or any sense would come in there looking to mate up, either. Tommy had long wondered if they laundered crime money or what, as they never seemed to be very busy, but had been in business as long as anyone could remember.

Over a few beers, the coaches agreed on a few things to try to help the Giants. More than his predecessor, Tommy tried to take his coaches' advice. They all agreed that the infield was their strength, and therefore they would concentrate on pitching and outfield in practice. Although only nine, Brian's boy, Derek, had the best arm of all the subs. They would move him from left field to center and give him more playing time. Without explaining his memories, Tommy told Brian to instruct his boy to run after every ball hit out there, and cut off the other fielders if he could, then throw it like mad to the cutoff man. Josh, then Rick, would get the next two starts at pitching. Coach Terry would work with Fred a lot in practice, and try to add a changeup to his fastball. Tommy also told them he intended to be much more aggressive with the base runners in the next few games, and would teach the delayed double steal to the few kids who could handle it.

The non-club talk drifted from the Orioles' chances, which they put at fair, to ex-wives, women in general, and the price of gasoline. Tommy noticed that Terry said little about his ex-wife, but when he mentioned her at all, Theo seemed to be very interested. All anybody seemed to know was that she had been no good somehow. Maybe it was drugs and many noted how unusual it was that a father had gotten custody. Tommy wondered if the ex was in jail.

They praised retired hero, now sportscaster, Brooks Robinson. They gave high marks to Johnny Unitas, for staying in the area and investing in businesses in it. Tommy told about taking Alex to see Brooksie, when he did a tour of gas stations for autographs. He had gotten the autograph on a '57 Robinson rookie card, and put it in a plastic sleeve, and given it to the boy, with an admonition to save it. There was some agreement that baseball cards were becoming collectible. Tommy wished he still had his childhood cards from the 1950's, and, like most guys his age, had no idea what had happened to them.

The Friday game was versus the A's, ably coached by a guy named Ross, and one of the two teams sponsored by Slim's Bar. Tommy knew that Ross was one of the club's best coaches, and his team would be well prepared for anything. However, he knew the Giants' chances were good since they had a good infield and a catcher who could throw your butt out if you tried to steal. Tommy put Alex in the batting order at clean up and wondered if he was being prejudiced in favor of his son. He asked Brian about it before the game, and Brian confirmed that Alex had been hitting the ball harder than anyone else had since Junior left the team. It was a high honor to bat fourth, or cleanup, and Alex knew he would have to deliver. He had the extra burden of being a coach's son, and needed to prove his worth, especially if he wanted to honestly make the all-star tournament team that the coaches would soon create. As silly as it might seem for children, the ten-year olds knew that with their best player gone, a new burden was on them, as the older, more experienced players.

The game was close, as the Giants' staff had expected, but the kids were hitting the ball better than the last time, perhaps getting over their missing star. Josh pitched with great confidence, smiling and having fun just throwing strikes. He would give up a hit now and then, but he never got in much trouble, and didn't stress out. His parents sat on the wall behind the bench, with hands clasped. Tommy prayed they would keep their praying silent.

By the fifth inning of the six-inning game, the Giants had a 6-3 lead, and Brian gave his opinion that another run or two might do it. When they batted, Tommy had a chance to play small ball to perfection. He had Fred on second and Stevie at the plate, with no outs. He gave Stevie the bunt sign, and he laid down a perfect, line-hugger right down towards third base. Fred ran over to third easily, and when the fielder panicked for a second, Stevie was safe at first. Now, with the bottom third of the order coming up, and all of them substitutes, manager Tommy decided to try to steal an insurance run. He didn't have much confidence that any of the next three batters would hit the ball.

In a rare instance, right after he signaled the key to the batter, his hand swiped across the chest, he grabbed his left wrist with his right hand, like a holding call in football. It was the take sign, meaning that the batter should not swing. He gave a couple more meaningless signs, and then stopped, bent forward, with his hands on his knees, waiting for the pitch. At this age level, since the runners could not take a lead, Tommy had decided that there was no reason to give the steal sign when everybody was looking at you to try to steal your signs. What he did for a straight steal came right as the pitcher let go of the ball. It was only natural for everybody -- players, coaches, and Buttinski parents, to watch the pitcher as he wound up. If Tommy wanted a runner to steal, he simply scratched his knee right as the pitcher let go of the ball. No one had stolen that sign yet, although many had tried. Now, he had added new twist. Checking out of the corner of his eye to see that both runners were still looking at him, he scratched his knee, and then scratched halfway up his left arm. It meant to steal half way, or the delayed double steal, a baseball strategy that Kirk always said you could not teach to kids this young.

Tommy knew that little Stevie gave away the farm every time he saw a sign, as his face would light up like a damn Christmas tree. It was some kind of secret bond between the manager and him, Theo said. Stevie treated a coach's sign like a secret initiation rite. As the ball crossed the plane of home plate, Stevie broke like mad for second. Coaches yelled different things. Some parents hollered “He's going!” to their kids on the A's, all to the delight of Manager Tommy, who now had dreams of a kind of organized chaos --

the Giants would be organized, and the Athletics would be in chaos. As the catcher stood up out of his crouch to throw, Stevie stopped halfway to second, and acted as if he did not know which way to run. Was he caught, and should try to make it back to first? Or, should he keep going to second, hoping to slide in beneath any tag? It was a question now planted in the minds of many. Meanwhile, Fred edged farther and farther off third towards home, unnoticed by almost everyone. The A's manager tried to holler to his catcher to just throw it back to the pitcher, but the kid couldn't hear him with all the noise and chaos. Besides, it was apparent that they had not practiced the play. The catcher threw to second, and the second baseman started to run Stevie back towards first. They had him in a run down, but, except for Manager Ross, they did not understand that it was exactly what the Giants wanted.

Fred crept more off third, and, when the A's second baseman threw a nice lob to the first baseman, two things happened. Tommy hollered, "Go!" and Fred tore off for home, while Stevie skidded to a halt and danced back towards second. Now the coaches and parents of the A's suddenly became aware that a Giants' player was trying to score (*damn him!*) and yelled even more. Fred slid in safely as the throw home was late. Stevie, now forgotten about, made it to second without a throw. The Giants players high-fived Fred and were happy. A couple of parents hollered "cheater," but Ross looked over to Tommy and tipped his hat. He was the victim, but he appreciated the play. Tommy knew that the next time they played the A's they would be ready for it.

Of course, when you teach your players an offensive play in any sport, it is always wise to teach the defense for it, in case someone tries it on you. Tommy had already worked on the defense for the double steal with his pitchers and catchers. At their age, it was simple. The catcher just looked the runner back to third, perhaps faking a throw, and then threw the ball to the pitcher, who immediately stood on the mound ready to pitch. By rule, once he was on the mound, the runners could not lead, hence would have to go back to their bases. In a worst case, the runner from first would keep going and steal second before this, but that was all right with the Giants' staff. They just didn't want to give up the cheap run.

The Giants went on to win 8-4. During the handshake ritual, Ross smiled but told Tommy, "Just try that again." The kids were happy and the coaches told them they still had a chance to win the league, but they would have to play their best. Tommy named Rick as the starting pitcher for their next game, on Tuesday. It was a surprise to some. He also said that Fred would pitch the last game of the half, and Josh was the relief man for both games. Beyond that, he was not sure who would pitch. They would practice tomorrow, Saturday and skip Sunday. Tommy called for two practices on Monday. He admonished the players not to miss practice if they expected to play much in either game. Some of the players wondered if he was going to become a hard ass like Kirk. Others, like Stevie and Josh, loved it – they would get to play more baseball than normal.

Tommy had Alex all day Saturday, and had a date with Maria for Sunday night, after he took the boy home. Maria seemed distant, and they ended up at Tommy's little apartment for an after-dinner drink. She drank more than usual and became aggressive. She practically ripped all of her clothes off, then did his, too, then pinned him down on the rug of the little living room, and went to work. Tommy had never seen her like that. He held on to those precious, harder-than-normal boobs while she did all the work on top. He wondered what the deal was, and soon found out during that quiet time of post-sex relaxation.

"Tommy, did you enjoy that, hon'?" she asked.

"Yeah, hell yeah, but hey, what's the deal, you're not usually that horny. Been watching movies or something?"

"No, I wanted it to be memorable, you know. It's the last time. Look, hon', we're not goin' anywhere really. I mean it's fun and great, and I love being with you like this, there's nobody better, but I have to look out for my future, and we're not in love, you know that."

"Who's the guy?"

"Look, right after my husband died I couldn't go out at all, you know? There's a friend, a carpenter, nice guy, who helped me out. The kids love him. Well, when you were out to sea he came around again. He wanted to get serious right away, but I held him off, and told him I wanted to be on my own a while, to see if that's what I wanted. That's when I met you. We're fun, Tommy, but I can't spend my whole life on fun. I'm sorry." She began to cry, and Tommy didn't know exactly why. Did she think he would be hurt? Maybe she would miss her independence? It didn't matter. He put his arm around her.

"I understand. You're right. I can't offer you a marriage, if that's what you want. But, I have to tell you I hoped that we would have the whole summer. I know you're a one-guy woman, and you have made a choice, and I'll respect it. Still, I'm going to miss all this," and he massaged her to emphasize the point.

It was over, and within a half hour, they were dressed and back at the driveway at her place. They kissed goodbye, but there were no tears, and everybody was acting grown up. Tommy stopped at a bar in Ellicott City on the way home, and closed the damn place. He shouldn't have been driving, but he took it easy on the two-lane, curvy, hilly ride home, and didn't hit any of the many trees that lined the road. He wasn't upset as much as disappointed. *Hell, just a few months of a regular thing -- just one summer, was that too much to ask?* He was so busy with baseball now, he wondered if he would have any time to even look for a new woman until sometime in August, when the season and tournaments were over.

On Tuesday, the Giants played the Reds, and they weren't too worried about it. The Reds were not much of a team, although they had one terrific pitcher, a big, black kid named Neal. The good news was that it wasn't Neal's turn to pitch. Tommy had checked with the other coaches, and knew that if they won their game, they would be tied with the Cubs, and play them on Friday for the championship of the first half. They had a head-to-head advantage over any other team that might also finish 5-3. He didn't tell the kids that.

Rick was on the mound for the boys in green, and did fine. He and Alex played catch, just like Coach Terry had taught them. Neal pounded the hell out of the ball, but he was the only Red who did, and it didn't cost them many runs. It did serve notice to all present that Neal deserved to make the tournament team.

They were up 7-2 in the top of the third inning when they had an injury. A Reds' batter took such a vicious swing that the bat wrapped all the way around his little body, then went flying behind him. It hit Alex on the side of his head. Alex went down, and Tommy ran out to see, thinking all the while how glad he was that he had bought a full helmet for him, and made him wear it. Alex's mask fit on the front of the helmet, the sides of the helmet extended below his jaw line, and he even had one of those new throat guards hanging down from the mask.

Alex was moaning and holding the side of his head. There was blood spilling out, and Tommy immediately saw what it was. He went back to the bench, reached into his duffel bag, and pulled out a wire cutter and needle-nosed pliers. He hollered to Josh's mom to get a clean towel with some ice cubes in it and bring it over.

Tommy checked his son again, noting that eyes looked fine -- no sign of a concussion. He had taken some EMT medical training for going to sea, and it gave him some confidence.

"Well, kiddo, you've got a busted wire from your braces, that's all. Problem is, the wire is sticking through your cheek, that's what's making all the blood. I'm gonna cut it inside your mouth, then pull it out from the outside, got it?"

"Dad, do you hafta? I don't feel too bad. Maybe we can wait . . . " Alex mumbled.

"No, I hafta. Don't worry. At sea they call me Dr. Painless. Now open up, and hold still."

"Doctor Doom is probably more like it," the kid spit out.

Tommy reached into the little mouth and snipped the wire as close to the teeth as he could. Then he used the needle nosed pliers to straighten it out on the inside. It needed to be straight to pull the wire out from the outside.

"Good job. Now comes the fun part, and then we're done." Tommy placed his left hand on Alex's cheek, with the wire protruding between his fingers. He grabbed the end of it with the pliers.

"On the count of three. One . . . two . . ." Then he pulled sharply and the wire came out cleanly. He handed Alex an ice cube, and put the clean rag with the ice in it on his cheek.

"Suck on this, you'll be okay. Want to come out of the game?"

"No, I want to stay. Anyway, who taught you to count, you said three?"

"If I waited 'til three, you'd flinch." For the first time, Tommy noticed that little Stevie was right at his side. He was holding Alex's mouthpiece, having picked it up from the dirt. Tommy always made his catchers wear them, especially catchers with braces.

"Mr. Tommy, is Alex goin' to be okay?" He was genuinely concerned. *Hmmm, the more I know about this kid, the better I like him -- shows honest compassion for his teammate.*

"Yeah, Stevie, he's a catcher and catchers are tough, you know? You want to do something, take that mouth guard over to his mom, you know who she is, and ask her to rinse it out with some clean water, then bring it back." Of course, he did it. Tommy had to give his ex a bit of credit for not rushing over when her boy went down, and letting the men handle it. Alex would have been appalled if his mother fussed over him in front of all the guys, but some mothers would have done exactly that. Within another minute the bleeding stopped, Alex put the helmet back on, and play resumed. Tommy took one more look into his eyes, and saw that they were clear. The small crowd gave Alex a cheer, and Tommy knew he would wear the blood on his game shirt like a red badge of courage for the rest of the game. Tommy made a mental note to call for an appointment with the boy's orthodontist. It helped the other Giants to see one of their guys tough it out. The nine-year olds took note of what the expectations were for a Giants' catcher, or one of the older players the team depended on.

The Giants went on to win easily. Alex even hit a home run, and most observers believed he was just full of adrenaline from his incident that he took it out on the ball. Tommy was glad to see his son regarded so highly by his own team, and some of the other kids, too. It was almost time to pick all-star teams for the tournament, and he didn't want Alex picked because he was a coach's son. Tommy and Brian went out of their way to find Neal from the Reds and tell him what a good player he was. They knew that a kid with such obvious talent who played for a weak team might get discouraged, and City Heights needed to keep all the good athletes it could.

There was no agreement to go to Slim's or anywhere else. Tommy was still saddened over the loss of his relationship (*had she been my girlfriend?*) and tired from staying out late drinking, that he actually wanted to go straight home. He told the others that he wanted to get home in time to watch public television, so he could improve his mind.

Parents and coaches took kids over to the ice cream truck, which, as usual, showed up right at the end of the game. It was amazing how much money a coach would spend in a season like that. Coaches made a point to shell out for kids who had no one show up to watch them play. Once a season, Tommy enjoyed asking his players how many of them thought the club paid the coaches. At least half the little hands would go up, and he would quietly explain how they were all volunteers, and the parents who helped were too. Then they would make their annual pitch for any kid who had a mom, dad, uncle, guardian or grandparent who wanted to get involved to come down to a game and talk to them.

Oddly, Bill Wilson, a lawyer with a small, two-member firm sponsored a team, and who sometimes came to a game or two, appeared and took Tommy aside. All Tommy knew was that Bill had his office in the same strip mall where Brian had his real estate office. He and Brian hung out a bit together.

"Tommy, you and Brian are close, right?"

"Yeah, you could say that."

"I just did. Kidding. Look, just between you and me, confidentially I'm saying, I am a bit worried about Brian."

"Whaddya mean? He's fine."

"Well, he seems depressed around the office, you know? I see him all the time, and he just isn't putting his usual effort into his business. Besides, and this is between us, he has asked me some questions about bankruptcy, and what could happen to him if Suzie divorced him."

"Oh, hell. Well, I know she's a bitch during baseball season, you know, all the time he spends with it. But his kid plays, you know. It's for him, too. Brian always says things are okay, or will get better. But, hey, I appreciate the warning. I'll pay a bit more attention to the big guy." That was how they left it, and the manager of the Giants went home and actually did watch some PBS on TV.

At Wednesday's practice, Tommy eased up with the kids. He did a lot of batting practice, throwing it right over the plate until his arm was sore. It was the thing the kids liked the best. He joked around and told the kids not to worry about the Cubs game. They knew the importance of it and he knew that if they didn't stay loose, if they were too tight and worried, they would not play their best. Besides, they were 9-10-years old, and summers and baseball should be fun, not work. Terry got off work early, came down to the field, and worked with Fred and Josh on their pitching. Alex's mouth was a bit sore, so Tommy gave Shawn some time working on his catching, for possible back up. By the time it was dark, they were as ready as they could be for tomorrow.

The crowd was a bit bigger than normal on Wednesday, in the park by the woods, behind the elementary school, the place where many dreams of inner-city kids played out. The kids would now act out all their baseball fantasies. Whatever they had seen their heroes in Memorial Stadium do, they could now act out on their own, in a game that was as important as any one they had ever seen.

The Giants were the home team, and, unlike Kirk, Tommy took the first base side. Less sun and closer to the woods for bathroom breaks, he reasoned. Fred took the mound, and did fine for the first three innings. Rick, Stevie and Joe hit singles, Alex and Fred pounded the ball into the outfield, and they went into the fourth leading 6-3. Then Fred got a bit wild, the Cubs slapped a couple of hits, and before you knew it, it was 6-5. Then, with a runner on, Shawn misplayed a ball in right, and it went for a home run. It should have been a single, but the all-you-can-get field belied that. The Giants were now losing 7-6, and all the Giants coaches could see that Fred had lost his confidence. The Cubs had the momentum. The game was rapidly turning away from what the Giants' coaches had hoped for -- a game of pitching and defense -- into a slugging duel. If things deteriorated enough, they might lose because of the mercy rule. Anybody who watched many games at this age level knew a team could get ten runs in a hurry. When things went bad, it seemed to snowball -- a few walks, an error, a hit and next thing you knew, you were worried about the ten-run rule. Tommy went out to the mound to get Fred.

On the mound, he called Josh in to pitch, and checked with Alex about the hitters. Fred went to third base, shifting Rick to shortstop for Josh. As usual, Josh's little face just lit up. He was the second smallest kid on the team, next to Stevie, but never showed any fear. He loved to pitch. He loved to play the game, and would not panic. He would throw strikes. While Josh was warming up, Tommy talked to the infielders. They had runners on first and third with one out. He wanted the out at home if they could get it. He trusted Alex to make a tag. In the big leagues, you might try to turn a double play, but that was tough at that age level. Other managers would tell the kids to take the easy out at first, but Tommy did not want to get further behind, and a throw to first was no guarantee of an out, either. Kids routinely threw easy outs over the first baseman's head.

On the walk back to the Giants' bench, Tommy wondered about his battery of Josh and Alex. They were both short kids, but Alex was stocky and strong. Josh looked like he was malnourished. When people met him, they wanted to feed him. Yet, Tommy knew that was not the case, he was just a skinny kid. Tommy had been a fat baby, and had been a skinny runt all through school, a fact that had held him back in baseball, he believed. Coaches back in the '60's didn't seem to give you much of a chance if you were weak-looking. And, Tommy had a younger brother who was skinny still, weighing maybe only 135 pounds, but he ate like a horse, and was quite healthy. *Josh will be all right.*

As usual, Josh threw it right over the plate, forcing the batters to swing. There was a grounder to short, and, as planned, Rick checked the runner at third. He was going home, and Coach Terry's boy gunned it home, as instructed. The kid slid into Alex, but he came up from the dust showing the ball to the umpire, and made the out. The Cubs did not score again, and the Giants came to the bench only down a run, with renewed hope and the top of the batting order due up. Terry, Theo, Tommy and Brian had a brief conference away from the kids. They all agreed to play small ball to tie the game right then. They did not want the kids to feel the pressure of getting into the late innings needing a run to tie. Tie it now -- bunt, steal, and do whatever they had to -- that was the consensus.

Stevie, the team's leadoff hitter, got on base with a bunt. In a rare move, Tommy gave the next batter the bunt sign also. The Cubs' catcher was very good, and he didn't want Stevie thrown out. Josh did it almost perfectly, but was out at first. Now the Giants sat back with the expectations that Fred and Alex, due up third and fourth, would drive in the tying run. It was just like the major leagues -- play small ball with the small guys, and then your big hitters could get the RBIs.

Fred hit a huge fly ball to centerfield, and Tommy, coaching at third, gave the hold up sign to Stevie at second. The center fielder was a good player, and might catch it. He missed it, but by the time that happened, Stevie barely reached third, and Fred held up at first. Just like the big leagues, the coach figured, I can tie the game with an out. He called time out and jogged down near the plate to whisper in Alex's ear.

"Just hit one to the outfield. Even a fly ball gets the tying run in, right? We don't need a homer, so don't try to kill it."

"I got it, Pops. No problem."

Tommy held his breath, wanting desperately for his own boy to show his worth in the most important game of the year. His mom was there, sitting on the wall, not interfering much, and Tommy, strangely, wanted Alex to do well for that reason also. Show the ex that all their time with baseball was worth it.

Alex hit the first pitch in the air to right field. Right field was where most teams hid their worst players, their substitutes, but Tommy took no chances. He hollered at Stevie to tag up. Amazingly, the kid caught the ball for the second out, but Stevie's speed served the Giants well, and he scored easily. Joe struck out to end the inning, but now the score was even going into the fifth.

Amazingly, neither teamed scored in the fifth, both going down 1-2-3. In the top of the sixth, the Giants turned a rare double play to end a threat, and they went to the bottom of the last inning still tied. Jason, a substitute right fielder, and ninth in the order, was up first. No one expected much of him, but he hit one in the hole at short, and the shortstop panicked and threw it over the first baseman's head into the woods. On the overthrow, the umpire granted Jason second base. The winning run was right there at second, with the top of the order coming up. Everyone in the park expected Stevie to bunt, now having seen him do it repeatedly, and the Cubs' coach had his corners play up, at first and third. The shortstop would cover third, in what many called the wheel play, and if the players at first, third or pitcher fielded the bunt, they would throw to third to try for the out on Jason. Tommy called time and took Stevie aside.

"You gonna give me the bunt sign, right coach?" Stevie asked.

"No. Listen, that's what everybody expects you to do. With their infield in like that, it's easier to get a hit. Besides, it's time you starting hitting more. You can't bunt all the time."

Stevie frowned.

"Stevie, I have faith in you. Tell you what. You go up there and I'll give you the bunt sign. You square to bunt, drawing everybody in. When the pitcher starts to throw, you pull the bat part way back. If the pitch is terrible, let it go. If the pitch is in there, take a short swing at it - just slap it around. With the fielders looking bunt, you can get it through the infield. Let's win it right now. You knock in the winning run for the team."

The prospect of faking a bunt and fooling everybody appealed to Stevie, as well as being the hero, and when Tommy gave him the phony signs, his face lit up. Now everybody, including the Giants players, was sure he was going to bunt. Tommy hollered over to Jason to be ready and watch him. The Cubs' fielders and bench players, hearing the warning to Jason, became more concerned about him. As instructed, their third baseman and first baseman crept in towards the plate, and their shortstop ran over to cover third. The maneuvers left a giant hole on the left side.

With no leading off the bases allowed, most pitchers never used the stretch, but took the full motion. It gave the smallest Giant time for his act. When the pitcher went into his full motion, Stevie waved the bat over his head as if he was going to kill the ball and then, with the most serious expression, he squared to bunt. As the ball came towards him, he pulled the bat halfway back, then chopped at it. It went between the pitcher and the third baseman, and, normally, would have been an easy play for the shortstop. He, however, was running to cover third, and when he saw the ball, tried to stop suddenly and reverse direction to go get it. He could not, and Jason went right by him on the way to third. The left fielder came running in to get the easy grounder, but Tommy knew that the kid was not their best arm in the outfield, and never hesitated. He yelled at Jason to "Go home!" with his right arm whirling like mad in the windmill motion. Coaches, players on the bench and parents now were all yelling, some for a run, some for an out. *The more noise the better for us,* Tommy knew. The pressure was on the kid in left to make a perfect throw. He did not. The throw was up the line towards first base. By the time the catcher caught it and tried to go back to tag Jason, he was already sliding across the plate with the winning run. Stevie crossed first base, as Brian coached him to do, then joined in the Giants' celebration behind the plate. Tommy had even more confidence in his little leadoff man.

All in all, it had been an exciting, close game, one where no one should feel too bad because they lost, or too cocky because they won. Tommy told the kids to meet out in left field for a quick team meeting before they went home. He and Brian packed up all the gear into the duffel bags and told the happy parents to hold off a minute. As usual for a post-game meeting, they had the kids sit down on the grass. Tommy told them how proud he was of all of them, especially how well they had played since they had lost Kirk.

"It shows what you can do if everybody plays their best," he told them.

Then he reminded them that there were no games the next week, for July 4th. The City Heights Boys Club always took a one-week break then, between halves of the season. There were many events going on -- some people took mini-vacations and went out of town, and some teams just needed a rest or time to practice. There were picnics, fireworks, BBQs and crab fests all over the city. July 4th was on Thursday, and many of the blue-collar workers in the Heights had taken a vacation day on Friday. Tommy told the kids they would practice in the mornings only on Monday, Tuesday and Wednesday, then be off until the following Monday. Then he told them that he and Alex would be down at the field on the Saturday after the holiday, and if anyone wanted to come down for unofficial practice, they could. He knew the serious ballplayers would be there, but he wanted to give them an excuse in case their families had plans.

As the happy group broke up, some adults came over to shake Tommy's hand and congratulate him. Brian reminded him that there was an important club meeting the next week. It was the traditional time that the club made plans set for post-season tournaments and the all-important crab fest fundraiser in August. Alex's mom was there to take him home. Tommy would pick him up the next morning. It was Friday night, his team had won a big game, and he should have been going out celebrating, but he didn't feel like it. He began to wonder if he had liked Maria more than he had realized.

Chapter 7: The Season – Second Half

The following Monday, Tommy had a short batting practice for the kids. He kept things loose. He took Alex home with him, for lunch, and then a trip to the orthodontist to get his braces fixed. He expected a hassle and he got it. It wasn't the first time they had gotten broken playing ball, and the good doctor had bitched about it the last time. After the repair, the orthodontist invited Tommy into the office, and closed the door.

"Listen, I can't keep treating your boy. He keeps breaking the braces, and he obviously isn't wearing his retainer enough. You will have to go somewhere else to finish his treatment."

"Well, you listen to me, doc," Tommy said, staring across the desk. "I have a contract for orthodontic services which includes emergencies and repair. This cost me $2,400 and I don't work steady. I told you he played baseball and was a catcher. I make him wear a mouthpiece and bought him a good helmet. He doesn't live with me, so you call my ex-wife to bitch about wearing the headgear at night. Now, if you refuse treatment, two things will happen. First, my lawyer will sue you, and his nickname is 'Mad Dog.' Secondly, I will tell everybody in the Heights, starting with every single player, parent and coach in the baseball league, what a jerk you are -- your call."

The doctor hesitated, and then offered to have his partner finish Alex's treatment, no matter how long it took, or how many times the braces were broken.

The regular Tuesday meeting of the City Heights Boys Club was anything but regular. It was one of the most important meetings of the year, and the basement room in the apartment complex was crowded. Parked cars and pickups lined both sides of the narrow street.

After the usual reading of the minutes of the last meeting and the treasurer's report, they got down to it. The July 4th break was time to settle many things of great importance in the Heights. They reviewed assignments for the annual crab fest, their biggest fundraiser of the year. They filled the gaps with a lot of cajoling and begging. There was a bit of the usual baiting, as in, "Well, I'll make the effort to do my part, what about you?" Tommy volunteered to work the crab room for an hour, which meant he would wrap and serve bunches of hot, steamed crabs. He also took an hour on the Big Six Wheel, a gambling device that was popular at such events. The club already had their annual permit that allowed them to have limited gambling just for that night. Only non-profit organizations could get one. There were no casinos in Maryland.

Then they addressed important matters related to baseball, which, after all, was the reason for the existence of the club in the first place. They had to pick their all-star teams in the next week, so teams could start practicing. The club always entered the Towson Tournament, which was a huge, double-elimination tournament of teams from all over Baltimore and its suburbs. It was played every year in August, after the Heights' regular season, and before any of the kids had to go back to school. There was some initial discussion regarding the availability of uniforms. The treasurer reported that he had paid the tournament fees. Then, they made coaching assignments. It was routine. Successful coaches kept their teams from year to year. The older teams did the best. For some reason, the younger teams had little success. In the middle of the discussions of post-season baseball, Brian stood up and surprised Tommy.

"Mr. President, I move that we make Tommy the manager of the 9-10 year old tournament team. He is not only the coach of the winning team from the first half, he's off duty from the merchant marine all summer, and can give the kids more time than anyone."

Tommy was surprised. Somehow, in his busy life, he had forgotten that Kirk had coached the 9-10 all-star team, and now they had to replace him. There was little discussion. Tommy suggested that Ross would do better, but he declined, saying that he had already agreed to help with the older kids. Tommy received the assignment, and secretly enjoyed the faith and hope the club was putting in him. The 9-10's never did well at Towson. He promised his best effort, and, in his mind, started listing the players he would want. The club rule was that every team had to have at least one player on the tournament team. The all-star coach would usually take two players from each of the eight teams. Typically, the tournament coach would ask each team manager who his two best players were, but the final choice would be up to Tommy. It was that way so you didn't end up with four shortstops and no center fielder. Tommy's opinion was that at that age level you could put a good athlete anywhere. He made a mental note to pick the best athletes, regardless of position. Hell, he was the manager now famous for having a left-handed shortstop. Often, the tournament manager would be a coach who had a son playing in the league, and usually there was no question he would take his own boy. Having a son who did well was one reason that guys would vote you a tournament team assignment. It was a high honor in the city neighborhood known as City Heights.

The meeting ended with the usual "50-50" drawing. The treasurer went around with his roll of tickets. Almost everyone bought some. As always, one winning number was drawn, and the winner split the money evenly with the club. Terry won it, and offered to buy the first round at Slim's. Tommy reluctantly agreed to go, hoping that his friends wouldn't start angling to put their favorite players on his tournament team. He checked with the equipment manager on the way out, and arranged to pick up the extra batting helmets, a dozen baseballs, and the uniforms. The equipment guy said that there were twenty uniforms in good shape for his team, and Tommy thought he might take that many kids. It was a lot to handle, and the club only required one kid from each team. It was normal to take two, but that was sixteen kids. Maybe he would take a few marginal players, in the hopes that the experience would help the club's tournament team the following year. It was unheard of to take any nine-year olds, but Tommy hoped there might be one or two who might be as good as any ten-year-old, and could use the experience.

Luckily, no one tried to push his kid on Tommy for the all-stars. Not until Nathan, Josh's father, showed up and sat down with them. He did not drink alcohol. The story went around that he had once been an alcoholic and had lost everything -- job, wife, you name it. Somehow, he had found Jesus, and had begun all over again. Little Josh on the Giants was the product of his second marriage. People who had been to his house said there were religious objects all over the place, and the couple would pray at the drop of a hat, or pray for your hat, or your soul, or a Giants' victory, or anything else that was handy. The skinny guy had always treated Tommy fine, though, and Tommy knew how much he appreciated his kid getting a chance to pitch. Tommy and Brian exchanged quizzical looks, but Nathan didn't hesitate. He asked what plans all the coaches had for the rest of the July 4th week. Ascertaining that no one would be out of town on Friday, he whipped out a stack of tickets for the Orioles' game on Friday night, and started handing them out to all the coaches, adding enough for their kids. They also knew that Nathan lived in a rather dilapidated row house, and didn't have a lot of money. The coaches tried to refuse, on financial grounds, and then offered payment.

"No, hey, I get these for a discount where I work, at the tire place. Look, they're upper deck, they don't cost much anyway. But, they're good upper deck, just inside third base.

You guys deserve it. And, don't bring anything to the game. I'm coming loaded with stuff. You'll see -- this'll be great. I'm just bringing Josh and me, not the wife. Guys' night at the ballpark, you know? And you guys drink if you want. That don't bother me no more, either." He smiled, and no one could refuse. Why should they? Hell, it was a perfect way to end the first half of the season, and bond the Giants coaches together a bit. They arranged some car-pooling, and Nathan left, a happy man. You never knew. Doing this was perhaps a huge deal to him, and it would make the son he called Joshua proud that his Dad treated everybody to an Orioles' game. Besides, Josh was a great kid, and he, Alex, Derek, and Rick were all friends. On the way out, Tommy said hello to Slim, who was on his usual stool at the end of the bar.

"Tommy, you no good. You hear the news?'

"What's that, Slim?'

"Gary Roenicke hit a grand slam tonight."

"Hey, that's great. He's not a bad outfield, either. O's win?"

"Yeah. But listen, that's only the beginning. He hit it in that 'Home Run Inning,' you know that contest they got. The one sponsored by the bank."

"Cool. Somebody win some money, then?"

"Some money? A fuckin' million dollars!"

"No shit? A million?"

"Yeah. Now listen, here's the part that gets me. You know those new bank machines, where you can get cash out?"

"Yeah, Slim. ATM's."

"Right. Well, you can send in postcards for the contest, that's what I do, but if you bank at their bank, you get entered every time you use your card."

"Okay. So?"

"So listen. This'll kill ya. I'm listening to the radio comin' over here, and they're talkin' about the contest, and they call the winner, some woman, up on the phone. First, she didn't even know she was entered in the contest -- used her bankcard thing. Second, she don't live in Maryland, she lives in D.C. Third, the guy asks her what she thinks of Gary Roenicke, and she didn't even know who he was!"

"Goddam, Slim. Don't seem fair, does it?"

"Fuck, no! That's my point. She ain't no Orioles' fan, knows nothin' about baseball, doesn't even try to enter the contest, didn't know they had picked her, doesn't know who hit it or what position he plays, wasn't watching or listening to the game - shit, Tommy, it ain't right! She oughta have to name the starting nine or something to win that. A million bucks for that moron? I sent fifty cards in for that, for God sakes!"

"It's a cruel world, Slim. I gotta go."

Wednesday was an easy day. He worked the Giants for two hours, mostly on defense, but did not wear anybody out. He made mental notes about his all-star team. Terry had the day off too, and came down to the field to work with the pitchers. Tommy appreciated his efforts tremendously. He was the best-natured coach of all and the kids responded to him. Still, there was that mysterious conversation about his ex-wife, and now, at practice, Terry mumbled something about his older son, Billy, going to visit his mom for a while. Tommy could not remember anything like that ever happening. He never talked about his ex, and Tommy could not recall his kids ever mentioning her, either.

Tommy took Alex with him for the night, as he had now made plans for the two of them for most of the holiday week and weekend. Alex was at the age where Dad could get him to go almost anywhere, but he was beginning to put up a fight against places he did not know about. He also sometimes argued over what he wore, what he ate, or what he was allowed to watch on TV. Tommy often wondered how many more years they would remain buddies. He knew, somehow, that the baseball time together was special, and he intended to make the most of it. After a spaghetti dinner, Tommy laid out the plans to his son. Thursday, the 4th, would be busy. President Reagan was coming to town to give a speech in the morning, and Tommy told Alex that they were going to Fort McHenry to see him when he left.

"Dad, you said you didn't vote for him."

"Yeah, that's right, but he's still the president, and you have to see at least one in your lifetime, in person. Besides, you'll like the fuss they make, with secret service agents, guns hidden under their coats, two helicopters, and TV cameras. It's quite a show. We're taking sandwiches and drinks with us. While he's talking downtown, we'll head out there and get a spot right by where the copters are. Besides, you've been to Fort McHenry -- it's cool."

Tommy went on to bait his boy to go along with the plan by telling him they were going to the fair in Dundalk after that, then to Brian's for a cookout for dinner.

"Brian's got some fireworks, too, he told me. I don't know what kind, but we'll have some fun there. Besides, you get along with Derek, and there'll be a couple of other kids you know there." Alex tried a small protest, but didn't get anywhere, and gave up.

"And, not only that for tomorrow, but I have tickets for the O's game on Friday, and Saturday we're taking a little trip in the van, maybe camp overnight somewhere."

"Just one night, Pops?"

"Yeah. I'm thinking of Harper's Ferry."

"Harper's Ferry? What the heck is that?"

"What's that? What do they teach you in school? It's a place about 60 miles west of here, in the skinny part of the state, near the Virginia and West Virginia boundary. There's a national park there now, and it's a famous Civil War site. It's near Antietam, where there was a huge battle, maybe you've heard of that, or Sharpsburg, it's near there too. Some rivers come together there, and there used to be a ferry. Anyway, a guy named John Brown attacked a weapons depot at Harper's Ferry to get some weapons to start a revolt of slaves in the South, but some soldiers trapped him there and there was a fight. I think federal troops captured him and later executed him by hanging. We'll go early, set up camp, then go down there and get a tour, and get the whole story. I don't remember it all. We'll learn something."

Now the boy argued with Tommy a bit, but he knew the boy secretly loved camping. Partly it was because Dad would let him pick out his own food to cook, be it over a fire or the little camping stove they always took. Dinner could be corn on the cob, steak, and roast potatoes -- whatever he wanted. In his mind, Tommy was already calculating the rest of the summer, and his financial situation, and did not know how many more opportunities they might have for a trip. They left some of the details in the air, but went to bed with the rest of the week arranged. It was the best he could do without trying to spend money he didn't have. Besides, it was a guy-thing weekend, and he felt it was his job to do such things with his only child.

The two boys slept in a little Thursday morning, then pulled their act together. Alex tried a little negotiating on the week's schedule, but Dad would have none of it. "Done deal," he told the ten-year old. "Get dressed." By 11:00 a.m., they entered the park around Fort McHenry and parked. There were cops around, and the two U. S. Marine helicopters were just west of the famous fort's walls. The road was marked off, and there were only a few people there. Tommy took out the cooler and he and the boy headed over near the copters. They set up right at the rope, and sat down for a little picnic. Tommy had a radio to listen to the speech. As soon as it was over, the presidential motorcade would be coming. They weren't there two minutes when a Baltimore cop came over and checked them out. He looked in the cooler, made a joke, and moved off.

About half an hour later, they noticed that the park was filling up. There were locals, tourists, more police, and some guys who were clearly secret service men. They seemed obvious because they were dressed in suits on the hot day, and had the run of the place. No one stopped or questioned them. Sure enough, about ten minutes later, they heard motorcycles, people moved forward and pressed against the ropes, and the cops were more active. There were cops on horseback, and others on foot. Everybody seemed to have a radio. One helicopter began to turn its blades slowly, and then the other one did too. A couple of marines were visible in the windows of the choppers, and one stood perfectly motionless at the steps of the president's chopper. *Regardless of your politics, it's quite a show.*

A couple of motorcycles roared into view from Fort Avenue. Two limousines followed, and pulled to a halt right in front of them. Tommy told Alex to watch all the guys who had suits and even overcoats on in the heat -- Secret Service, he told the boy. He recalled his own experiences seeing presidents. While a boy in Wallingford, Connecticut, he remembered that everyone in his elementary school walked down to the local railroad station to see former President Harry Truman. He arrived on a train and gave a short speech.

When he was a freshman in high school during the 1960 election, he had gone down to the little park in the center of Jacksonville, Florida, with his dad, to see and hear candidate John F. Kennedy. He recalled that during the speech, he had slipped away with his little box camera and gone out to the street. He had looked around and found the limo that was to take Kennedy away. He went right over to it, and no one stopped him. Sure enough, when Kennedy came over, the crowd pressed him right up against the car. He was the closest one to it on the curbside, had gotten a close up picture, and had shaken his hand. The events of 1963 flashed through his mind just then, too, but he pushed them away. There was no way to get that close to Reagan. The country had become so dangerous that access would never be the same.

Still, after a couple of guys looked around and gave the okay, Reagan emerged, smiling, and made a great show. He stopped and waved to all sides. More guys in suits stepped out of the second limo, and Tommy told Alex that the second car was the "gun car."

"Dad, what the heck are you talking about?"

"See all those guys in suits? See the guys with overcoats? Hell, it's about 90 and humid. They have machine guns under those coats."

If nothing else, that seemed to impress the boy.

Both helicopters now revved their rotors faster, a couple more marines appeared, and within a minute, Reagan had taken a salute from the marine at the bottom of the steps to his chopper. Then he walked up, stopped again, turned around and, smiling, waved to the whole crowd. "Damn, he's good," Tommy said out loud. *Years in Hollywood have taught him how to play to an audience.*

From there, the two City Heights guys drove over to Dundalk, on the east side of the city. Tommy had sailed into the Dundalk Marine Terminal many times since the advent of the modern container ships. The Bethlehem Steel plant at Sparrow's Point wasn't far away, and Dundalk had a lot of blue-collar workers from there, or the nearby GM car plant. A lot of them were Polish. The small, downtown area of Dundalk had a great July 4th fair every year. There were rides, food, and bands. Steamed crabs were everywhere, as was beer. Alex did some rides, while Tommy preferred to sit at an outdoor table with a beer and a Polish Dog, listening to the live music and watching the girls go by. There were a few girls he would like to talk to, but he knew how tough it was with your son with you, and he didn't even try. *Damn – the arrangement with Maria had been perfect.*

After a few hours, too many dizzying rides for Alex and a couple of beers for Dad, they headed out through downtown, past the bad neighborhoods along Frederick, and back to the familiarity of City Heights. It was still light when they parallel parked in front of Coach Brian's townhouse. It was a typical summer evening in the Heights, with kids playing in the street and on the tiny, well-manicured front lawns. There were a lot of American flags hanging from the small front porches, and there were smells of steamed crabs, with their overpowering scent of Old Bay seasoning, as well as that of BBQ'd steak or burgers, in the air. Guys with beer bellies stood on their lawns and watered their patches of grass with hoses. Some wore the ever-popular sleeveless tee shirts, but no one then called them muscle shirts. A couple of the guys waved to Tommy. He was a coach in the neighborhood, and people in City Heights knew the coaches.

The door to the townhouse was open, and Tommy could hear several people inside. He and Alex went right in. There was a ballgame on the TV in the little living room. The dining area next to it had a table with numerous dishes of food on it. There were hamburgers and dogs, chips, pickles, beans, potato salad, and some dip mixes. Terry and his younger boy were there, and a couple of Brian's neighbors Tommy didn't know. Brian was out in the backyard, cooking more burgers and dogs on the grill, and loving it all. He was, perhaps, the most friendly person Tommy had ever known, and he loved having all his friends and their kids over. Suzie was polite, but busy in the kitchen. Things were clearly not right between the two of them, but it had been this way for a long time. Some couples just seemed to be at each other's throats, and then would make up. Suzie pointed out the coolers with beer and those with soda. They grabbed their drinks and went out to the tiny backyard.

Brian had set up a few rows of folding chairs in his backyard, and told Tommy they were for the kids' fireworks show that he was going to put on. A couple more people from Brian's street came by with small children. They seemed to be people Suzie knew more than Brian did, and the kids were friends with his daughter, not Derek.

Sure enough, about nine, Brian made a big show of getting everybody into the tiny backyard. The kids sat in the chairs. The adults stood around with their beers or mixed drinks. City Heights wasn't much of a wine-drinking place -- you had beer or whiskey, but a mixer for the gals was okay.

He had a box of fireworks. One neighbor asked how he could have them, since it was illegal in Maryland -- illegal, but they weren't hard to get. The response was typical. He knew somebody who had driven to Florida on vacation, something many Marylanders did. When you passed through Tennessee, you bought your fireworks. Tommy had given the guy money and a wish list. Some entrepreneurs went down there as a business. They bought a truck load, smuggled it back into Baltimore, and then sold the fireworks illegally. It was like a drug business that was only good for a few weeks a year.

The show didn't last long, and the older kids would say later that it was "kinda hokey." The little ones loved it. There were strings of firecrackers, some of which Brian lit and threw in an old washtub, making a huge racket. Roman candles were popular, and Tommy wondered why the whole damn neighborhood didn't burn down every July 4th, as there were fireworks all over the Heights. The finale came when Brian nailed two pinwheels to his small tree and lit them off. They spun around, shooting showers of sparks out as they went faster and faster. As they broke up, someone had the idea to go upstairs and watch the fireworks from downtown, at the Inner Harbor. You could see some of the higher shots from Brian's upstairs windows, as his house was on the crest of a small hill. Overall, it was a successful day, and he and son went home tired.

Friday was a quiet day until late in the afternoon. Tommy carpooled with Brian and Derek, and they took the van out to Memorial Stadium early. They parked in the stadium lot on the first base side. Tommy had grown tired of the street parking hassle. They went in early to watch batting practice, and help the kids hustle autographs. Tommy brought a foul ball he had gotten the previous year. It hadn't been a clean catch. He and Alex had been in the upper deck when there wasn't much of a crowd, and he had grubbed for a foul ball that was rolling around an empty row of seats. A fat woman had tried to grab it too, and Tommy had beaten her out for it. Alex took the ball down to the field, on the third base side. He wasn't having any luck until right before the game when Eddie Murray walked by on his way to the dugout. Alex held the ball out with a pen. Murray quickly signed it and went into the dugout before any other kids could get down to the fence. It was a terrific autograph to get.

Nathan and Josh showed up about ten minutes before the game, hauling baggage. They had two coolers and a grocery bag. Memorial Stadium allowed you to bring in coolers provided they could fit under a seat, and you opened them up for inspection. There were rumors that some of the new stadiums were going to try to prohibit the bringing of food into a ballgame. Baltimore fans understood that no one would go to a baseball game with such rules.

During the National Anthem, all the City Heights boys took pride in shouting out the "O!" in "Oh, say can you see. . ." As they sat down to watch the game, Nathan propped up the coolers and took food orders. He had everything, and it was most impressive. He had one cooler that had insulated heat bags in it, and he had hot dogs for everybody. The cold cooler had mustard, ketchup, onions, and relish. The grocery bags had all kinds of chips, napkins, and paper plates. It was like a damn picnic, right in the upper deck of the baseball stadium. He joked about "Nathan's Hot Dogs," and took orders. Dogs went around the whole game. No one went hungry, and when the O's won the game with a home run in the ninth, all went home happy. Tommy declined offers to go out after the game. He and Alex had a trip to take in the morning.

The camping trip to Harper's Ferry was a quick one, but a good one. Once on the road, Alex would settle in to riding with Dad in the van, and he could actually help with road maps or signs. They were lucky with a camping spot and set up. They would use the van to drive over to the National Park for their tour, so they rigged up a self-standing tarp over the picnic table. When parked for the night, Tommy would rig another one out from the side door of the van. The campground even had a recreation hall of some sort. Maybe they would check that out before dark. Tommy had a six-pack of beer for himself, but, keeping to his rule for camping trips, did not drink alcohol until he finished driving for the day.

The tour of Harper's Ferry was better than Tommy expected. Many of the original buildings were still there and a tour guide took you around. The tour ended at the brick firehouse. It was the little building where the feds trapped John Brown and his men. You could still see the bullet holes. Men died right there, and although it was not clear if Alex understood the issues that had brought them there, he understood the dying part, and became quiet. Standing in the same spot where someone died could do that to you.

They had a small campfire, but cooked over the two-burner camp stove. Tommy always kept a few pieces of dry firewood in the back of the van, but he was not opposed to cheating and using a Duraflame log as well. Another trick he used was to put some charcoal briquettes in the bottom of a fire ring, and start a fire from them with lighter fluid. It wasn't Boy Scout approved, but it worked, and he wasn't working on a damn merit badge. He had been camping in places in the Smoky Mountains in the pouring rain, and had rigged a campfire under the side tarp, being the only one in the campground with a fire going. *Screw methodology.*

The campground manager, a guy who spent the whole summer living there in a trailer, came around right before dark to see how everybody was doing. The loquacious old man told Alex that the ditch that ran right beside their van was once a trench dug by Union Civil War troops. He said that every so often somebody would find a relic -- a tunic button, musket ball, something, right there. Tommy wondered if he was blowing smoke, but enjoyed the story. The manager also invited them to Saturday night bingo in the recreation hall at 8:00. It seemed like a joke, but by eight, the boys were actually bored, and drifted over to the hall. They bought a few cards and sat down to play with the mostly-retired crowd. The old women fussed over Alex as they enjoyed having young people in there. On their third game, Alex had a bingo, but Dad had to make him holler the word out. The boy liked it better when the manager came around, verified his card, and handed him $8.50, the prize amount for that game.

The two camping buddies slept in on Sunday, as much as anyone could with campers all around. By nine, they had coffee for Tommy, juice for Alex, and some eggs and bacon going. They decided to go straight back to Baltimore. They drove off about noon. After a couple hours of watching football on Tommy's little TV, Dad drove Alex over to his mom's and dropped him off. He purposely drove off before the ex could come out of the house and talk to him.

Back home, Tommy made a few calls. July 4th week had been great, but now he had to concentrate on baseball again. He called his own assistants, then a few of the other 9-10 coaches. He was looking for recommendations for the all-star tournament team. He kept a list of the names and positions. He knew the players, so there were no real surprises. He also called the club's equipment manager, and found out that there were indeed twenty uniforms available for his tournament team. He wanted to pick his team right away, and spend the week notifying the kids and coaches. He wanted to do that in person. He also worked out a practice schedule that would not interfere with any of the teams. Not working made the usually difficult task easy. He would work the tournament team every morning, starting a week from Monday. He would work with the Giants on all the days they did not have a game, in the afternoons, except on Sunday. There would be no practices on Sunday, although he knew some of the kids would come down to the field with their dads or friends and play anyway. By the time he went to bed, he had a probable list of players, a tentative practice schedule, and a headache.

On Monday morning, he picked up the tournament uniforms from the equipment guy's house. He wasn't home, but his wife was, and she knew the drill. Back home, he inventoried everything. He would need to use Alex's catcher's helmet. The batting helmets looked terrible, but he had an idea. The helmets were plain green, one of the club's colors, but they were scratched, dirty, and old looking. He went down to the hardware store and bought some green spray paint, clear polyurethane spray, and a bunch of press-on letters. The letters were three inch-high "C's" and "H's," and they were white, the other club color. Back home, he obtained permission from his landlord to use the shed out back, and he went in there and cleared off a shelf.

After cleaning the helmets off and letting them dry, he sprayed on a coat of green paint. A few coats of this, then make 'em shiny with the clear spray, and put on the club's letters, "CH," slightly angled, right in the front, and the helmets would look new and terrific. Drinking a beer and thinking about it, he wondered if the shiny clear coat would make the sun shine off the helmets and blind the pitcher for the other team. Then he realized that he was thinking too much about it. Still, kids from the Heights rarely got new equipment of any kind, and making their batting helmets look sharp would inspire them.

He had also received an allotment of tournament hats from the club. He had begged for 25 and gotten them -- enough for all the kids and coaches, and a few extras. All the City Heights teams wore the same tournament hats -- green and white, with black letters of "CH" in script, right in the front. The kids kept their hats, as usual, the only part of the uniform that was theirs. Tommy made a mental note to get new white wristbands for the whole tournament team, and give them out right before the first game. If nothing else, things like the helmets and the wristbands would make his little team feel special. And they were special -- they were the best City Heights had at their age level. They were the all-stars of their neighborhood, and he was going to make them feel like it.

True to his plan for the second half of the season, he had practice for the Giants at 2:00 p.m. The earliest any other team could get together was 4:30, when some of the coaches could get home early from work. As usual, he had their game field to himself. Tommy took stock of his team. *Things are going well.* He worked on pitching with Josh, Fred and Rick. Alex begged out of that, and Tommy gave up the idea of making his catcher into a pitcher.

Theo showed up, and Tommy had him throw some batting practice. When they broke up, Theo and Tommy stepped aside for a talk. Tommy told him that he had to pick his tournament team by Friday, to start practicing the next week, so he wanted Theo's opinions. They discussed some players, some obvious choices, and a few that were not. Theo never put up his boy, Stevie, although, with his improvement and attitude, Tommy was thinking about him. He could take more than two kids from some teams, maybe as many as four from his own. He had the uniforms, and no one doubted that he had the Giants playing championship ball. Then, out of earshot of the kids, Theo told him a story.

"Tommy, did you know that Terry's oldest boy, Billy, took off?"

"Whaddya mean? He left home?"

"Yeah. He's only fourteen, and we're sure he ran off to live with his mom. She's somewhere just outside of D.C."

"What the hell, I thought she was no good somehow, although I don't really know why. And you say 'we' like you mean the police, right?"

"Yeah. Look, I told you I used to work vice, and now am on narcotics. Well, I've seen a lot. Tommy, the drug problem is getting huge, and it's moving out of the inner city. It's here, in the Heights, and out there, in the suburbs. There's too damn much money involved, you dig? It's all about money."

"Hell, isn't the Heights blue-collar straight, you know, for the most part? But what does that have to do with my assistant coach, and why are you telling me all this?"

"I like you, man. You're a real hero to my boy. But your buddy, Terry, I'm not sure about him. This is a warning. If he ever tries to do any funny business deals with you, back off. Never mind the quick money. The neighborhood needs guys like you and Brian. In fact, you can warn him, too."

"You're saying he's dealing? Right here in City Heights, right under everybody's nose?"

"Maybe. Lookkit. Divorced dads don't get custody of their kids. Almost never happens, right? You have a shot at that? No. He did. Why? When he split up with his wife, he was on a list of people to watch out for here on the west side. We think he was on to us, and next thing you know, somebody drops a dime on his ol' lady. She gets busted in her car with a shopping bag full of shit. Good shit. High-grade Panama Red, in fact. Odd thing is, her fingerprints are on the shopping bag, but not on the bags of dope, get it? So, she plea bargains, and as part of it, agrees to a divorce and Terry getting custody. Further, that she won't contact the kids for two years. That time is up. Now, Billy has looked her up, gotten her side of it, and has gone to live with her. She called us is how I know. She realizes Terry has legal custody, and she doesn't want to get in trouble with interfering with that. Doesn't want us to think she came and kidnapped her boy. We're probably going to let the boy stay there, at least for now."

"Hell, Theo, I always thought Terry smoked a bit now and then, but I never heard this. What do you want me to do?"

"Stay out of the dope stuff as it comes around. Talk to your boy and your team. Stay clean. I'd bust you if I had a reason to. Got to. We gotta fight it in the Heights. Terry can 'get Jesus,' or that hairy mother-fucker will go down if he goes back in business."

"Ok."

They left it like that, except that Tommy then asked Theo if he had any interest in helping work with the 9-10 tournament team.

"Maybe. You need a brother on the staff, huh?"

Tommy wondered if he had offended his assistant, but assumed honesty was best. He stared right into Theo's eyes.

"Damn right. That's right. I need a 'brother,' or a 'soul man,' or an 'African-American,' call it what you want, that's right! The kids on the team need to have minority fathers working with 'em. Role model, damn your hide! You in or out, brother?"

Theo smiled for the first time in the intense conversation.

"Take it easy, man. I'm in, and that's with or without Stevie on the team. He'll come along with me and be the damn water boy if you want him to, just to be near more baseball. You have us both, 'brother.'"

The cop then reached out and shook Tommy's hand, with the thumb lock shake, and stared into his eyes. Tommy could feel the power in his grip and arm, and thought about the fact that all Baltimore off-duty cops had a piece on them, somewhere. Maybe Theo's was strapped to his ankle. Theo was one tough S.O.B. and Tommy was glad he was on their side and lived in the Heights. As they left, apparent friends, Tommy wondered about how the city needed honest cops, and how tough it would be for Stevie if anything ever happened to his dad. In a few years, Stevie would learn more about his dad's business, and Tommy hoped the kid would be proud of his father. Then he went home and sprayed another coat of green paint on the tournament batting helmets.

During the week, Tommy planned to hang around some other games, taking one last look at his all-star picks, then talk to each coach and invite the players to join the tournament team. He had a line-up roughed out already, but would fine-tune it in the five weeks he had before Towson. No one would refuse. It was a big honor for the kids and their parents. Sometimes a kid would go on a vacation in August, when the Towson games were, and just as often, the player would stay home with a relative or neighbor to play in the tournament. As he talked to each team and the all-star players, he gave each of them a schedule of practices that he had copied at a Kinko's. He knew that being manager of the Giants and the tournament team would keep him busier than ever, but he didn't have much of a life besides baseball. *Anyway,* he reasoned, *this is the one year I committed to doing it, and it is already half over.* When the Giants' season ended in four weeks, he would have more time for the all-stars.

The eight games in the second half of the Giants' season began and ended with the Red Sox. On Tuesday evening, the team began its defense of first place. They had lost to the Sox in the first half, but Tommy and the coaches knew that they hadn't played well then. Tommy had decided to keep the Giants' pitching rotation and batting order the same for the rest of the season, if he could. Fred and Josh were the starters, with Rick as a reliever. The first five in the batting order would be the best players, and probably play the whole game, unless they had a huge lead or were way behind. Stevie, Josh, Fred, Alex, and then Joe would be his 1-5 hitters -- speed, then a combo of speed and power, then raw power. The last four hitters would rotate with the subs.

By Friday night, the Giants had won their first two games, and looked like a good bet to win the second half, and become champs of their age level for the second year in a row. One change he was making was that he wasn't giving Stevie the bunt sign much, forcing him to swing, and he was. Conversely, he gave the bunt sign in close games to his four and five spot hitters, something no other manager did. Tommy's answer was that those kids might be power hitters now, but when they were older they might not be, and learning to bunt would help them.

By Friday night, Tommy had his tournament team picked. He ended up in Slim's with his tournament coaches, Theo, Brian, Terry and Nathan. He had asked a couple of the other managers he respected to help him, but they were all already committed to other teams. The older teams usually attracted the better coaches, it seemed. Not only did the club do better with their older players, it was closer to being big time baseball. Pitchers threw more than one pitch. Tommy had asked Nathan about being a coach, even though he knew little about baseball. Nathan, to Tommy's great delight, had offered to be more of the "equipment and refreshment coach."

"Hey, Nathan, does this mean any more of your famous hot dogs when we're on the road over in Towson?" Tommy had asked.

"You bet. And water and Gatorade, too. The wife and I know what's good for the kids, you'll see. We have a first aid kit and everything -- towels, ice, we'll bring everything. You just worry about baseball. We'll carry the equipment and everything."

Nathan didn't stay long, probably because they were meeting in a bar, but Tommy was glad to have him on board. Then he reviewed his picks with the coaches. He had eighteen players. Ten were white, seven were black, and there was one lone Hispanic, or was the proper term Latino? There were fourteen 10-year olds, and four 9-year olds. They had five kids with pitching experience, and two catchers, plus a 9-year old apprentice. There were twelve kids who played infield regularly and six from the outfield. Five players had playoff or tournament experience. Overall, Tommy was pleased, although he knew that in a bigger organization half those kids would not make a true all-star team. Most of the other towns or neighborhoods that sent teams to Towson would not take any nine-year olds. Tommy figured he could have taken one or two more.

They set a practice schedule to begin the next Monday morning. As soon as the regular season ended, it would be twice a day, six days a week. Without rainouts, they should have three weeks of practice during the City Heights' season, then two weeks after the season with only the tournament team. Tommy asked Terry to work with the pitchers and catchers, and get every pitcher to learn to throw a changeup. He also took him aside and told him that he knew why he didn't like a cop on the team, and to "stay cool." Then Brian reminded everybody that their first job was to get the Giants the championship. That was how they left it.

Tommy's life settled even more into baseball - practices and games with the kids' teams, watching the Orioles on TV, and discussing both with his assistants and all the experts at Slim's or Max's or anywhere else he went in the Heights. His Giants beat the White Sox the second week of the half, but lost to the A's in a close one. Still, they were 3-1, and he was happy. The tournament practices were tough at first. He kept moving kids from position to position, and some of them didn't like it. "I play center field," one would say, as if he had a right to it, and that settled the matter. "If you want to play for me, you'll play wherever I put you," Manager Tommy would answer. Then he would try to explain how it needed to be a team effort, and what was best for the team had to come first.

By the end of the next week, he needed a break from kids and baseball. On Friday night, he cleaned up and even threw on a sport coat, one of the few he owned. It was an old tweed he had picked up in England when he had been there on a ship. He knew it was summer, and the tweed was typically a fall coat, but it was the best he had. He had bought it years ago, but had hardly ever worn it, and it looked new. *Tweed never goes out of style.* Even if it did, he didn't care. Guys from the Heights didn't try to keep up with any damn style pushed on them from Madison Avenue. He did not wear a tie.

Tommy drove on the Baltimore Beltway, I-695, and headed north away from the neighborhood. A casual acquaintance had told him that the night club in the Hilton Hotel, at the Reisterstown Road exit off the Beltway, was a good place on Friday nights for divorced guys in their 30's. Tommy had popped in there only once before, and knew it had a dance floor. That seemed to be an attraction for divorced women. It let them get close to you without the commitment of a date. It had worked before, with Maria and the gals from PWP. He also knew that Reisterstown was an upscale neighborhood, had a fancy private school nearby, and a high percentage of Jewish residents.

The oval-shaped bar was crowded, but he took a seat where he could view the dance floor and the tables. As his eyes adjusted to the dim lighting, and his ears to the loud music of a four-piece band, he saw that indeed there were some women without dates. Some sat in groups at tables, and guys came over to talk them up, or asked them to dance. *Christ, it's just like high school, that's why people my age are here -- it's a comfort zone.* If the dance goes well, you offer to buy her a drink. It was sexist, but it was what the "D" crowd understood. If the female wasn't interested, she begged off, or had to go to the powder room. He had two mixed drinks, vodka 7's, and, feeling like some kind of desperate, lonely loser, was ready to leave. Then he noticed her.

She was kitty-corner across the bar from him. She seemed to be alone, which he found interesting. He watched as she turned down a couple of offers to dance. Maybe she was a bitch. Maybe she was one of those married women who came to places like this just to tease, and pump up her self-esteem when guys hit on them. She was short, brunette, and had long hair. She had dark eyes, and what Tommy called a spaghetti catcher blouse. That meant it was low cut, and showed a lot of cleavage. He wondered if he was becoming a boob man, and could that be? He had always thought he was a leg man, but he couldn't even see her legs, and was interested. She had a lot to show. Or, was the chest attraction because of his experience with Maria's charms? *Damn, she probably has legs like four by four's.* He decided to check 'em out anyway.

Soon they were dancing, which pumped up ol' divorced Tommy's esteem, since he had seen her turn others down. Better yet, her legs did not resemble the framework of a house. She was apparently tanned all over and she actually smiled at him. He sneaked a look or two over the top of her low-cut blouse, and saw that her boobs looked real and tanned (did she sun bathe nude, he wondered?), and had some freckles.

"You're staring," she told him.

"Huh? Excuse me? Whatever do you mean?"

"You know what I mean, babe, we're not kids here. It's okay. I like it. C'mon, I'll buy you a drink." He could not believe what he was hearing. She did buy him a drink, too, and refused all offers of payment.

"Look, I'm not poor, and things are changing, she told him. Women can stand on their own you know. I work, I have income, own my own house, and if I like a guy, I can turn the tables a bit." She was smiling as she said it. They quickly established that they were both divorced, she had no kids, lived nearby, and she was in advertising. *Boy, are you ever in advertising.* She was Jewish and he was Polish, but neither went to synagogue or church regularly. They danced some more, took turns buying drinks, and before they knew it, it was closing time, 1:00 a.m.

"Walk me out to my car, will you?" she asked. Tommy wondered now if they would need two cars, or just one. Maybe he could follow her to her place. After all, it was a lot closer than his was. Out in the parking lot, she unlocked her Accord and turned to face him.

"I like you Tommy, but I'm going straight home tonight. Still, you might like to know that I have a hot tub room in my house, right off the bedroom. Maybe you'd like to check that out some other time?"

"Oh, yeah!" He leaned into her, put his arms around her waist and kissed her. She did not pull away. It seemed a good sign. Then she gave him a better one.

"Here, you've been staring at these all night, check 'em out." She took his hand and guided it inside the blouse. She felt warm, large, and terrific, but the sample didn't last long.

"Tommy, I know this is like high school or something, you know, making out in the parking lot. We're older than that. So, I'll give you my number, and you can call me or not. Either way, it's okay -- I'm a big girl." She pulled away from him, wrote down a number, stuffed it in his hand, gave him a quick kiss, and before you could say anything, was gone. Tommy took the long drive home around the Beltway very carefully, considering the drinking. He wondered if she was some new kind of woman, one still apprehensive about men, but more aggressive than he had grown up with. He had gone to high school in the Deep South, and he had already learned that the northern girls played the game differently. Baltimore was on the border, but his new friend, Rachel, was playing with the faster, northern team. *Hell yeah, I'll call you.*

Tommy slept in a bit Saturday. By the third cup of coffee, he remembered that there was a special meeting down at the field in the afternoon. Big John somehow had arranged for a couple of the Orioles to come down to the field and do some kind of talk for the kids. There would be autographs later. The only problem was that they did not know who the Orioles would send. The kids were supposed to wear their uniforms. Tommy checked with Alex, and he said he wanted to go and see who was there.

Tommy and son arrived at the field on time. There were about a hundred City Heights kids, of different ages, standing around, most with their uniforms on, waiting to see which of their heroes would show up. Big John was there and in charge of it all. To keep the kids from getting antsy, he divided them up into age groups, and had them play catch. He had been smart enough to bring some baseball gear with him.

Only one car arrived behind Simpson School with any Orioles in it, and they weren't the ones the kids were looking for. There was no Jim Palmer and no Eddie Murray. It was the bullpen coach, Elrod Hendricks, with the pitching coach, Ray Miller. They did show up in full uniform, however, and had some baseball gear with them. What happened next impressed all the adults.

They rounded up the kids and had them sit around the first base bench, in the shade. Kids sat in rows, on the grass and dirt in front of the bench, and on the wall behind it. The adults now expected a ten-minute talk from former catcher Elrod or former pitcher Ray, followed by a quick autograph session, and a quick exit. *Hell, at least somebody from the real Orioles showed up for the kids.* What Hendricks and Miller did was amazing. They gave a talk and then divided the kids up into groups, and began drills. They taught infield, outfield, pitcher and catcher skills, and they worked hard at it. Miller threw pitches, and showed grips. He even threw some BP to the kids, and they really enjoyed it when he threw a major league curve ball. They stayed for a couple of hours, and by the time they sat down for autographs, they were both sweating. The kids were impressed, too. They had just gotten a professional workout and coaching session from two guys who, after all, were on television. It was a big-league experience.

Alex was able to get both autographs, and Tommy thanked both coaches. He also told Elrod that "the tag," from that World Series game, was one of the greatest moments ever captured on film in baseball history. Clearly, Elrod had heard about it a thousand times, but he still smiled. "Yeah, that was somethin'," was all he said. Tommy had the replay firmly in mind. Elrod, the Orioles' catcher, tagged a runner out at home, in a close play in a World Series' game. It wasn't until after the game, when someone played the film back in slow motion, that the real play was apparent. Elrod had reached to his right to catch the ball, with glove and free hand. Then, he had swung his body and left arm towards the third base side, to tag the runner with his catcher's mitt. The umpire was right there, to see that the glove hit the runner before he crossed the plate. All of this was fine, except when you stopped the film at the right frame, you could clearly see the baseball still in Elrod's right hand, nowhere near the runner.

The Giants next game was versus Big John's Dodgers. In the first inning, Tommy had to pull the now standard trick of swapping a pitcher for another position player, then putting him back as pitcher later, without taking him out of the game. The Giants' opponents had seen this trick so often they didn't even bitch about it anymore. The double steal was another matter. Tommy used a few bunts, and gave the take sign a few times when their pitcher was struggling. Alex blasted a home run, a legitimate one this time, over the left fielder's head, and Tommy couldn't be prouder. He had taken Alex, Josh, Rick and Stevie on the tournament team, and had told them all to "make me look good."

They won again, and other coaches were starting to concede the title to Tommy's team. With a 4-1 record the coaches agreed that they probably needed two more wins to clinch it, although one more might do it, like in the first half. Tommy also noticed that there were more parents coming to the games, too. It was the usual division. There were those who were supportive and positive, and those who used the City Heights baseball club as a free baby-sitting service. When these parents bothered to show up, they bitched about everything. The club didn't allow profanity, but you heard a word or two here and there. Most of the coaches tried to discipline their own fans, and protect the umpires from too much abuse. "Hey, it's just a game for the kids -- shut up or leave," was a typical comment. At times, fans had to separate a couple of fathers, but it was rare. In spite of the fact that kids going down into the woods next to the field to pee sometimes saw a used needle, there were no organized drug gangs in the Heights - not yet. The summer was one of the last of almost pure baseball, one during which the kids and coaches could suspend worry about weightier matters and concentrate just on baseball.

Their Friday game was against the Reds. Josh pitched, and Tommy was happier that he had picked him for the tournament team. The kid just threw strikes. You had to hit him, and the better players did, but he did not panic, and did not help you with walks. He also fielded his position well, and made several putouts from the mound. At the end of four innings, the Giants were ahead 14-3, and the umpire invoked the ten-run rule, also known as the mercy rule, and ended the game. There was no mercy rule in the Towson tournament, however, and Tommy worried a bit that Josh would face better hitters, and get tagged. He put those negative thoughts aside, however, convincing himself that Josh was one of the best City Heights had, and he, the manager, could do nothing about the talent pool except work with it as best he and his helpers could.

Tommy had changed arrangements with the ex for the weekend. He was spending so much time with Alex and baseball, he told her he wanted Saturday night off, to relax away from it. In reality, he had a date with his new friend, Rachel. Although they had been completely divorced for over two years, Tommy knew that if the ex knew he had a date she would try to mess it up by making him take Alex. She had done it before.

Tommy didn't wear the tweed this time, but dressed "casual nice," and picked Rachel up at her place at seven. She made a joke or two about his having a van instead of a real car. He took her out to a restaurant he knew near Westminster, in the country, about fifteen miles from her house. It was an Italian place, and located in an old farmhouse. He always figured an Italian place, with its choices of meat, fish, chicken and pasta, had something for everyone. They also had an appetizer that was Tommy's favorite -- clams oregenato -- stuffed clams with spices, baked to perfection.

Dinner went just fine. Rachel laughed at Tommy's choice of food. He had the clam appetizer, and then ordered clams and shrimp oregenato for his entrée, then, later, instead of desert, ordered another half-dozen clams. "I love this stuff, and you can't get it many places," was his defense. They ended up back at her house.

For a while, Tommy thought he had died and gone to a single guy's heaven. She not only fooled around, but she had taken him to her bedroom right away. In it there were sliding doors that led to an addition built onto the house. Real wood lined the walls of the extra room. It had plants all over the place, like a jungle, and there was a hot tub. She set the timer, starting the pulsating jets, suggested that he get naked, and disappeared. She lit some candles, turned out all the lights in the bedroom, and reappeared, nude, with towels. She was aggressive and sexy, and memories of Maria were far away. The warm jets of pulsating water not only eased the soreness of baseball workouts with the kids, but added to the excitement of what Rachel could and would do right in the tub. Images of his next assignment at sea dissipated, too. He began to see why guys might give up the crazy life of sailing around the world in the merchant marine. He spent the night.

She seemed happy that he did not go to church Sunday morning, and confirmed that she did not attend synagogue regularly. He also now thought it was true, what he had heard many times, that Jewish girls were sexy and liberal, and not just politically liberal. He recalled that there had been one Jewish family in his neighborhood when he was in high school, and the daughter was his age and very attractive. Although his best male friend in high school was Jewish, it was different than dating a Jewish girl. It just wasn't done, not in his neighborhood, family, church, or circle of friends. His euphoria over finding Rachel, and her being so damn good, didn't last. His visions of a new steady girlfriend, one without kids, evaporated too. At a breakfast of bagels and scrambled eggs, he tried to arrange another date. She started talking about her hot tub, and how she liked to have parties.

"What do you mean, have some people over, right? Then, you and me later?"

"Not exactly. Look, Tommy, I like you, you know, but I like some adventure, too. When I say 'Let's do a party,' I mean other couples, in the tub and in the bedroom, you know. I know a couple that is perfect. You'll like her. She has a better body than I do."

"Christ. And you make it with the guy right there, too, right? I mean, a group sex scene, that's what you want me for?"

"Well, yeah. Look, you'll like it. You're not goin' to fall in love with me anyway. Live a little. What do you think?"

"I'll have to think about it. I'll call you." That was how he left it, but he knew he would not go for it. *I'm too straight maybe*, he thought, on the ride back to Paradise. *My God, have I met a woman who is too sexy for me? Too open, too much?* He hadn't imagined that was possible, but the prospect of being in her bedroom while she and another guy . . . it wasn't him. Even if he had an arranged date at the same time, it was wrong somehow. *Old-fashioned, that's what you are.* Now he didn't know if he wanted to go out with her if she agreed to just another date with the two of them. Was she so wild she was fooling around with other guys, or groups? Was he at risk for some kind of disease? Damn, was he okay now? She was so pretty, why the hell did she have to screw it all up with this group business? *Wasn't that just for losers who read weird magazines?* He reaffirmed his commitment to a summer of baseball, and if a woman showed up in his life, okay, and if not, that would be okay, too.

Sunday morning he went out to the shed and put one last coat of green spray paint on the tournament team batting helmets. The landlord came out to see what he was doing, and seemed to appreciate his efforts. Mr. Walker was over 80, but he and Tommy got along well. He figured it was partly because he didn't have parties in his apartment, was quiet, and Mr. Walker liked his work with kids. Within a couple of days, the helmets would be ready for a couple of coats of clear, acrylic finish, then the press-on letters. They would look sharp and new.

Tommy picked Alex up at ten, and they went to the little racquet club for a quick game. When the game ended, Tommy bought the boy a soda while he had a beer. Then, they made a quick trip to the supermarket, and a return to his apartment. They watched a game on TV and did little else. Tommy hated to admit to himself that he was tired from his date, a little housework, and a racquetball match with a ten-year old, but it was true. He made a mental vow to work out more and get in better shape. He was still too young to feel old. He took Al back about six, and reminded him that the coming week was the last for the City Heights league, and to stay rested. "I'm counting on you, pal -- both for the Giants and the tournament team."

Tommy ran a tough practice with his tournament picks Monday morning, but an easier one with the Giants in the afternoon. The reason was simple. He had his discipline and assignments straight with the Giants. He was still establishing himself as boss with the tournament kids. He hadn't made any final decisions on starters, batting order, or positions. Besides, the little Giants had proven themselves, and were one win away from repeating as champs. Tommy wanted that badly, but he knew he needed to stay loose with those kids to get it. He also knew that much of what those kids knew about baseball they had learned from Kirk the Jerk. *It was too bad that the guy couldn't ease up with little kids, and too bad that he had taken his kid away from the neighborhood team.* However, if

Tommy did win it all, it would at least be partly because of his efforts, the time he spent with the kids, if nothing else, and that would be something. Nothing else in his life -- work, money, or women, was right, so he felt that he needed some success in baseball.

Tuesday's game was with the Cubs. Fred was pitching well, and throwing harder than usual. He was a big kid, and told Tommy that his father had told him he should "hum it in there more." They didn't argue. The Giants had a nice lead, and, by gathering information from the other team's members who were hanging around the park, the coaches knew that if they won this game, no other 9-10 team could catch them. The only potential problem was that there were dark clouds overhead, and it could get ugly. They had to finish four complete innings for the game to count, by club rule.

By the third inning it looked like hell itself was overhead, but there was no lightning or rain, so they kept playing. The Giants' coaches met with the Cubs' coaches, and they all agreed that if they saw lightning nearby, they would call the game off, rain or no rain. They made it to the top of the fifth inning, with the Giants comfortably ahead, 9-5, when it began. There was lightning, thunder, and huge rain pellets that seemed as if they had been thrown down from above. The ump called the game finished, the players just waved to their friends on the other team, and the coaches and parents scrambled to jam the bats, balls, and helmets into the duffel bags. Coach Tommy did not want any of his players walking home. He had Brian scoop up the Giants' equipment, while he ran over to his van, unlocking the sliding side door, and hollering for all the Giants to get in. The kids ran and jumped in, soaked, but happy. They had won the championship, with a game left to play. They liked the van, and now knew that Tommy would "ride them" all home. Brian threw the canvas bags in the back, under the fold-down bed that also worked as a seat, hollered to Tommy to meet him at Slim's, and ran off, into the wet, dark, early evening.

Tommy sat in the driver's seat, looked around to take stock of his team, and figure out who lived the closest. He had to ask a couple of kids where they lived, since they always walked down to the field. There were some parents at the game, but they were also running to their cars. Tommy rolled down his window enough to tell them that he would bring all the kids home. To send them running, under the trees, to their parents' cars, with lightning and heavy rain drops pelting them wasn't worth it, he figured. Besides, there was a jumble of happy, wet Giants sprawled all over his van, like an impromptu party of nine and ten-year olds. Tommy reached into the glove compartment and came up with a couple of large packs of bubble gum, which he threw in the back and told the kids to pass around. There was a scramble for the gum, and some shouting, but it seemed like everybody got a piece or two. Then he put the V-8 Chevy into gear and pulled out of the parking lot, through the already-forming deep puddles of water. It was a happy group, and some of the kids were yelling, "We beat, we beat," or, "We're the champs, you got no chance," and other kid yells. In spite of the weather, it was a rare, happy time for many of the hard-nosed kids from the blue-collar neighborhood of City Heights. Times like these that make it all worthwhile. His own boy's happiness, as one of the leaders of the team, made it more special to him. He doubted if any of the boys knew how rare the day was, but he also knew that the time would come, many years hence, when they would understand it.

He started dropping kids off with the ones who lived closest to the field. The routine was simple. Tommy pulled up in the street parallel to the curb, double-parked. A kid would open the sliding door, and everyone would yell, "Go! Go!" and the player would run like hell through the storm and into his house, usually a row house. Mostly it was a house where someone was already there, with the front door open, smiling and waving, already knowing they had done it, and happy that his or her boy was safely home.

Josh was next to last, and then Tommy took Alex home. As he pulled up in front of the wood frame structure, it was obvious something odd had happened. Alex's mom was standing on the front porch, waiting. There was an ambulance in front of the neighbor's house on Hillview Road, just two doors away. Red lights were flashing, and there were neighborhood residents all over, some on their porches, and some with umbrellas near the house on Hillview. It was a house where two young boys lived, kids eight and ten, who didn't play baseball, but kids Alex played with. As Alex prepared to bolt from the passenger's seat, his mom came out and ran around the van, in the pouring rain, to Tommy's side.

"What the hell's going on?" he asked.

"Oh, Tommy, I'm not sure, somebody was hurt bad playing behind the neighbor's house right there." She pointed to the house kitty-corner to her house, and just below the crest of the hill.

"Where? Who?"

"Down in the woods, I think. Somebody said it was that kid who comes over here to play sometimes. Alex knows him. He plays baseball with the club. Jimmy something, I think he's eleven."

"Jimmy Cavaretta? The Italian kid, from over on Chapelgate Road? He plays in the 11-12 year-old league."

"Yeah. Oh, God, look!"

Tommy turned to look at the neighbor's house, and saw two paramedics carrying a stretcher from the side of the little clapboard house. A plain blanket covered the stretcher, and the form underneath it was small. The woman who lived there was standing there watching, soaking wet and crying. Tommy jumped out of the van.

"Stay here. I'll see what's going on."

He ran over in front of the house just as the medics shut the doors to the ambulance. It drove off, but no siren was on. There was a gathering on the front porch of the house, and Tommy knew everybody there. They were all neighborhood people. Some of them were crying, while others just shook their heads. He heard their story and then ran around by the side of the house, down into the woods. It wasn't much of a woods. It was an inner-city version. There was a slope behind the houses on Hillview where a bunch of trees grew. Below that was the back alley of the row houses along Frederick Avenue. You could get out of sight of the houses behind Hillview Road, but you would then be in sight of the row houses. It wasn't much for woods, but there were a bunch of large, shady trees there, and all the kids in the neighborhood played there.

The story was simple, but brutal and unbelievable. Indeed, it was little Jimmy in the ambulance, and he was dead. When the storm struck, he had been playing in the woods with some other kids. According to one of the Hillview kids, there had been a huge crack of lightning, and the next thing they knew, Jimmy was down. He had squirmed a moment, then was still. The kids had run up to get help. Their mom had called 911, and then run down to the tree. She had done CPR. She had no chance. Tommy walked down to the tree, and saw it. There was a black, burned mark on the truck of an elm tree. The other kids said Jimmy had been standing right there. He fell to his knees in disbelief. If the boy had been a foot away one way or the other, the lightening would have missed him, and he would be home now. Instead, somehow God had allowed him to die right there. No one could have helped. Tommy prayed and he was not alone at the tree.

Back up the little hill, he tried to comfort the woman who had tried CPR. She could not speak. He went back to Alex's house, and told the boy and his ex what had happened. In a rare moment for the three of them, they huddled up on the porch and said a prayer for Jimmy. *Just because we don't go to church regularly doesn't mean we don't have any spirituality.* He comforted Alex as best he could, but it seemed the boy did not fully comprehend that Jimmy, a kid he knew and occasionally played with, was gone. Tommy realized that so far in his son's life he had not had to face the death of anyone close. All his grandparents were still alive, and Alex had never been to a funeral. Tommy forgot about Slim's. After a while, he went home, and, remembering that the dead boy was a club member, called Big John, the club president, and broke the news to him. John was distraught, saying "Oh, my God," over and over. Tommy finally made him realize that the club would need to send something to the parents, and members would need to know where and when the viewing, if there was one, would be. John recovered enough to say that he knew the parents, and would find out and let everybody know.

Tommy had practice for the tournament team and the Giants on Wednesday, but his heart wasn't in grueling practices. He just talked to the kids about Jimmy, and asked them what they wanted to do. As he expected, they all wanted batting practice. They trusted Tommy and the other coaches to just dump it in over the plate, where they could hit it, and that was fun. It was like going to the batting cages. Brian made it down to the Giants practice, and helped talk to the kids. He was damn good at it -- as good as he was selling you real estate, or talking you into sponsoring a team. Tommy, as usual, had been alone with the all-stars in the morning practice.

The A's lost their game on Wednesday, and that officially clinched it for the Giants. There wouldn't even be a one-game playoff. Tommy's team had won both halves. Thursday's practice for the Giants was different. Tommy knew it was the last practice for most of the kids, except for those few who had made the tournament squad and would play baseball through most of August. He fooled around a lot, and even disciplined himself with a lap around the pole. The kids all yelled and jeered at him to run faster as he jogged out into center field. He also took his best players aside, and explained to them that they would not play much in the last game. He could afford to play the subs more, and, in fact, would start all of them in the game. He expected his best players to root for all of the subs from the bench, however, and tried to remind them of the team concept, and how many of those kids had gotten a key hit or a putout during the season, and how they all deserved recognition. He emphasized to the players that Friday's game was the end of the season, and how they should invite everyone they knew to come watch them play their last game.

The Friday game versus the Red Sox was different. The kids who had played their two required innings each game all year, and not much else, started the game. Tommy used only pitchers as starters, as he did not want anyone to get ten runs ahead of him. It didn't matter if they lost the game, but he wanted the full six innings to play his backup kids as much as possible. The usual starters would be limited to the two required innings, a fact not lost at all on the subs, who loved the fact that they were in the starting lineup. Their parents loved it too. Tommy, Brian, Theo, Terry and even Nathan received several congratulations from parents, and offers to buy them beer.

They did lose the game, 12-6. It featured numerous strange plays, one of which was a classic. In the third inning, a Red Sox batter had hit what should have been a routine single to right field. Lee, the Giants' fielder, a nine-year old who didn't play much, ran in and scooped up the grounder, a fact that made Tommy proud. Then, the Sox batter, also a sub, rounded first and kept going towards second, in spite of the coach putting up the stop sign. Lee then panicked, and instead of throwing the ball to the second baseman, kept running in to the infield, after the batter. The Sox kid rounded second, and, with both benches and all the fans yelling loudly, had no idea what to do, so he kept running. Lee, in a similar fix, kept chasing him. The Sox kid rounded second. Lee chased him, and, possibly remembering his base-running instructions, touched second on his pursuit. The Sox kid reached third just ahead of Lee, who was gaining. The third base coach put up his hands in the classic stop sign, but the Sox kid was inspired, and headed for home with his head down. He apparently had no idea where the ball was, perhaps thinking it was still way out in right field, and clearly had no idea that Lee was five feet behind him and in furious pursuit. Lee caught the kid five feet from home plate, tagging him on the butt with the ball, which caused the kid to tumble into the catcher at home, who had been hollering for the ball for what seemed like hours. The three players went down in a pile, but Lee held onto the ball, and the umpire, stifling laughter as best he could, called the runner out. The Giants all high-fived Lee as he ran towards the bench, with the ball and the third out secured. He had no idea he had done anything wrong. He had gotten the batter out, hadn't he? It was the kind of thing coaches of young kids lived for -- those great plays you could not script.

There was a variety of emotions in the post-game comments. There were parents and older brothers and sisters of the Giant players, all happy. Then there were the adults who passed around the information that the viewing for Jimmy Cavaretta would be the next day in the afternoon. It killed any plans for celebration, and Tommy just reminded his coaches that he was taking Saturday off, but would work the tournament team in twice-a-days, starting Monday. He expected all of them to make the evening practices, and the mornings if they could take the time off work. It was Friday, August 2nd, and the opening round of the Towson Tournament would begin just eight days later, on Saturday, the 10th..

Chapter 8: Tournament Time

Saturday's viewing at the funeral home was tough. It was clear to Tommy that he had to go, to pay his respects to the boy, his parents, and to the City Heights Boys Club. Tommy told Alex that he had to go, too, and even wear a tie, but then he showed some mercy for the ten-year old and told him that he didn't have to go right up to the body. Further, if there was more than one room, he could stay in another one, or out in the hallway, and not even go in the room with Jimmy's body.

The parlor was right on Frederick Avenue, about a mile east of Simpson School, and not far from Mount Olivet Cemetery. Coming from City Heights to the viewing, you drove right past Loudon Park National Cemetery, and the long rows of crosses seemed to set the somber tone of the day, even before you pulled into the parking lot and saw the attendants in their dark suits waiting outside. Alex was quiet as they walked up to the front door, and Tommy, knowing his boy was too old to hold a hand, just put his arm around him and patted him on the shoulder. Alex had a long-sleeved white shirt and one of his dad's ties on. Tommy had his only suit on, a dark blue one with pinstripes. He referred to it as his "wedding and funeral" outfit.

The first person they recognized was Big John. He was coming out, and wiping his eyes with a handkerchief. There were tear streaks down both cheeks. Tommy had never seen the rough truck driver in a suit, let alone crying. They hugged, in as manly a fashion as possible, but John could barely speak. He mumbled something about it being "not right" or "too young," or something, and went out into the parking lot for a smoke. Alex was silent. John was one of the toughest guys around, and it probably shocked the boy to see how much emotion and compassion he could display.

Luckily, there was a reception room just inside the building, with no bodies in it. There were some people Tommy didn't know serving punch or soda, and he took some to Alex. They sat in the back on a couple of metal folding chairs. Tommy went to look for the parents, to pay his respects, and also to see what room Jimmy was in.

"I'll be right back," he told the boy.

"Dad, stay right here, you know?"

"Look, I know this is rough, but you can stay right here. I'll find the parents and pay our respects for both of us. Just hang out. Drink your soda."

On his way down the hall, Tommy flashed back to his first funeral home experience. He vaguely remembered it. He had been only five. It was his grandpa, his father's father. He had hardly known him, but he still remembered his little brick house with the grape arbor in the back. The viewing had scared him, and he remembered most of the people speaking Polish instead of English. He recalled that the women had doted on him, finding him things to eat, and smothering him with kisses he didn't want.

He asked around, and found Mr. and Mrs. Cavaretta just inside the viewing room, where they were greeting people. They look so young. In fact, he would find out later that they were indeed younger than he was. It seemed incredible to be so young and have lost a son. They both looked sedated. Tommy introduced himself and shook their hands, not feeling comfortable hugging either one, since he did not know them. He told them he was a coach at City Heights, and that his boy, who knew Jimmy, was in the next room. Tommy then went over to the coffin. It was open. You would never have guessed the extent of the boy's injuries. Little Jimmy looked asleep, like he would wake up at any second and shout "April Fool's" or something, and go back to being a kid in the baseball league. Tommy bowed his head and prayed. After a talk with a couple of the other coaches, he went back to Alex.

"Sorry I took so long. We can go anytime. I spoke to the parents. They know you're here, and that you're sorry for them."

"Dad, I'll do it."

"Do what? We can leave, I said."

"I'll go in the room, you know, where Jimmy is."

"You don't have to, you did fine coming this far."

"Dad, sooner or later, I'm going to have to do this, right?"

"That's right."

"Well, might as well be now. Just tell me, he . . . he looks okay, right? I mean, they 'fix him up' to look okay, right?"

"Yeah, Al. He looks like he's asleep. You won't see any injury. You just walk as close as you want to, and stop. I'll stop with you. We'll bow our heads. Say a silent prayer. On the way out of the room, I'll introduce you to his parents. Just say 'I'm sorry,' or 'Jimmy was a good friend,' something like that."

"Okay."

Tommy then became prouder of his boy than when he hit a home run. The kid walked right into the viewing room, and right up to the casket. He held up fine even talking to the parents. He started to choke up on the way out, and Dad handed him a Kleenex. "Here, blow your nose," he told him, but they both knew he needed it to wipe away tears. Tommy did too, and they left. Tommy did not attend the funeral itself, as he did not know the family at all, and they had quite a few people to attend it. He just dropped Alex off, and went back to his place to change. He stayed home. It would be a quiet day.

The next day, Sunday, Tommy had tickets to an Orioles' game. He didn't feel much like going, but it was a special day, and Alex wanted to go. It was the day of the annual Oriole Wives' Auction, and Tommy had tickets to that, too. All year long, the players' wives collected items to auction off. Many were baseball things -- balls, gloves, spikes, and autographed pictures, things their husbands contributed or begged off their friends from other teams. Others were from local businesses, things like having your portrait painted, or dinner for two somewhere. Several hours before the game, you entered the stadium from behind the left field fence and scoreboard. There was a complete BBQ set up, and your ticket entitled you to as much as you wanted, mostly burgers and dogs. They gave you a list of the items in the auction. All the proceeds went to a children's hospital.

Tommy and Alex thought it was cool just to be back there, in a part of the stadium a fan never sees. Then, while they were sitting on the grass and eating, several of the Orioles, apparently under orders from their wives, came through the crowd, shaking hands and signing things. As the auction part began, it became clear to Tommy that he probably would not get anything. There were not only a lot of the players' friends there, but also many doctors and their wives, in support of the hospital. They seemed to overbid on everything. They paid incredible sums for a used glove. Alex seemed to understand, but Tommy could see he was feeling poorly. With his usual, "What the hell, I'm going broke anyway" attitude, Tommy started to holler in some bids on baseball items. Alex was proud of his dad, and seemed to understand when Tommy dropped out of the bidding. Then, they had some luck. Towards the end, when many people were leaving to find their seats for the game, or had already won some items, Tommy had in interest in an item. It was a group of autographed baseballs, each one autographed by an Oriole rookie. The players were the new guys, the unknown ones, and not too many people were interested. To his great surprise and Alex's delight they won the bidding at $35. Tommy sent Alex to pay and pick up their prize. There were five brand new American League baseballs, each with a neat, clean autograph. Tommy checked them out, but he didn't recognize all the names and two of the players were already back in the minor leagues. At least he knew one name, third baseman Cal Ripken. "Maybe he'll amount to something," Tommy said, giving the baseballs to Alex.

The City Heights 9-10 year-old tournament team now had one last week of practice to try and become as good as teams from neighborhoods and towns all over the Baltimore metro area. They met Monday to Friday at 9:00 a.m. and again at 4:00 p.m. Tommy worked them for two hours each practice. He worked them hard Monday to Wednesday, and then eased up. He lectured them on getting enough sleep and not eating junk food. He told them to be especially good around the house, and to do everything their parents told them to. This was no time to be grounded. They would play their first game at Towson on Saturday, August 10th, and they needed every player. He told them how the older kids from City Heights sometimes did well at the big tournament, and now it was their chance to show that the nines and tens could, too.

"Kids from City Heights are tough," he reminded them. "I expect you to play smart baseball, and concentrate on every pitch. That's what I expect."

Morning practices were the usual combination of fielding and hitting. In the afternoons, they added side work with pitchers, when Tommy had help from Terry, Brian, Theo or Nathan, all of whom tried to get off work early to come down to the field. One good thing, since the club season was over, was that they had the 9-10 field to themselves, anytime they wanted it. Tommy even ran the kids a bit after practice Monday and Tuesday, making them run around the bases a few times. He did not expect he could get a kid in better shape in one week. He wanted them tired on Monday and Tuesday, so they would stay home and sleep well. Then he would allow their energy level to build up again towards Saturday morning's big game.

On Wednesday he caught a break when his friend Brian took the whole day off and came down to practice. In between practices, they went back to Tommy's little apartment. They finished off the batting helmets, and they looked sharp as hell. They were not only brand-new looking, but different from all the other club teams. Before the afternoon session with the kids, they stopped off at the local sports shop and bought white wristbands for the whole team. It was amazing how much little things like that were worth to the blue-collar kids from the Heights. Brian also bought a couple of new bats, even though Tommy tried to stop him.

"You spend too much of your own money, Brian. We have enough bats."

"Ah, hell, the kids need some new ones. It'll psych 'em up, you'll see. Just like your helmets and wristbands. This team is special. I can feel it. We're not gonna lose and be out in one day this year. We have a chance."

On Wednesday, Tommy eased up some more on the physical work, and spent more time on the mental part of the game. He used the same signs he had with the Giants for hitting, taking, bunting and stealing, and went over them again and again until the kids were sick of it, but knew them all. He went over the rules repeatedly, and special circumstances: the delayed double steal, tagging up when a fly ball is hit in foul ground, when you could call time out, and so forth. He worked them repeatedly with different possible double plays. He changed kids around and did it again and again.

On Thursday, Tommy concentrated on the pitchers, with different people taking turns throwing batting practice. In the evening practice, he had the other coaches go over anything they had seen in games that caused confusion. The outfielders practiced throwing the ball in to the cut-off man, who was the second baseman for right field, and the shortstop for center and left. He had them practice relays from the outfield to the cutoff man to the plate. He had subs run the bases while the kids threw it around.

Thursday night, Tommy and Brian drove over to Towson for the pre-tournament meeting. It was in a giant recreation center. The Towson folks were very organized, as they had been hosting a little-league level tournament for years. They gave each coach a bracket sheet, time schedule, maps of all the fields, driving directions to hand out to parents, and more. Tommy went up and drew for City Heights. There were sixteen teams in each age group, and it was double elimination. When you lost a game, you went into the losers' bracket. When you lost a second game, you went home. He drew "Towson," which meant his team would play the host team Saturday morning at 9:00 a.m. They were always one of the better teams.

"Way to go, coach," Brian said, smiling.

"Fuck you, we can beat those guys. Gotta play the good teams sooner or later."

Friday was an easy practice day. There was no running. He did fielding in the morning and let them go early. He let the kids hit batting practice all they wanted in the afternoon practice. He had the coaches field the balls and throw them in. The kids got a big kick out of seeing their coaches miss a ball or make a bad throw. They would holler out the same things the coaches had to them, like "Stay in front of it," or "Move your feet," and "Keep your glove down on the grounders!" Tommy even persuaded a couple of the moms who were there to play outfield, and the kids howled even more. It was great fun, and that's how he wanted to end it. Tomorrow would bring a lot of pressure. For most of the kids, it would be their first game anywhere outside of the neighborhood. He wanted them loose and happy. It would be their only chance.

There was a last coaches' meeting after practice. Tommy had insisted everybody be there. He had even called Slim's and asked them to reserve the table in the far back, where it was quieter. He bought the first pitcher of beer, and a soda for Nathan, and took out his notes. The team would meet at the parking lot behind Simpson at 7:30 a.m. sharp. He would take all the kids in the van with him, unless a parent objected and wanted to drive their own kid to Towson. It was to develop and foster the team unity concept, he said. Nathan would bring all the equipment plus Gatorade, water, and first aid stuff. Tommy told the others what he had done with the batting helmets, and he would bring them bagged up. Nathan would keep the surprise until right before warm-ups. He would then line up the five sparkling helmets in a row. Right before the start of the game, Brian would hand out the brand new wristbands.

The flyer he had sent home had stressed to the parents that Towson was a double-elimination tournament, and you would typically play two games a day, at least in the early rounds. When you lost a game, you went into the losers' bracket, where you tried to stay alive, to play the winner of the winners' bracket. The goal was to win early, and stay out of the losers' bracket. Some parents might not understand all that, so Tommy told the coaches to talk to the parents when they could. He wanted them to understand things. They would drive back to Simpson after the game, and meet there again in the afternoon for their second game Saturday. On Sunday, if they played twice, they had a special offer. Alex's mom, to her credit and Tommy's surprise, had offered to host the whole team at her house for a lunchtime cookout. She had also offered to wash the kids' uniforms while they were there. When they figured out their Sunday games, if they were still in it, ("and I damn well expect to be," Tommy added), they would tell the kids to bring an extra pair of shorts over to Alex's house. It was a terrific idea, to keep the team together. By Sunday, if they had a second game, they would be deep into the tournament, with its sixteen teams in their division, and the team concept was crucial. Plus, they would be tired by then, and at least they could try to make them rest.

Tommy told them that Alex's mom would try to have a naptime, like in kindergarten, without calling it that.

Tommy would coach third base, Brian first, with Theo the bench coach, Terry the pitching coach, and Nathan the equipment manager. Tommy emphasized that he wanted any of them to talk to him if he saw something; that is, was the pitcher changing his delivery, and not throwing strikes because of it? Did the other team look weak in any particular position, so perhaps Tommy would be more inclined to send a runner to the next base when that kid had the ball? Who looked tired? Were any of their players not paying attention in the outfield? By the second time around the batting order he wanted Theo to remind him of what the opposing kid had done the previous at bat. Was he aggressive, swinging at anything? If so, they would instruct the pitcher to throw to the corners. Was there a batter who stood there, trying to get a walk? If so, we'll just lob it over the plate, nice and easy, Tommy told them. His coaching style would not change much from the Giants, he told them. We'll run if we can, or if the game is close. If they can't field, we'll run some more. If the catcher can't throw, we'll steal every chance we get.

Then he went over his starting lineup. He had been discussing it informally with all the assistants, all week long, but it was time for final decisions. Nathan's wife would keep the scorebook for City Heights. Tommy listed the starters:

1.Jim, from the Red Sox, CF
2.Eric, from the White Sox, LF
3.Ronny, from the Cubs, P
4.Neal, from the Dodgers, 1B
5.Alex, from the Giants, C
6.Bobby, from the A's, RF
7.Matt, from the Orioles, 3B
8.Josh, from the Giants, SS
9.Rick, from the Giants, 2B

Overall, he told his friends that it was the best they could do. They had speed at the top of the order, power in the middle. He expected a lot of RBI's out of the 3, 4 and 5 slots. Josh and Rick, at the bottom, had little power, but they had speed and were smart. He would bunt them to start a rally if he could. The subs were: Stevie (Giants), Pete (Cubs), George (Reds), Brad (Reds), Doug (Dodgers), Roberto (A's), David (White Sox), Barrett (Orioles), and Will (Red Sox). The killer rule in the tournament was the fact that there was no two-inning participation rule. You could play your best players the whole damn game. Only pitchers were limited. They could throw seven innings in a week, but could not pitch on consecutive days. This was because of the weekend nature of the tournament. A kid could not pitch on Saturday and come right back on Sunday because it was a new week. But he could pitch Sunday, then again the following Saturday, with whatever innings he had left out of the seven, the organizers feeling that five days' rest was enough. Tommy told his coaches that he intended to play everybody if he could. He told Theo to have kids ready to pinch hit, especially in late innings if they were far ahead or far behind.

He ended by thanking them all for their efforts all summer long. "Stay positive around the kids, all the time," he added. "They don't realize how tough this is, and how much better most all-star teams are. That's what I want - I want them to feel that they are just as good as anybody, and play that way. City Heights kids are tough - City Heights kids can do it, that's the message. And keep it fun. Don't let them get uptight because we are. We keep our worries to ourselves. That's what I want tomorrow. You know, people who don't live in the city wouldn't understand how important this club is to the kids and the neighborhood. A lot of these kids don't have much else to look forward to except the baseball opportunities we provide for them." Tommy sat down, and wondered if he had said too much, and if it was too much like a speech, but the other guys applauded, for chrissakes, and ordered more beer. Then Brian stood up.

"Hey, we all know that whatever happens tomorrow, the kids and their parents owe a lot to my friend Tommy, here. I've lived in the neighborhood for years, and I'll tell you, no one has ever put this much time into a 9-10 team as he has. And that starts with the Giants, champs again even without Kirk, and now the all-stars. Lemme tell ya, these kids are psyched up for tomorrow, and we don't care if we are playing Towson we're going to kick some Towson butts!"

Some guys commented that Brian had enough beer and should shut up, but he wasn't done.

"And hey, one more thing! Tommy had the whole summer off thanks to the merchant marine, so let's toast -- Here's to the goddam merchant marine!" He raised his glass, as did the others, except for Nathan.

"Hey, I'm sorry, Nate," said Brian. "How's this? God Bless Tommy and the whole merchant marine!"

Nathan smiled and sipped his coke, but didn't stay much longer. He begged off with the true statement that he still had a lot to do to organize all the stuff for tomorrow.

Theo was the next to leave, but took Tommy aside on his way out.

"Look, man, you have a good look at Terry tonight?"

"Yeah. I mean, no. Whaddya mean?"

"His little eyeballs ain't right. I can tell. I bet you can, too. Look, if he's gone back to being a casual user, you know, just a little smoke now and then, okay. But, if he starts dealing like I think he did before, I'll take him down. Got to. You understand?"

"Yeah I do. Look, I'll talk to him after the tournament and see if he'll open up to me. Thanks, Theo. I know your heart's in the right place. And you make sure Stevie gets enough sleep tonight."

"Sleep? Hah! He thinks tomorrow is the World Fuckin' Series, Tommy. You should see it. He runs around the house in his underwear, practicing what he'll do if you put him in. He throws an imaginary ball up in the air, hits it with an imaginary bat, and runs through the house like each room is a base. He doesn't care that he's a sub, he's part of it, you know. He won't sleep, but you get some. You're looking a bit stressed, man."

Theo sauntered out of the bar, eyes darting this way and that, noticing who was at the video poker machine, and who he knew, and who might be a problem someday. *Christ, I couldn't be a cop*, Tommy knew, watching him leave.

Terry begged off next and only Tommy and Brian remained. They moved up to the bar, to free up the table. Waitresses appreciated such a move. In conversation, Brian let on that his wife wanted to move out of the neighborhood. "Far out," he added, "to the suburbs." They were the kind of places that Brian hated. None of them had the grit of City Heights, he told his friend. Tommy wondered if this was the kind of thing driving the two of them apart, or what the lawyer friend had noticed. In his experience, it had to be more than just where you lived, or how much time you spent with kids' baseball. Within minutes, though, Brian was back, acting like the big family man, the successful businessman, and the coach. He told Tommy that he knew Ronny's situation, and he would take care of him.

"No father at home, mother unreliable, but he is clearly the toughest kid we have, and maybe the best athlete. You should see him play pee wee football. He's a halfback and he likes to run into kids, not around them," Brian said.

He would make sure he was at the parking lot on time by just casually showing up outside his house. Between games he would even clean his uniform if necessary. There were no more revelations, personal or sports-related, and eventually, it was time to go home and get some sleep. Handling eighteen kids for at least two games Saturday and maybe more Sunday would wear anybody out.

On the drive to the game on Saturday morning, Tommy reminded himself that they had to stay loose and just play. If they could just win the first game, they would get their confidence up, and have a chance. Historically, most City Heights 8-year and 9-10-year-old teams lost twice the first day and were eliminated. Tommy wanted to stay alive until the second weekend. Do that and they would have another week of practice. Hell, do that and they might win it all.

The Towson Recreation Center itself was imposing, with eight ball fields back to back to back, all of which would have games going on, in different age levels, at the same time. There would be larger crowds than his kids were familiar with, and most of them would be rooting against them. As he drove up the Beltway with a van full of excited City Heights kids in their green and white uniforms, Tommy kept most of these thoughts to himself. They pulled into their assigned parking lot at 8:00 a.m., right on his schedule. There was plenty of time to loosen up little arms, take a little fielding and hitting, and get the kids acclimated to the big time. And, to them, it clearly was the big time. As the kids piled out of the van, cheering and yelling, Tommy noticed a couple of the kids with big eyes. They had never seen so many baseball fields, or so many people and players in one place. The coaches' main job today, especially Theo's, would be to keep them calm and keep their concentration on the game.

Before they had time to worry about anything, both teams were warming up, taking turns in the field. Tommy had drawn home team status, and City Heights would bat last, something he always preferred. That way, if the game was close in the sixth, you knew whether to play small for a run or two, using a squeeze play, perhaps, or if you needed a lot more, and would play to put lots of kids on base then get big hits to score them.

The new batting helmets were a big hit, and looked great all shiny and lined up in front of the bench. Coach Nathan also lined up all their bats, in a fan pattern, with a rosin bag, a towel, and a doughnut weight next to them, just like the Orioles. Brian handed out the new wristbands while Tommy exchanged lineup cards with the other manager and the home plate umpire. There was another good change from their own league -- they would have a second paid umpire in the field, not a volunteer. The kids tossed balls back and forth on their side, but kept stealing looks at the other team. Tommy knew that they were trying to see if they had a lot of big kids, or tough kids. They didn't have nearly as many black kids, being more of a suburban team, and that, in itself, was a lesson to his kids. Coach Terry had Ronny Brown, their starter, warming up way behind their bench, apart from almost everybody. The kid had a wicked fastball, and they didn't want anybody to see his speed.

Right before "play ball," Tommy gathered all the coaches together with Ronny and Alex, their battery.

"Okay. You two just play as if we're behind Simpson School. No different. All fastballs unless we give the signal for a changeup, right?" Two little heads nodded, but emitted no sound. "We'll start with 'smoke,' or 'smoke 'em.' That's the signal for the changeup, got it?"

"Yeah," two little heads nodded.

"Now, you guys know what to do with the first two pitches?" Brian had an idea what to do with the first batter they pitched to, but Tommy was unsure about it. He knew that teams from Towson had played hard baseball in the past, and he wasn't afraid to do it too. "Ronny, what are you going to do?"

"First pitch, I throw it over the umpire's head, into the backstop. Second pitch I throw it way behind the batter's back." He was smiling. Ronny was clearly the toughest kid they had, and the hardest thrower. The idea was to make the Towson kids think he was completely wild, and would hurt them.

"Right, then three down the middle and strike the bum out. Let's go. Huddle up with the team." Then they all did a little "City Heights baseball -- let's go, let's go, let's go!" cheer and took the field, nine little hearts beating wildly with excitement, and nine more on the bench watching with envy and encouragement.

It could not have started better. Ronny took a bigger windup than normal, playing up the charade, and hurled two missiles, one over everybody's head, and the other six feet wide of the plate. Alex went part way out to the mound, motioning down with his mitt, like he had seen the major league catchers do when the pitcher was high and wild. It was a great act. The Towson kids on the bench were pointing and talking, just what they wanted them to do. Their little leadoff batter had hit the dirt twice, and had his uniform dirty already. He did not swing the bat until he was 2-2. "He'll get the 'K,'" Tommy said to no one. Ronny struck him out and Tommy and Terry exchanged looks that meant, "He has it -- Ronny's on his game today."

Towson did not score in the first inning, and Tommy knew that the Giants would fight it out. They were anxious but not nervous. He felt like using the story of how the kids from other neighborhoods and towns "put their pants legs on one at time just like you do," but figured they wouldn't get it. There was no need for any Knute Rockne style speech. In the bottom of the first, Jim led off with a walk, and Tommy gave him the steal sign. He made it easily. Eric grounded out, but to the right side, so Jim made it to third with one out. Ronny nailed a line drive over the shortstop's head, and City Heights scored its first run. Ronny made it to second, and the CH coaches now hoped for a big inning. Come-from-behind victories were exciting, but a good coach wanted a lead -- an early one, and a big one. If you didn't hope for that, you were a fool.

They scored three runs, and took the field in the second with confidence. Brian could hear some talk from the Towson side, coaches and parents, saying things like, "This City Heights team isn't like the others." *Hell yeah,* Brian thought, *these kids can play ball, and have been practicing hard.* Once or twice an inning, Tommy or Brian called out to Ronny to "smoke 'em," or, later, to "give 'em some heat," which were code words for a changeup. It worked well. Tommy used the steal sign a couple of times and a hit and run once, to good effect. No one stole his signs.

In the fourth inning, Alex reached second base. Bobby smoked a liner to center field, and Tommy immediately waved his son over to third. Then the center fielder made an incredible play, running straight in at full speed. He did not play the ball safely, and made a shoestring catch. Tommy could not believe it, and Alex was halfway to third. "Back, go back!" he hollered, but it was too late. The kid not only made the circus catch, he knew enough to fire it right in to second base. They caught Alex off the base, and the inning was over.

"Way to go, Pops," Alex said, unkindly, on his way back to the bench.

"Hey, the kid made a fantastic play. I'm not perfect, you know." He was a bit pissed, as he expected more support from his own boy.

It stayed close, as a tournament game should. The dream of a big lead never materialized. They went into the sixth and final inning ahead by only one run, 7-6. Ronny was still pitching well, and they were only three outs away from a crucial opening round victory. Then, it became apparent that the players were, after all, from nine to ten-and-a-half-years old. They made errors. A couple of simple grounders slipped through the infield. There was a bad throw to first, and Ronny got mad about it and walked a batter. Tommy sent Brian out to settle him down, thinking that Brian was closer to him.

"Nobody's getting any good hits off you," Brian told him. "We need you to settle down, just throw strikes. Okay?"

"Yeah." Ronny Brown didn't say much. He didn't smile much, either, which said a lot about where he was from, and who he was. He struck the next two kids out, and Jim, in center, made a great catch of his own to end the inning. City Heights, however, was now losing 8-7, and had only one more at-bat.

Their number seven hitter, Matt, was first up. He struck out. Then, Towson put in a relief pitcher, which surprised the City Heights gang. Tommy whispered to Josh, the next hitter, to remind him that they needed a base runner. "You're smart, take a walk if they offer it." Josh worked the count and earned the walk. Then Tommy pinch-hit Stevie for Rick. He gave him the take sign on the first pitch, then the bunt sign. He had noticed that the Towson third baseman was playing back, and guarding the line. Tommy also hoped that Towson had never seen a kid as fast as Stevie, and he could bunt for a hit. He did it beautifully, and the City Heights bench came alive. They had the tying run at second, and the winning one at first, and only one out, with the top of the order coming up. Josh was smiling at second, staring at Tommy for any sign he might give, while Stevie was going crazy on first. Brian had to talk to him. It was high drama, and the parents in the stands now became more excited, too. The opposing parents outnumbered the City Heights parents, but the Heights' gang made up for it with noise.

Jim came up and tried to kill the ball. *You're the leadoff guy, for chrissakes. Just work your way on base. You're not the big hitter.* He was just a boy, though, and trying to help. He popped up to the right side. The Towson first baseman caught it, in foul ground, and now Towson was one out away from victory, and had the momentum. Their bench and fans came alive. Eric was up next, and the relief pitcher walked him, loading the bases. Josh was on third, Stevie on second, and Eric on first. Ronny was up next. Tommy again called time, much to the dissatisfaction of the Towson manager, but Tommy didn't care. "Hey Brian, talk to him," and Brian knew he needed to calm Ronny down. After a brief talk, the City Heights pitcher stepped to the plate.

The first pitch was a ball. Ronny tried to hit the second pitch to D.C., and fouled it off. The third pitch was a ball, and the fourth a called strike. Then Ronny got madder, waving the bat over his head as he had seen on TV. Tommy had no time to calm him. He gave no signs. It was two outs and the game on the line, and their best player at bat. The pitch came inside and hit him, and Ronny went down.

Their toughest kid was hurt, and squirming. Tommy and Brian reached him at the same time, Brian bringing along some ice wrapped in a towel. Ronny was crying. It had nailed him right on his little hipbone. It would bruise, but he would be okay. Brian rubbed ice on it, and reminded him how he gets hit worse than that in football, and they needed him to tough it out now, too. Tommy now tried to think ahead. The hit batter would force in the tying run, and Neal was due up. Good deal, no worse than a tie, and extra innings. Then the umpire spoke.

"Coach, I can't give him first base."

"Excuse me? He was nailed with an inside pitch!" Tommy hollered.

"He stepped across the plate. Rules say that's strike three. He didn't try to get out of the way."

"The hell you say," Brian broke in, "he tried to avoid it any way he could, plate or no plate. You gonna decide the game like this?"

"No, I'm calling ball three. Count now 3-2. I'm not gonna decide the game. The kids are."

He put his mask back on. The Towson coach, hearing all this, changed his tune from being happy that Ronny would not get first, and walk in the tying run, to thinking that he should be out, and the game over.

"Hell, ump, he's either hit by a pitch and gets first, or he's out for crossing the plate," he said. It was true, but the ump would have none of it, sticking to his decision not to decide the game on such a call. Tears streaked down Ronny's dirty cheeks.

"Ronny -- this is it, buddy. They're giving you another chance. Show this pitcher where you're from," Brian told him, pulling him to his feet, and wiping some tears away with a dirty towel. Tommy went back to the third base coach's box, now expecting Ronny to get so mad he would strike out.

As the Towson kid wound up, indeed, Ronny waved the bat over his head again, like a maniac. There was nothing to do but watch. What everyone saw was incredible. Ronny ripped the pitch into right-center, and it was clearly going to get down. The great Towson center fielder would not catch it. Tommy started wind milling his right arm, sending Josh easily home from third with the tying run, and waving Stevie over towards third with his left arm. By the time Stevie was near third, the cutoff man had the ball, but Tommy didn't care. He wanted to take his chances right then. He waved Stevie around third.

"Go home, go home!" he shouted, and as his speedster neared the plate, and the ball did too, it was, "Slide, slide!" Stevie slid in, kicked up a bunch of dust, but was safe. The City Heights kids went berserk. Some of them started a cheer, "Downtown, Ronny Brown, downtown, Ronny Brown!" It took a lot to get them lined up for the handshake. Remembering that they were the home team, and had supplied the baseballs, Terry went over to the ump and retrieved the game ball and the extras. Baseballs cost money, and in City Heights, you saved the used ones for practice.

Tommy then took his coaches and players aside, away from everybody. He told them what a great game it had been, and then handed Ronny the game ball, something never done in their league play. It was a high honor. It was also clear no one had ever handed him a ball like that. Then Tommy told them to stay put and have something to drink, while he went over to the tournament center to find out when their next game would be. "Damn it, Brian, we're in the winner's bracket!" It was exciting stuff. The goal of every team was to stay in the winner's bracket as long as possible. If you survived in the losers' bracket with only one loss, you then had to play an undefeated team from the winners' bracket, and beat them twice.

Nathan and Sheila came over with drinks for thirsty kids, ice and sympathy for bruises and sore arms, a Band-Aid or two for those who had slid into a base, and some munchies. The parents who had made the trek from the inner-city neighborhood to watch their kids came over, too. They shook all the coaches' hands. Beating Towson? No one expected it, they said. "I did," Tommy answered.

Inside the recreation center building, there were tables for each age group. You went up and reported the score of your game, and were given field and time assignments for the next game. It was very well organized. There was a guy who was the head umpire, and he would explain rules or local ground rules, and settle you down if you bitched about your umpire. There was a paramedic there, who would treat minor injuries, or radio for an ambulance if necessary. Tommy was impressed until he walked up to the 9-10 table. There, he met "GOD."

Seated at the folding table, with papers all over the desk in front of him, was a white-haired guy with a baseball cap that had the word "GOD" in large, capital letters on it. He was in charge of the 9-10 age level. Tommy reported his score, but the guy hardly answered him, did not congratulate him, and never looked up at him.

"When's my next game, then?" Tommy asked.

"Hang on, or come back later. I'm not sure," GOD answered.

"Whaddya mean, you're not sure? There's a bracket. I have a copy here. I'm just here to officially report in and make sure. According to this paper, we play at three this afternoon on field #11. Is that right, and do you know yet who we play?" GOD didn't answer or look up. He was getting red in the face, and suddenly, Tommy "got it."

"I got your number now, pal. You're from Towson. We just beat your boys, the home team who's supposed to win it all in every age level, and you don't like it. You're a Moron. And your hat? That's offensive. Down in the Heights we believe in live and let live, but there are limits. You come down there with that hat and I guarantee you two things. One, you'll go home alive, but your hat won't be on your head. Now give it up!"

Tommy's euphoria over winning his first game had degenerated into a merchant seaman approach to solving this particular problem. His blood was up, as they say.

"Yeah, yeah, City Heights, I have it here. Three on field eleven, versus Eastside." He still wouldn't look up.

"Thank you!" Tommy hollered, sarcastically, and left, knowing that if he stayed much longer, he would drift back into some kind of maritime justice thing, only he couldn't take the old guy 'back aft' and settle it, man to man. On the way out, another coach, from the small town of Westminster, who had overheard the whole thing, pulled him aside.

"Hey, man, he's always like that. You put him in his place and that's cool. He's been here forever, and thinks the Towson kids should win it all every year. You should see it -- he has a golf cart, and rides around to all the fields, checking on the scores. Don't let him get to you. Your city kids are tough and deserve to win."

It was a high compliment from a peer, and it helped put the smile back on his face. "Hey, thanks, man. Good luck to you."

It was a happy group in the van on the 25-minute ride back to the parking lot behind Simpson School. Brian gave the "Go home, eat some lunch, something good for you, and rest up," speech. "Be back here at 1:30 for a ride to our next game." Tommy told them again how proud he was of them. He told them their next game was against Eastside, who had beaten Randallstown in their morning game. When the kids were all gone, walking or running home to tell their parents,

"We beat," Tommy huddled with his coaches. Eastside was tough, he told them. The neighborhood was larger, but similar to City Heights. Neal would pitch for the Heights. Batting order would stay the same, although he said he was going to try to work in more subs. Brian promised to pick up Ronny Brown at his house again. Everybody went home for a rest that would last only a couple of hours, and the afternoon game would be in the heat of a humid day, on a dusty field. *Tough kids -- that's what I need now more than skilled players.*

He dropped Alex off and went home to shower and eat lunch. A noon TV show, *The Richard Sher Show*, a local production with some guy named Richard Sher and his sidekick, Oprah Winfrey, came on, and he watched it for a while. It was pure Baltimore -- the white guy and the more personable black woman, talking, giving some news, and interviewing people. *These shows never amount to anything.*

The City Heights group took off for Towson again just after 1:30. Brian had whipped his car into the lot late, with Ronny Brown running for the van with his shoes in his hands. But, the van full of kids was also full of optimism, and it was clear they were no longer very scared, or felt that they didn't belong because their neighborhood wasn't very fancy. Tommy saved his "let's get serious" speech for just before game time.

During warm-ups, the Heights kids couldn't help but notice one of the Eastside players - he was huge. He couldn't be only ten years old, they wondered out loud. Tommy told them that the tournament people check birth certificates, and anyway, he looked out of shape and probably couldn't run worth a damn. Privately, he wondered the same thing, and thought the kid would hurt the ball if he hit it. Checking the lineup card from the other manager, he checked the kid's number and saw that he batted fourth. *Maybe he can hit.* He talked to Neal, and told him to watch the fat kid. "If he hits you hard the first time up, stay away from him the rest of the game, especially if there are any runners on base," he told his tall, black athlete. Neal was quieter than Ronny. Although his fastball wasn't quite as fast, he never seemed to lose his focus, and was very coachable. City Heights again had drawn home team status, and took the field first, with higher expectations than they had in the morning.

There were minor differences with the morning game. The home team had drawn the first base side, not the third, so Tommy would be in enemy territory when his team was at bat, as he was in the third base coach's box. Eastside parents were all over the area with their lawn chairs, rather than sitting in the little bleacher section behind the plate. The City Heights parents sat in the bleachers, or strolled behind their bench. Tommy noticed that there were a couple of new adults there he had never seen. *Maybe winning brings out the fans at this age level, too.* It was also a lot hotter. He talked to Nathan about keeping the kids hydrated, and making sure that they drank only Gatorade or water, not soda. His wife said she had several facecloths, and would dip them in cool water and press them on the back of the kids' necks, to keep them cool. Tommy had no idea if that would help, but the effort was outstanding. As Neal wound up to throw the first pitch, Tommy saw Nathan cleaning the dust off all the batting helmets, and lining them up, for effect. *Hell, I've got a great group of adults here.*

Neal did fine in the first inning. The big kid batted but popped out. Eastside did get a run, on a walk and an error. In the bottom of the first, thanks to big hits by Ronny and Neal, City Heights scored two runs, and took a 2-1 lead into the second. It seemed like it would be a low scoring game, but it didn't stay that way for long. Maybe it was the hot sun, or the high humidity, or the fact that both teams had played a game in the morning, and little bodies were getting tired, but there were more walks and errors by both teams, interspersed with some hits. Tommy watched Alex closely, as he would suffer the most from the heat, being the catcher, with the full helmet on, and squatting down all the time. Mentally, he began to think he would use a lot of substitutes, regardless of the score. They took a 7-5 lead into the top of the fourth.

Eastside had two kids on base, with two outs, but the big kid was up again. It seemed clear he was the team's leader, as Tommy noticed their whole bench coming alive whenever he was up. "Remember what I said," Tommy hollered out to Neal. Neal nodded, but his first pitch was right over the center of the plate, and Fatty didn't miss it. He knocked a shot to dead center that went over the center fielder's head, something you did not see much at that age level. "Damn, he's strong for a flabby kid," Tommy said. The Eastside bench and fans clearly knew it would be an easy home run, and they would take the lead. With no fences, however, the Heights kids had a chance.

Jim, in center, had great speed and a terrific arm, which was why he played there. It was no accident, Tommy having played center as a kid for the same reasons. Josh went out to get the cut-off throw, while Jim ran like hell to get the ball. Fatty rounded second and headed for third, but he was slow. He rounded third base too widely, and ran into his coach. The coach grabbed the kid and pushed him towards home. The correct call would be interference, and the kid called out, but the umps missed it completely. Josh now had the ball and fired a strike to home. The collision at third had given the City Heights kids the extra time they needed. Alex was holding the ball while the Eastside slugger was still ten feet from the plate. He came in anyway, and people cringed. He was literally twice Alex's size. Tommy prayed that his boy would not get hurt. Alex held the ball in his mitt with his right hand still wrapped around it, and again impressed his dad with his knowledge of catching. He stayed low, blocking the plate, but with knees bent, not standing straight up. As the runner came in, Alex tagged him low and flipped him over. Alex went backwards with the impact, and Alex on his back, the big kid on his belly, mitt, ball, and umpire all descended on home plate at the same time. He was out if Alex still had the ball.

After a couple of seconds, Alex wormed his way out from under the pile of flab, and came up, showing the ump the ball, just like on TV. "Out!" the umpire yelled, and the City Heights side went crazy. Alex was not only alive, but he had made a great, tough play. The coach's son had come through again, and Tommy had to hide a small tear that somehow formed in one eye. It was also the third out, and Alex came over to the bench to high-fives and backslaps from his teammates. Tommy recalled his own boyhood baseball, and knew he had never experienced anything like that. He wondered if Alex knew how special that tag had been, and how long he would remember it. Tommy made a special show of congratulating Jim, for his efforts and great throw, and Josh for the relay. Tommy thought that the Eastside folks should be happy. They had just tied up the game, and could have had the lead if the third base coach had been watching things. Plus the ump should have called the kid out for the coach's interference. However, they were downcast because their Hercules was out.

There are those who say that there is no such thing as momentum in baseball, but you could not tell the City Heights coaches that this day. At least kids feel it, they all agreed, and the Heights kids smacked the hell out of the ball in the bottom of the inning. They took a huge lead. The 7-7 game became 14-7 in their favor before you knew it, and the Eastside group was quiet. Tommy made a point of talking to Neal, telling him not to let up, and not to walk anybody.

The score held up through the top of the fifth inning, and as they came to bat in the bottom of the fifth, Tommy talked to Brian. "Sneak over to the Eastside manager, and tell him that I'm going to use a bunch of subs. Make sure he understands that I'm just trying to get some kids into the game, I'm not being a wise ass and delaying things or anything." Brian understood, and later, Tommy saw the

Eastside manager wave to him. *Good coach.* He understands and has the same problem. He might play more subs, too, being way behind, and now knowing in advance what Tommy was going to do. Tommy warned his starters what he was going to do, but not the subs. As each batter came to the plate, Tommy called time out. Then he announced, in a loud voice and dramatic fashion, who was pinch-hitting for whom. "Mister umpire, we have #22, Pete Smith, batting for Jim Johnson," and so on. He used five pinch hitters in a row before they made three outs, and they even scored a run. The only danger was that for the last inning, he had a bunch of kids in the field that had not played in a tournament game before. No lead was ever safe. Coach Tommy believed that every kid deserved to play. *If we can't hold a huge lead like this, we deserve to go to the losers' bracket.*

When they had one out in the top of the sixth, Tommy brought George in to pitch, then Will. The kids gave up a run, but got the final two outs and it was over. The handshake routine was now becoming routine, and Tommy hoped that his kids were now getting used to winning. He wasn't sure if that was good or not. "Don't get cocky," he told them in his post-game speech, then had to explain "cocky" to some of them. They had their own words for it. Again, he went over to the recreation center to see GOD, report in, and verify their next game. The kids were quieter than after the morning game, and all the coaches thought it was because of the heat, and how tired they were. Even energetic kids run out of gas eventually. Brian told Tommy that his two-a-day practices had gotten them in better physical shape than a City Heights 9-10 team had ever been.

GOD didn't have much to say this time, and Tommy checked in and out quickly. Their next game was Sunday morning at 10:00 a.m., against Ruxton. Ruxton, a Baltimore suburb just west of Towson, had just beaten Linthicum in their second game. The happy group from the Heights drove off in a caravan, Tommy in the lead with the whole team crammed in his van, and several cars of coaches and parents behind them. Some parents blew their car horns when they pulled into the lot behind Simpson, and again driving around the neighborhood, taking kids home. It was an uplifting experience for the whole of City Heights, but the coaches knew that the longer you played, the tougher the competition would get, as the weaker teams lost their second game and dropped out. Still, being in the winners' bracket after two games was terrific, and improved their chances. *Maybe people would start being fearful of the kids from City Heights for a change.*

When the last kid was gone, and Brian had Ronny in his car to drive home, the coaches all decided to have a meeting at their usual place. With nowhere else to go but home, and no romantic interest going, Tommy agreed. Nathan went home. It would feel good to stroll into the bar and have the locals ask how the tournament kids had done.

"We won both games today," he proudly told them.

Brian observed that the beer tasted better in victory than it did in defeat. It seemed to be true, and Tommy even ordered a sandwich platter for his supper, in spite of the fact that he knew what the kitchen looked like.

Tommy took out his bracket sheet and showed it around the table. City Heights had now won their original group of four teams -- City Heights, Towson, Eastside, and Randallstown. Their next opponent, Ruxton, had won theirs. Four teams had already lost two games, and were out of the tournament. There were twelve teams left, but only four undefeated ones, and they were one of them. The guys would never talk about it in front of the players, but they could see that they were just two wins away from the championship game. If they stayed in the winner's bracket their opponent from the losers' side would have to beat them twice in a row. It was heady stuff. More than one father came around in the bar to congratulate the coaches, and most of them bought rounds of beer. The manager also told Brian, Theo, and Terry that they had two kids who hadn't been in a game. He was going to start them in the Ruxton game, then yank them after an inning. That way, he would have had everybody in a game so that all the kids will all feel a part of it, and he wouldn't have to wait until the late innings to see if he could afford to use a sub. "The longer we go, the better the competition," he told them. "Remember, all these teams have wins, too."

Tommy also told his gang that they looked sharp. Before the tournament, the coaches had agreed to dress alike: blue jeans for pants, since everybody had those, and a City Heights club polo shirt. The shirts were white with a green collar and trim on the short sleeves, with a pocket, and "CHBC" stitched above the pocket, in green. They topped off with tournament hats, just like the kids had. Tommy had reminded all the kids to get their uniform washed overnight, and he now mentioned it to the coaches. Then he remembered that he didn't have a washer or dryer, and would have to go to the coin Laundromat. His buddy, Brian, remembered that, too, and saved him.

"Hey, Tommy, you got an extra shirt in the van?"

"Yeah, probably something lying around from my last camping trip."

"Good. When we go outside, change shirts and give me your club shirt. I'll wash it with mine. Don't waste your time going to the Laundromat tonight." Tommy knew he was lucky to have such good friends and assistant coaches. They were doing just fine without Kirk.

Home and alone, Tommy thought about Rachel. Should he call her? *Baseball is not enough.* When he was home and was alone, he missed having company. When Alex was with him, he was busy with the boy. He hadn't met a woman that he was serious enough about to combine dates with his custody time. He was tired -- maybe during the week? He needed to find out about her offer. Was she that wild? If he could get a date with just her, would it be worth it? He poured himself a glass of vodka and realized he had nothing to mix with it. No matter. He used tap water, just like you would at sea when you couldn't get to the damn grocery store and buy mixer.

They all met again in the parking lot again Sunday morning, this time at 8:30 a.m. for a 10:00 a.m. game. The kids were happy, but the adults could tell they were a bit tired, too. None of them were used to playing twice a day, except for some of Tommy's twice-a-day practices. However, the kids from Ruxton were in the same shape, and they were the same age. It wasn't as if they would have any particular advantage. Of course, he knew that the City Heights All-Stars were maybe half all-stars and half regular players, and maybe it would hurt them eventually. If they played with heart they could overcome it.

Tommy's main problem was pitching. Ronny and Neal were terrific, but they could not pitch today. He had Josh, Will and George left. Will was only nine years old, but Tommy was going with him. He was a big kid, and could throw harder than the other two. He would use George in relief, and hold Josh for the second Sunday game. Roberto would start in right field and David at second base. Then Coach Tommy would have every player with game experience. He kept thinking that was important, even though he didn't have to do it, and even the kids would understand if he only used his best players. Tommy reasoned that if you gave a kid a shirt, you were telling him that he can help this team, and you ought to use him. Besides, small programs like City Heights don't get better unless you develop as many kids as possible, and drag as many parents into things with them. That was his philosophy.

City Heights drew the first base bench, but was home team again. The initial signal for a change-up was "rifle it." Tommy did not change any of his signs to the batters. No one had stolen them yet, and he had new parents and coaches opposite him every game. Alex started as catcher, but he looked tired. He told him to give him four good innings, and he would bring in Brad as backup. If the score was still close at that time, he would put Alex out in the field, to keep his bat in the game.

Ruxton was good, but they seemed to have the same problem with pitching that City Heights did. They had used their best kids to get this far and now hoped for the best. Both pitchers walked a few guys, and neither had a lot of smoke. However, they hung in there and they made it to the third inning in a 4-4 tie. It seemed more like tournament or playoff baseball -- a close game, with good defense. In the bottom of the third Tommy had Rick, the leadoff batter, on first, with Jim up. As he went through his signs, he couldn't help but hear the parents from Ruxton, in their lawn chairs by his third base box, yell out to their kids. "He's bunting, he's bunting!" they yelled. He had not given the bunt sign. Tommy gave the key, the familiar swipe of his right hand across his chest, at different times. Sometimes he did it right away, with the next sign the message to the batter, followed by meaningless motions. Sometimes he went through a whole series of nonsense before giving it. The parents kept yelling out different things about his signs, and Tommy was pissed.

"Why don't you let the kids play the game?" he yelled over to them. "You can't steal my signs anyway!" *Fuck them.*

To emphasize his point, he gave the steal sign. It was successful, and he had a go-ahead run on second. Then, perhaps because he was pissed at the Ruxton parents, who now were yelling at him and challenging him, and because the third baseman was playing deep, he gave Rick the steal sign again, and gave the batter the take sign. Little Rick stole third easily, and Tommy turned to the Ruxton group and smiled at them. A fly ball to right drove the run in on a tag-up, and City Heights had the lead.

They went to the bottom of the fifth with the Heights still ahead by one skinny run. Alex was on third after a double and an out to the first base side. Matt was up. With the last inning coming, one more run would be huge. As Matt stepped into the batter's box, a strange thing happened. A man Tommy did not know suddenly appeared out of the stands, and was standing right behind the backstop. After Matt swung and missed, the guy grabbed hold of the fence, and yelled at Matt so loudly that everybody could hear him. "You're stepping in the bucket! Keep that foot down!" he yelled. Tommy looked over to Brian and made a motion with his hands. Brian hustled over to the backstop before the next pitch.

"Hey, you can't stand here like this, go sit in the stands. Who are you, anyway?" Brian asked.

"I'm Matt's father, and I'll stand wherever the hell I want to," was the defiant reply. Matt's dad didn't seem to realize that Brian wasn't afraid of too many people.

"Well, asshole, you're probably the reason he strikes out sometimes. You make him too nervous. Now, you're coming with me." Brian peeled the guy's fingers off the fence, putting one hand behind his back and twisting it upwards 'til it hurt. He dragged him way out past first base, grabbing a lawn chair in the process. Brian set the lawn chair down and threw the guy in it.

"You sit right here, and cheer for all the kids. No negative shit from you or you'll have me to deal with. We don't see you all fucking season, now you're gonna show up and tell people what to do? No way. Just sit here and I am not kidding!" The guy stayed put, and the game went on. The game went on, but Matt was shook up and struck out, emphasizing Brian's point.

Luckily, Josh was up next, and he understood the importance of an insurance run. Even though Tommy had poor speed at third, he took a gamble. He gave Josh the bunt sign, and made sure Alex had seen it. "Two outs, Alex," Coach Tommy reminded him. "Run on anything." It was a rare squeeze play. Perhaps its rarity at that age level helped it work, because Ruxton was not looking for a bunt, and the runner was safe. Rick popped out to end the inning, but City Heights took a 6-4 lead into the last inning. Tommy took his pitcher out, and put in George. He took Alex out of the game and put Brad in as backup catcher. The little black pitcher was a lot like Josh. He didn't have the fastball that Will did, but was more accurate. "Just throw strikes," Tommy told him, knowing it was easy to say.

George overthrew to start off, and Tommy had to call time and go out there to calm him down. He contemplated bringing in Josh, as he could throw one inning and still be ready to start the next game, but that was a risky move. "Slow down. You don't have to throw it a million miles an hour, just over the plate. Play catch with Brad."

Ruxton managed to get the leadoff hitter home, and, with two outs, had the tying run on second. There was a sharp ground ball to Ronny at short. He went to his left to get it, then spun all the way around and heaved a bullet over to Neal at first. It was over, and the kids from the Heights were one game away from playing for the championship next Saturday.

GOD was not at the table, much to Tommy's delight. He came back to the group, now in their familiar pose of a bunch of kids drinking water from bottles and snacking, and waiting to hear about their next adventure. "This afternoon at 4:00 p.m." he told them. "We'll go back to Alex's house now, all together in the van. Parents can come along, too, or meet up with us back here, on the same field, at 3:00 or so." As everybody packed up, Brian took him aside.

"So, who are we gonna beat next?"

"Cockeysville."

"Oh. Well, cool. That's cool. We can beat them, no problem."

His look belied his statement. Cockeysville was a wealthy suburban team that won numerous tournaments. Many of the professional Orioles lived there. City Heights and Cockeysville were now the only two unbeaten teams left of the sixteen teams. The loser would go down to the losers' bracket. The winner would be one game away from winning it all.

Tommy pulled up in front of what he still considered his house, with Alex and all his teammates. To her credit, Alex's mom had the picnic table out back and the BBQ ready to go, with burgers and dogs for all the kids. Tommy cooked them up, just like in the old days when he and the ex and Alex had been a family. It was a happy group, and why not? They were 3-0 against some good teams. Tommy still hadn't told them who they were going to play next.

Most of the kids had remembered to bring a change of clothes, but the ones who hadn't borrowed shorts from Alex. Soon, the washing machine in the basement was full of small-sized baseball uniforms, socks and wristbands. After eating, Tommy and Brian had all the kids go into the living room. They gathered up all the pillows they could find, and had the kids lie down for a rest. Some of the kids bitched, until Brian told them that the Orioles took naps between games of a double-header. Most of the kids had no shirt on, thanks to the heat, and the fact that the house had no air-conditioning. Tommy noticed how skinny some of the kids were. He also noticed that none of them cared what color the little chests were.

When the team was dressed in their clean uniforms, Tommy huddled them up in Alex's living room. He and Brian talked to them about doing their best, and who they were going to play. A couple of the older kids knew the reputation of their opponent, but the younger ones didn't. It didn't matter to them who they played, and that was good. They took off again, the players all packed into Tommy's van. The lunch and rest had served them well, but they would now play their fourth game in 32 hours. *Maybe I'll use more subs,* Tommy mused, *and keep some kids rested.*

The City Heights bunch arrived at the field first, settled in on the third base bench, and began easy warm-ups and batting practice. A few minutes later, they all noticed a chartered bus drive up to the parking lot. It wasn't a school bus -- it was one of those luxury buses, and it contained the Cockeysville team. As they piled off the bus and moved, almost in formation to the field, some of the Heights kids starting asking questions. "All their stuff looks new, huh coach?" was a typical comment. "Man, they have a lot of coaches and fans," was another. "They got a lot of big kids on their team, huh?" Of course, their uniforms were brand new, and they had their names printed on the back. It seemed like each player had his own batting helmet and bat. Others noticed that every kid on the Cockeysville team wore cleats. About half of the Heights kids still wore sneakers.

As game time crept closer, Tommy sent Terry over to exchange lineup cards and talk to the umpire. When he returned he showed the Cockeysville card to Tommy.

"Lookkit the sixth player." The name was Belanger.

"Is this . . . you mean, Mark Belanger, the Orioles' shortstop, this is his kid?"

"I asked them, and yeah. He plays shortstop. And, Dad comes to practice sometimes and works with the infielders. That's not all. There are two more sons of Orioles in the outfield."

They all knew the elder Belanger. He was in the twilight of his career, and wasn't hitting much, but he was one of the best defensive infielders in the game. Tommy leaned over to whisper in Terry's ear.

"Fuck 'em. Bigger they are, harder they fall." He said it, but he wondered if he believed it.

Josh was their starting pitcher, with Rick in reserve -- two Giants pitchers who had been instrumental in them winning their league. But, this wasn't the Heights. He counted on them to throw strikes, but he couldn't teach them to throw harder all of a sudden. If the Cockeysville kids hit them hard, it could get ugly. Josh would have to pitch to the corners, if possible, while the team played great defense to keep the score low, and managed to score some runs, probably by playing small ball. Tommy could help with that. He had a great reputation for getting a run in with almost nothing: a bunt, a stolen base, a kid taking an extra base on a hit, whatever it took.

Teams from the wealthy suburbs, like their opponent, drew a tournament team from many more players than City Heights did. It meant that they would have a fourth pitcher almost as good as their first -- not much of a drop off in talent, unlike the Heights. The Heights kids took the field with high hopes. If they felt inferior, they didn't show it. *Hell, they have so much heart and emotion, which has to count for something. Just one more time, just one more win, and on to the championship game next Saturday.*

Tommy was able to use his subs early, but not as he had hoped, just to give his kids a rest. Cockeysville was killing them. Reality hit City Heights, and hit hard. Heart, emotion, and desire don't always overcome superior talent, equipment and coaching. It was great to be the underdog and win, but it didn't usually happen. Tommy recalled all the fans that loved the come-from-behind victories, but didn't understand that every coach wanted the early lead. You would win most of the time.

By the third inning it was already 14-3 Cockeysville and the Heights was lucky to have the three runs. In spite of the huge lead, Tommy had played small just to get a couple of runs, so his kids wouldn't get shutout, and feel even worse. Josh threw it over the plate like he always did, but these kids hit it. Tommy had gone out to the mound twice. Josh wasn't upset, which might have been because of his upbringing -- it was baseball, and there were more important things in his life. "Try to hit the corners, you know? And pitch one low, then one a bit high, see if they'll go fishing," Tommy told him. It didn't make much difference.

By the bottom of the fourth, it was worse. Cockeysville looked like a pro team compared to City Heights. Brian pointed out to Tommy that some of their kids were developing an attitude, and he immediately substituted for them. The right fielder threw his glove at the ball, and Tommy took the unusual step of replacing a fielder during an inning. "You talk to Bobby when he gets in here," Tommy told Theo. "We've got at least one more game in this tournament, and I won't have any of that!" Their starting center fielder went out in the top of the fifth inning, and promptly sat down on the grass, apparently tired of chasing hits. Tommy sent Stevie out to play center. "You tell Jim to come in here, and sit way down on the end of the bench, away from me," he told Stevie. Stevie ran out as if he was on "Mission Impossible," and would help the team make a remarkable comeback. He hollered to the others as he ran out to center, "You don't give up! We gonna do it!"

By the bottom of the fifth, City Heights was losing 17-5, and every sub Tommy had was in the game. Even Alex, Ronny, and Neal, his three best players, were on the bench. Tommy needed them for the next game, which now would clearly be in the losers' bracket. He went up and down the bench, telling them things like, "It's just not our game," or "Hey, we're 3-1, if the Orioles won 3 out of 4 games they would win it all every year!" In his heart, Tommy felt just as bad as the kids, but he couldn't show it. *Dammit, just one game from going to the championship!* Brian and Theo worked the bench, too, Theo more with the kids who had behaved badly and were now in the coach's doghouse. They would have all week to prepare for their next game, on Saturday. Win that one, and they would go to the championship, against Cockeysville, and have to beat them twice in a row, but hey, you never knew. He would come back next weekend with Ronny and Neal as his pitchers. *Yeah, that's it. Let 'em prove they can hit those kids! The tournament is not over!*

By the time the game mercifully ended, Cockeysville had all their subs in, too. Even the subs could hit pretty well, and, even without trying very hard to score more runs, they did. The final was 20-6. Brian and Terry monitored the lineup and handshake, as they knew that inner city kids, when they felt bad, could be less than sportsmanlike. The kids did okay, though, just shuffling through and tapping hands. Tommy heard one or two, "Nice game" comments from his kids, but there wasn't much heart in it. The Cockeysville coach complimented Tommy, and told him that he had a few terrific players. "Hey, that's nice of you to say, and you're right. My problem is you have a terrific kid at every position. Good luck -- we hope to see you again next weekend."

This time, it was a quiet, somber ride back to Simpson School. Brian gave some kids a ride home as all the coaches did. A couple of kids walked, and Tommy could see their heads down. He had meant what he said -- 3-1 is terrific! The problem is that they had been just one game away from playing for the championship. Now they were two. There was one advantage to staying alive in the winners' bracket as long as they had – they would not have to play again until Saturday afternoon. The other four teams left in the losers' bracket would play Monday night, and the winners of those two games would play Saturday morning. Whatever team City Heights faced Saturday afternoon might be a bit tired, and maybe would not have their best pitcher available. Their opponent would be Reisterstown, Lutherville, Highlandtown, or Dundalk.

Win that game, and then they would have to play Cockeysville again and beat them twice, since it was double elimination and the "Cocky kids" had not lost a game. Well, two wins and it would truly be a championship, winner-take-all game. Who knows? He could pitch Ronny in the next game, then Neal against Cockeysville. He wouldn't have to pitch Josh. He could try Will again, and maybe even Alex. Rick, too, might work. He'd try every kid on the team! By the time he was back in his apartment, however, he realized he was dreaming big.

Tommy gave his kids Monday off, having told them, "Stay home and rest up. Watch TV or something. Stay out of the hot sun." On Tuesday and Wednesday, he worked them hard, twice a day. On Tuesday, he told them that Reisterstown and Dundalk had won their Monday games, and would play each other Saturday morning. One of the City Heights coaches from the 13-14 age group, whose team was still in the tournament, had gotten the results for him. "We get the winner of that game, guys," Tommy told them, and more than one kid recalled that Reisterstown was Kirk and Junior's new team.

Thursday and Friday, he eased up on them, and had just one practice. Friday's practice, in keeping with his philosophy, was easy and fun. Again, he had coaches and parents in the field while all the kids took batting practice. He had all the coaches -- Brian, Terry, Theo, and Nathan, give the kids a quick pep talk and reminders. He had the last word, but thought Nathan's, strangely enough, as he knew the least about baseball, had been the best. It was more inspirational, with comments about "doing your best and not hanging your head." Nathan avoided mentioning God, but made it clear to the kids that the sun would still come up, win or lose, and how all of City Heights was proud of them. Brian, ever the salesman, had taken a different approach. The old fullback gave them a psych-up, motivational speech that would have gotten Baltimore native Babe Ruth out of the grave and suited up. Manager Tommy knew it was a bit much for ten-year olds.

At the end, Tommy reminded them about clean uniforms, being on time, and other mundane things, and he declared their last practice finished. He told them that there were only four teams left in their age group out of the sixteen who had started out - City Heights, Cockeysville, Reisterstown, and Dundalk, and how it was special that they were very much in it. That's what he said, but he was thinking that a summer's hard work would either end tomorrow, if they lost a game, or sometime Sunday, if they kept winning. It could end with a championship. Tommy saved his season over speech for whenever the season was over. *You didn't need too many words for nine and ten's anyway. Ice cream or pizza would help them get over things better.* He reminded the coaches to bring some cash for food for all the kids, win or lose. He knew some of the parents at the game would also chip in. All that remained for the kids' baseball season after the weekend would be the Awards Night ceremony.

The City Heights gang met, again behind the elementary school, at noon on Saturday. Their game time was 1:30 p.m., and they would not know who their opponent would be until they showed up. Local radio announcers didn't report the scores of youth baseball games. Tommy hoped for Dundalk. He didn't want to see the suburban kids anymore. Dundalk was a blue-collar neighborhood that his city kids would match up with better. He didn't get that break. As he parked the van near field #9, he could see that Reisterstown was already on the field, warming up, and there was Kirk, hitting fly balls to the outfielders.

Oh well, we can beat those guys. They've lost a game, too. The problem with that was he already knew their loss was also to Cockeysville, and only by two runs. Kirk tried a feeble wave at his old friends, but Tommy, Brian and the others pretended not to notice him. As usual, the City Heights kids noticed that every kid on the other team had on new-looking baseball shoes with rubber cleats -- no tennis shoes.

The Heights crew settled in on the third base side, and Tommy arranged to split the field-practice time with the other team. Nathan did his thing arranging all the shiny helmets again, and fanning out the bats. Theo worked the tough kids, like Ronny and Neal, trying to get them settled down a bit, and ready for baseball. As Terry took Ronny away from the others to warm up his pitching arm, Tommy noticed that Terry was avoiding him. He followed him over towards the trees behind the bench, and stared at him. He didn't like what he saw in his eyes -- they were dilated. He yanked his friend aside by his shirt.

"Christ, you're fucked up! What are you thinking? You're smoking dope? Again?"

"Hey, just a toke or two, you know. And whaddya mean, 'again'?" Terry mumbled, smiling.

"Look, there are people around who know you used to use it, and they think you used to sell it. We can't have that on the team, or in City Heights. I won't lie for you or protect you, either. I'll warm up Ronny. You just get a fucking lawn chair, and go sit out beyond the bench, and stay there. I'll tell the kids that you don't feel well. Got it, asshole?"

"Yeah, okay, cool. You know, man, you just oughtta chill out. This ain't no big deal. But I'm goin', doan worry, you don't have to get your enforcer Brian over here, ha ha."

"I don't need an enforcer for you. I'll kick your ass right in front of your boy if you fuck with me! I'm being as nice as I can. We'll talk later -- I've got work to do." Terry, fortunately, meandered away from the team, and settled into his own world in a folding chair. Tommy was fuming, but tried not to show it. *Christ, he's smoking dope on the day of our biggest game.* Then, right before the game began, Theo caught Tommy's eye. The cop just put his index finger up to his eye, pulled his lower eyelid down slightly, and cocked his head slightly in Terry's direction. It was a silent signal, like, "Have you seen that?" Tommy just nodded his head. At least his best friend, and main coach, Brian, was in form. He was everywhere, encouraging the kids, talking up defense and hitting, shaking the hands of all the parents, City Heights coaches, Reisterstown coaches, everybody. Well, everybody except Kirk. He would not go near him, and Tommy wondered if, after the game, there might be trouble. His friend was too big for him to keep off Kirk, and it could get ugly and be a terrible example to the young ball players.

"Hey, listen -- win or lose, never mind Kirk," Tommy whispered to Brian. "Don't get upset, big guy, remember we have kids here. We play our best and hell with it, right?"

"Yeah, I know. But if he gets loud, or acts like an asshole, you know what I mean, I'll take him down into the woods right there. I'm not gonna put up with his holier than thou, 'my kid's a superstar' bullshit!"

Tommy huddled his team up right before they took the field and gave them words of encouragement. He told them that there were now only three teams left, and how proud he was of each one of them. "All of City Heights is proud of you guys," he said. "Now get out there and play hard!" Nine and ten-year-old bodies scattered and ran out to their positions and Tommy could not get over it. No matter how many times he had seen it, the eternal hope that existed in every kid on each team, at the beginning of a game, was inspiring. Before anybody threw a pitch, anything was possible. It was part of the beauty of baseball. Every kid out there had a fantasy, like Tommy had in his youth, of making the game-saving catch, or getting the game-winning hit. The kids looked loose and happy, and that was a good sign for the Heights.

Junior was a starter for Reisterstown, but curiously, he played left field, and batted seventh. Tommy asked Brian what he made of it.

"I hate to tell you this, but it means they have several better pitchers and hitters than Junior, who used to be our best player," was the honest but depressing answer.

"Ah, fuck 'em," Tommy whispered.

Per instructions, and now tradition, Ronny wound up big time. He was supposed to throw the first pitch behind the batter. It was a bit off track, and nailed the kid right in the helmet. The Reisterstown players, not intimidated as much as some others hooted and hollered at Ronny and vowed to get even. "You wait 'til you come up," they yelled. Ronny fumed and decided to show them who was boss. He nailed the next batter on the first pitch. The umpire warned the City Heights bench, and Tommy went out to the mound. Ronny's actions fired up the parents from the other team, and the City Heights coaches could hear comments about "damn city kids," and other things. Some of them were racial.

"This isn't football," Tommy said. "You're not supposed to hit the other kids. Your job here is to throw strikes, and get people out. If you hit any more batters, the ump will throw you out of the game, and I can't stop him. Then you don't get to play. We need you in here. Cut out the shit." It was a rare cuss word from Tommy to a kid. *Christ, I've got a coach who is stoned and my best pitcher is so mad he may never settle down, both in the biggest game of the year. Maybe there's just too much pressure. Maybe I didn't prepare them correctly.* Ronny went back to work.

Being extra careful not to hit anyone, he walked the next guy, and the bases were loaded with no outs. He struck out their clean-up hitter, but gave up a single to the fifth batter, scoring two runs. The sixth hitter popped up behind the plate, and Alex made a diving catch. He also remembered that there was a runner on third, and ran back to the plate to cover it. Ronny had not come in to cover home, as he should have. It was rare for kids that age, but you could tag up after somebody caught a foul ball. Tommy had scored runs that way and he was sure the Reisterstown coaches had, too. He was proud of Alex.

Junior was up next, and the City Heights bench came alive. "Strike his ass out, Downtown Ronny Brown!" some kids yelled. Tommy didn't stop the hollering as long as it wasn't too profane. He knew that his players considered Junior to be a traitor. He also knew that the situation was not Junior's fault, and told his kids on the bench that. The leftie nailed a line drive, but it was right to Rick, at second, and he caught it in the air for the final out. *Two to nothing. Not bad for how we started.* They had a game.

As City Heights prepared to bat in the bottom of the first, Tommy suddenly remembered something. Kirk would certainly remember Tommy's famous signs. He quickly talked to Brian and Theo, and they agreed that Kirk would steal his signs if he could, and tell his players what Tommy was doing. He had to change them immediately. He huddled the team up away from the bench and explained the problem.

"I'm sorry. I just realized this, but you guys are smart, you can remember new signs."

He needed to change everything: the key, hit away, take, bunt and steal signs. It was a lot for young players to learn in a minute or two. Tommy was horrified that his lack of experience had now hurt the team's chances. Certainly Kirk, or a better manager, would have thought of this long before the game started. They had just finished a week of practice when he could have changed things. Now there was no time. He changed the key to a grab of the bill of his baseball cap. Whatever the batter saw after that was his sign. The take was Tommy holding his elbow. Hit away was clapping his hands. Bunt was pulling on his right ear. He still wouldn't give the steal sign until the pitcher wound up. That way even if Kirk read it and tried to holler out, it would be too late. Instead of scratching his knee, Tommy would kick the ground with his foot. The kids broke the huddle, and Jim went up to bat. Tommy wondered how many of the kids would remember all the new signs. He wondered if he would. He told Brian and Theo to take the kids, a couple at a time, away from the bench and go over them. Then he jogged down to the third base coach's box.

Tommy let the first two kids just hit away, giving only the new hit sign after the key. They both struck out. Ronny was next, and everyone in the park wondered if the Reisterstown pitcher would dust him off, or hit him in retaliation. Tommy could see that Ronny was still angry, and was crowding the plate, daring the pitcher to hit him. He felt bad for any kid who, because of his living circumstances and upbringing, could harbor such feelings at the age of ten. *My God, this should be fun.* His parents should be there, cheering him, but they weren't. He shouldn't hate the opposing players, but he did.

The first pitch sailed right under Ronny's chin. The players on both benches and the parents in the stands made noise, but Ronny hardly moved. *My God, he's tough. No wonder he's such a great football player. He won't back down for anything. He's daring that kid to hit him!* The pitcher came inside again, but not as close, and the tension eased somewhat. Tommy wondered if their pitcher was so good that he could throw a threatening pitch without hitting the batter, a rare skill for a young kid. But, he was in the hole 0 and 2, and now came in with strikes. Ronny hit the next pitch to right center, and took off running, like a madman. He rounded second and headed towards Tommy at third without ever looking at his coach. He would make the triple easily, but not home, and Tommy threw up the stop signal. Ronny pretended to ignore him, and rounded the base. Tommy hollered, "Stop, hold up!" to no avail. The toughest ten-year old in City Heights flew home and slid into the catcher. He was out, and there was no doubt about it.

"You talk to him!" Tommy told Theo. "I'm too mad!"

Theo took Ronny aside and told him how he should have stopped at third, and how the game wasn't all about him. He told him that the fourth batter always had a good chance of knocking a run in, and the game could be 2-1 right now. Ronny never answered, preferring instead to look down, scowling. Tommy saw it, and knew it was about the end for his star player. He wanted to show those rich kids something, but didn't quite know how to go about it. He used his anger at the world as motivation, but in the finer parts of the game of baseball it was working against him. Worse, it worked against the team, and Tommy could not let it continue. As Ronny passed him going out to the mound, Tommy just said, "Stay cool out there, or this is the end for you. You can't hurt the team."

The kids from the suburbs continued to hit and hit. It quickly became a 6-0 game. Then the umpire called ball four on a close pitch, and little Ronny threw his glove down. Tommy heard a low level "mother-fucker" coming from the small body on the mound. The ump called time and yelled over to Tommy, who was already on his way to the mound. "Coach, I can't have that, you know."

"I know. He's done, just give me a second." Ronny didn't seem too surprised that Tommy told him to give him the ball, but was shocked to learn he was coming out of the game. Tommy just told him to go see Coach Theo, and talk to him.

He put Neal in to pitch, and brought Pete off the bench to play first base. After a quick talk amongst Tommy, Alex and Neal, Neal took a few warm-up pitches, and the game resumed. Back on the bench, Tommy could see that the high hopes of the inner-city team were fading. *We don't have enough experience to weather all this properly.* They, like Ronny, felt it was "Us against the world," and the only thing that mattered was "who beat." He and the other coaches could not overcome all their problems with a summer of baseball. It had to help, but it wasn't enough. A clever stranger could walk along the City Heights bench and, just by their expressions, pick out the kids who had love and care in their lives, and those who didn't. The "didn'ts" would begin with Ronny.

Neal did okay, but he had to pitch with runners on base and the top of the order up again. He got the three outs but gave up two runs, and the kids in green and white came to bat in the bottom of the second down 8-0. Brian worked the bench, trying to psych up the team, knowing that they had to score some runs right then to have any chance. All the coaches, well, perhaps except for Terry, who sat alone, knew it. Their kids were too down on themselves. Only closing the gap would help. Words of wisdom could come later.

In spite of the score, Tommy played small ball. He started bunting and stealing. He was playing for a run -- any run, any way he could get it. Down by eight in the majors you might play for home runs, or a big inning. Here, Tommy's approach was that their only chance began with just one run, to prove to themselves that they could score on this team. It was only the second inning. If Neal stayed focused on the mound, and they started scoring runs, it could happen. *To hell with the odds.* They scored their first run on a risky play at the plate. Then the center fielder made a great catch on a blast Alex hit, and they finished the inning down 8-1. Tommy, Brian and Theo worked the team with the usual sports platitudes: "Okay, gang, we're on the board! That's one, here we go now! Let's hold 'em right here, and we'll catch up!" That's what the City Heights coaches told their players. What they believed in their hearts might have been more realistic. They were getting to the point of no return, the stage of a game where one team knows it is going to lose no matter what they do, and because they feel that way, they help make the negative prophecy come true. Some would say you could manifest your own demise, but people like Tommy didn't believe in such bullshit.

The batters from beyond the Beltway kept hitting the pitchers from inside the city limits. Neal did his best, but Tommy had to yank him after five more runs scored and they were still in the top of the third inning. He sent Neal back to first base, Pete to right field, took his right fielder, Bobby, out of the game, and brought George off the bench to pitch. It was a tossup with George, Josh or Rick. All three were smallish kids who threw strikes, but didn't have the speed or ferociousness of a Ronny or Neal. Reisterstown would not get many walks, but the danger was that they would pound his pitchers. There was no ten-run rule to end the misery. It would take a miracle, but Tommy still hoped for one. He silently hoped and even prayed his kids could just come back and make the score closer. He told George to try to locate his pitches up and down, in and out, as Alex gave him different targets. "No matter what, don't walk 'em. This situation is not your fault. Just do the best you can."

George did fine, but another run crossed the plate. Tommy noticed that even his own son was getting discouraged. He hadn't even bothered to take off his mask or block the plate, even though the relay throw might have gotten there in time. It was defeatist – he assumed the throw would be late, and it was. After a fly out to left, the Heights team came to the bench slowly. Some were hanging their heads. Before Tommy could speak, Brian called for a team huddle far away from the bench. Tommy gave his friend the nod of the head to go ahead. Brian then gave his best, "We're from the Heights and we never give up," speech. It was full of football analogies and trite expressions, since Brian was, after all, a former football player. And, there was no doubt that the going was tough.

Reisterstown changed their pitcher and a couple of outfielders. Tommy wondered if maybe their second tier pitcher wouldn't be very good and they could rack up a bunch of runs. But no, he was almost as good as the first kid, and even threw an occasional curve ball. He did throw a changeup to Neal, who promptly hit it over the left fielder's head for a home run. The City Heights kids at least had that to cheer for. Neal was a popular player, and at least "one of ours" had hit "one of theirs" out of the park. However, the score was 14-2 when they took the field for the top of the fourth. Tommy told Theo and Brian to warm up all the kids on the bench, as he intended to play them all before it was over.

Uncharacteristically, George gave up a couple of walks along with two hits, and Tommy yanked him. He put Josh in to pitch, moved George to left field for Eric, and brought David off the bench to play shortstop. He gave the same talk to Alex and Josh that he had to George. "Move the target around a bit. You can't just throw it straight over to these guys," he told them. Alex looked tired, and Dad made a mental note to take him out after four, unless they performed a miracle in the bottom of the inning. He also noticed that Junior was due up next. "If he gets on base, don't let him steal, whatever you do. Kirk will send him, just to rub it in. Screw him if he goes!" Junior slapped a single to left field. Kirk was coaching third base, and giving signs. Tommy didn't steal his signs, but hollered at Alex, "Remember what I said." Junior took off for second on the first pitch. Alex came up throwing so hard that his helmet flew off his head. David put the tag on, extra hard it seemed, and Junior was out for the final out. Alex pulled out his mouthpiece and spat on the ground in Kirk's direction. Tommy saw it, but said nothing. *These tournament games will age you a bit.*

The city kids had some small thing to cheer about again. In a brief chat with his assistants, Tommy told them, "This is it -- bottom of the fourth, now 16-2. We have a big inning here we keep our best kids in and try to come back on 'em. If not, we make substitutions all over." Theo volunteered to have a party at his house after the game, win or lose. Brian volunteered to pick up pizza at Mario's for the whole team. Tommy knew it was defeatist to be discussing that – the game wasn't over, and if they came back and won, there would be another game to prepare for. But, he knew it was realistic, and he appreciated their efforts.

"Cool. Theo's after we win," he answered with a wry smile. "Tell the parents in the stands. We'll call the others from Theo's."

As he went out to the coach's box, he told Alex that he was done catching. If they scored a bunch of runs, he would put him in the outfield to keep his bat in the game, otherwise he was done. He told Doug to get his catcher's gear together and go in to catch in the top of the fifth. He told Stevie to go in at second base for Rick, and Will to go in at third for Matt, all after this at bat. That would only leave Brad, Roberto and Barrett to get in the game, and he would pinch hit all of them in the bottom of the fifth. That way those kids would get to play the field in the top of the sixth. Unless, of course, they executed a miracle right then and scored about ten runs.

Unlike the fantasyland of Hollywood movies, there was no miracle. There was no Angel in the Outfield, or Bad News Bear to save them. They scratched out one more run, on another risky play at the plate. Tommy sent Josh home when he should have held him up. The kid was smart, and slid away from the catcher, feet first, but touching the plate with his gloved hand as he slid by. It was a beautiful slide, and even some Reisterstown fans cheered it. Tommy felt good that people could see that he had some kids who knew how to play. He also thought it was easy to applaud the other team when you had a huge lead. *Those fans weren't saying nice things about my team in the first inning,* he recalled. Stevie ran out to high five his teammate. He pounded him on the back as if he had just hit the game-winning home run. He was a kid who never gives up. Again, a small victory to cheer for a brief moment, but the well-heeled suburban team was marching on to a victory, and a rematch with Cockeysville. There didn't seem to be a damn thing Tommy, his assistants, or his players could do about it. There was pizza at Theo's, and a reminder that they could keep their hats and wristbands. That would be the end of their season, in about an hour.

Reisterstown changed pitchers again, probably saving the other kid's arm for a few innings against Cockeysville. *At least that's what I would do.* He sent his subs out, as directed, putting his arm around his own boy as he sat on the bench. Josh stayed in to pitch and did fine. The other team now was emptying its bench, too. At least their manager had some class, Tommy figured. Kirk would probably have played the starters more. For the first time in the game, City Heights gave up no runs. It was the first zero next to the other teams' score. Again, a small victory, but that's how you build a program they thought, on the green and white side.

As promised, Tommy stopped the game in the bottom of the fifth, and, as he had done before, made a huge production out of announcing his pinch hitters. Brad, Roberto, and finally Barrett, batted one-two-three, and he had used all his players. He had to get some help from Brian to figure out where to put them all in the field for the top of the sixth inning. He hadn't cared much about that. He just wanted everyone in the game. Barrett hit a double, and scored when Will drilled a pitch into right center. The Heights' subs outscored theirs, but it was little consolation to most of his kids. Stevie, of course, was right there, to yank the dropped bat out of the way so Barrett could score. He high-fived him, too.

They went out to the last inning down 16-4, but somehow it didn't seem as bad as it did a few innings ago. There had been a few bright spots. Tommy heard Brian make a threat to Kirk, something about, "No more goddam stealing with the score like this," but he said nothing. *To hell with Kirk -- if he wants to be a jerk, he can deal with the consequences.* Tommy wondered if Kirk would dare try to steal a base, and if Brian would then beat the hell out of him after the game. Nathan had the post-game drinks and snacks lined up on the bench. His wife was ready with the ice packs for the bruises. *Can't put ice on an ego, though.*

Will replaced Josh as pitcher, and became the only nine-year old to pitch in the game. He did great, and Tommy hoped they would have him to work with next year. That was one thing the club needed - a way to maintain consistency from year to year. Neither team scored in the sixth and, mercifully, perhaps, the game ended without it getting worse --16-4. Tommy voiced his appreciation that his subs had held Reisterstown scoreless for two innings and how this might be a portent of next year. *If the nine-year olds on the team could learn from this and come back next year better prepared, who knew?* Perhaps he was dreaming.

The handshake line went better than he had predicted it would. His kids did not like shaking hands after a loss, but they had lost so badly they did it without saying much.

Tommy swore he heard Stevie and Josh going through the line saying, "Wait 'til next year - we be back," and things like that. *Amazing kids. Give me a team of 'em, and I'll show you City Heights baseball!* Brian monitored Ronny's moves through the line. It wouldn't have shocked any coach to see him spit on his hand before offering it, or to swear at the other kids, or challenge them to a fight right there. It was what he knew. It was how the poor examples he had in life taught him to deal with adversity. Tommy didn't think a couple of months of baseball were enough to counteract all that, but he played peewee football, too. Who knew? Perhaps his mom would straighten up, and some man he respected could become his mentor. That's what he needed.

A bit embarrassed by the defeat, and the sudden end to their season, the City Heights crew huddled one last time out towards left field, beyond their bench. Brian, then Theo and Tommy, then gave their best "Don't worry about it" speeches. *The kids are so young,* Tommy mused. *How much of this do they understand?*

"We were beaten by a better team," Tommy said. "They had better coaches, better equipment, and more players to get their all-star team from than we did. That's the truth. They have more money to spend on equipment, and nicer fields. But, here's the deal. You guys did great to get this far, and yes, we'll be back next year, and the year after that. We're going to keep coming back here until we win it all. Kids from City Heights never give up!"

There were some cheers for that, but the announcement about the free pizza party at Theo's house went over better. As they split up to go to the cars, little Stevie tugged on Tommy's shirt.

"Yeah, Stevie?"

"Coach, Reisterstown now gonna play Cockeysville for the championship, right?"

"Yeah, that's right."

"Well, then the winner of that is the champ, and the loser is second place, so we in third place, then?"

"Uh, yeah. Right. Third place. Not bad, you know, you guys did better than any previous City Heights nine and ten team."

"We get a trophy for third place? In my school, sometimes third place gets an award too."

"Uh, you know, I'm not sure. I'll call the . . . uh, the tournament people tomorrow to see about that. You bet. I'll give them a call. Maybe."

That seemed to satisfy little Stevie for the time being, but Tommy made a mental note to see about doing something. Third place was good and it ought to have an award, but he already knew that the Towson Tournament didn't award anything for third place, and any other team that finished with a W-L of 3-2 could also claim to be third.

As the kids piled into Tommy's van for the ride to Theo's, Ronny didn't join them. Brian took him in his car. It seemed the ferocious kid somehow blamed Tommy for his lack of success, along with the umpire, who he referred to with some words not usually heard from such a young boy.

An hour later, you could have walked up to Theo's little row house and never have guessed it was full of kids who had just lost a playoff baseball game. There was pizza all over and kids running through the house and around the house. It was a miracle they didn't run over the house. Stevie was in heaven -- he had the whole team to play at his house. Well, it was all except Ronny. He had insisted on going straight home, perhaps because his mom had told him to do that, or perhaps he felt guilty and didn't know how to overcome it. Brian had stopped at Mario's, ordered the pizza, taken Ronny home, and then gone back to pick it up and get the mass of doughy food to Theo's.

Theo had beer for the coaches. His wife was happy to have them at her house. Tommy could see why Stevie had such a positive attitude. *Dammit, every kid in the Heights deserves support like this.* In coaches' discussions about what had gone right, and what wrong, Tommy mentioned Stevie's "third place" comments. Brian knew a guy in the club who worked at a trophy place, and made them their plaques for the sponsors for a good price. He promised to pick Tommy up on Monday and go over to the trophy shop. The annual awards night was next Saturday, in the Simpson School auditorium, so if they were going to do anything at the last minute, they had to get on it.

Awards night would end the season for the kids. A week later was the club's big crab fest. That would officially end the season for the adults, and determine how much money the club would have to start the next season with. Naturally, Brian was heavily involved in both crucial events. It was his forte, more than coaching baseball.

Chapter 9: The Wrap Up

On Monday morning, the two coaches drove up the Beltway to the trophy shop. They found the City Heights guy and took him aside. They explained the situation. They had no money from the club for this, but the kids deserved something for taking third place. They knew it was short notice and did not expect charity, but could he help them out? The guy took the two beggars into a backroom. There were shelves with boxes full of odd pieces of trophies, plaques, and awards for almost any kind of sport or event you could imagine. Tommy was impressed with how cheap most of the parts looked when scattered all over, and how great they looked when assembled. The trophy guy rattled around box after box.

"How many kids on the team?' he asked.

"Eighteen," Brian answered.

"How about these? Left over from a St. Patrick's Day order, some marching group. They're green, which I know is a club color." He held up a medal, like the kind you pin on a soldier. The fabric part was green, and a round, plain disc of cheap brass-colored metal hung below it. "I can make up a stamp of some sort for the medallion part. Maybe put 'CH' on one side, and "3rd Place" or something on the other. Can't put too much on 'em, they're small."

"How much?" Tommy wanted to know.

"I gotta charge you something to keep my boss happy, even if I work on 'em on my own time. Three bucks apiece, he'll go for that. Whaddya think?"

"Hey, who's your boss?" Brian asked. "I'll go talk to him, tell him about the kids and all."

"No. We'll take it. Don't butt in with the guy's boss, Brian," Tommy said. "Just have to have them by Friday. I'll come around and pick them up, okay? Eighteen of 'em. Put whatever you can on 'em. And, nobody tells the kids it was for an Irish parade. We really appreciate this."

He dragged Brian out, with his friend protesting that he could talk the boss into donating them, and he could talk anybody out of almost anything, it was what he did for a living for chrissakes.

"Shut up and drive, we did fine. Leave it alone," Tommy told him.

On the drive back to the neighborhood, the two coaches joked about the black kids on the team getting a medal meant for St. Patrick's Day.

"Yeah, you know we don't have a nickname in the tournament -- we could be the City Heights Fighting Irish or something," Brian joked.

"Hey Brian, you hear who won Towson?"

"Yeah, Cockeysville beat Kirk and the boys, 12-4. Bit of his own medicine, too. They had a kid steal third in the last inning, when they were up 11-4."

Tommy arrived at Simpson School on Saturday night an hour early. He knew there would be something to help with at the last minute. He helped set up the lobby. Per club tradition, each coach would be out in the lobby with a large cardboard box labeled with his team's name. Admission to the program for a player was to turn in his uniform. They kept the hats. Some of the coaches brought their wives or girlfriends. Sadly, coaches met some of the parents for the first time all year, and worse, many kids had no adult with them.

Big John was the emcee, and he loved being the center of attention, even when coaches took the mike and made jokes about his height or age. Tommy's favorite was, "I won't say John is old, but his social security number is two."

Per tradition, all the sponsors were invited, and most came. The club gave each business a plaque with a picture of the team and an engraved plate with the name and the year on it. They did this first, as some owners had to get back to their bars or restaurants. Also per club tradition, each coach had a minute to speak, and then read off all the names of his kids. They went from the youngest age group, eight, to the oldest. Each kid was to stand when they called his name, then the audience applauded the team at the end. This way every kid was recognized whether he or she was any good or not. It didn't matter if his team had finished first or last. Then there were awards for teams from the club's season. Tommy accepted the small trophy for the Giants, and promised to give it to their sponsor, after all the kids had a chance to have their picture taken with it.

The club did not give out Most Valuable Player awards and things like that. A coach could say something about his best players, however, and most did. Then they went to the all-star teams, and talked about the tournament. Big John called the tournament coaches up, and again, they read off names and had the kids stand. These players now had two special moments, and, if their team had won awards at tournaments, they came up on the stage to get them. Tommy already knew that the 15-16 year-old tournament team was the only one to have taken first place, and they would get trophies. He also knew he was cheating a bit with the third place awards, but Big John had okayed it. John knew how tough it was to have any success with the younger kids, and agreed that this would encourage them and the eight and nine-year olds coming up. Luckily, there were no other teams that finished second or third but had no awards to hand out, or they would have had to get those medals or something, too.

Tommy started his tournament presentation by inviting all his coaches up on the stage. He coerced the audience to applaud them, and made a plea for more moms and dads to help next year. "You don't have to know anything about baseball," he told them. "We'll find something you can do to help, don't worry about that!"

Then he proudly called each of the eighteen kids up, and told them to walk across the stage and get their award for the great third place tournament finish. He had Theo shake their little hands, and Brian hand them the medals. There was no sign of Downtown Ronny Brown. "I'll take care of it," Brian whispered, putting his medal in his pocket. A couple of kids asked what the award was, apparently never having seen a medal. Terry or Nathan would whisper to them that it was a medal, like a soldier gets, and they could pin it to a shirt, or maybe to their baseball cap. All the kids smiled, and some went off the stage holding their tiny medal up over their heads as if it was the damn Stanley Cup or something.

The evening ended when Big John stood up and said that he had a bit of a surprise for the little neighborhood gathering. He brought a guy out from behind the stage curtains to talk to the group. The guy was Baltimore's leading television sportscaster, and everyone in the place knew of him. He was a real celebrity around the city, and the crowd in the Simpson auditorium felt special that he would come speak to them. John knew some guy on the docks who knew somebody at the TV station, and had arranged it. The sports guy didn't give a canned speech. He talked for a few minutes about the importance of community, kids and baseball. Then he invited folks to stand up and ask a question.

Before long, many adults and even a few kids walked down close to the stage, and asked questions. Mostly they asked about the Orioles, or the Colts, or what this player or that player was really like. One woman asked if Jim Palmer looked as good in his underwear in person as he did in the ads, and the place roared. Before the guy could compose himself to answer, she added, "Well, hon', I gotta know, because I like that man!" The sports guy nearly choked. He claimed he wasn't a good judge, but he knew many women who liked Palmer, and others who thought the quieter Eddie

Murphy was cuter. John ended the meeting by thanking everybody for attending and reminding them it was their last chance to buy their tickets to next week's crab fest.

The evening ended with punch and cookies out in the auditorium, brought by moms from all over the Heights. It was a tradition with the wives of the coaches and mothers of the players, and they never had a year when there weren't enough cookies to go around. Tommy rated the night their best Awards Night ever, partly because of the sports guy, and partly 'cause he had given out medals to seventeen smiling kids, including his own. Big John put a damper on things by going around reminding everyone who had volunteered for the crab fest what their duties were, and what time to be there.

During the next week, the worst job in the club was that of the equipment manager. Coaches came by his house all week, dropping off stuff, and promising to get the odd uniform back from the kid who forgot it, or who hadn't been at Awards Night. There were minor disagreements about the condition of the catcher's gear and so forth. There were those who took the time to wash all the uniforms and clean the dust off the gear, and there were those who did not. Tommy had.

Tommy spent most of the week trying to balance his money problems and decide what to do now that his baseball season was over. He wondered if his boy knew how special it was for the two of them to not only work on the same team, but also a tournament team, and one that had done well. He doubted if there would ever come a time when they would be closer.

His finances were a mess. His vacation pay had run out in the middle of July. He was now on union leave. That meant he earned no money, but could not ship out. It was what they did when jobs were scarce. You had to stay on the beach longer before you could ship. The idea was to try to spread the work around more evenly. Every mate knew it -- if there wasn't enough work, there just wasn't enough work. Tommy figured he would be legally eligible to ship in the middle of September, but would have little chance of getting a job. Maybe he would go to New Orleans and try the union hall there, or even out to San Francisco, where he had a brother who might put him up for a few weeks. There was almost never a shipping job called in Baltimore. Another thought was to get a shoreside job, anything to pay the bills, and wait several months, then go to New York. It was part of the negative side to shipping out. When it was good it was the best, but when it was bad you starved, and no one gave a damn. He put off any decisions for a couple of weeks, not wanting to deal with the reality of it.

Tommy drove over to the Arbutus Fire Hall at five in the afternoon on the Saturday of the big City Heights Boys Club Crab Fest. He felt sad that he had no date for the damn thing, and he would work it most of the night. He had pondered about Rachel, and had even called her once to talk, leaving a message, but she had never called him back. *Probably found the wild man she was looking for,* he figured. Worse, there were hardly ever any singles at these events, even though they had music. You paid $25 per person for a ticket, but that included all the steamed crabs and some side dishes you could eat, all the beer or soda you could drink, and a live band from nine until one. You could bring your own whiskey and get free setups. The club had many games of chance to take more money out of your pocket. There was a cakewalk, and a Big Six gambling game wheel. They sold 50/50 tickets every hour for a drawing. There was also a silent auction of many items that people and businesses had donated. They hired the required policeman to watch over everything.

It was a big social event in the Heights. Guys brought their wives to it, but single guys usually came only if they had a date. Some people brought their teenaged kids, but no one brought little kids. It was a night for City Heights parents to party. *Except for old sailors like me. I'll just work it and drink beer.* Brian was bringing Suzie, and Tommy hoped that was good. Maybe she would be civilized to all the guys who worked so hard partly so her son could play baseball all summer. Maybe it would help her "get it." Nathan would have his wife with him, but they would leave early, not drinking or approving of the rock music. Terry was coming drag with some woman he knew from work. Theo had told him at Awards Night that he had his tickets, but might have to work that Saturday. If he did his brother would bring his wife.

By the official crab fest starting time of seven, Tommy was back in the kitchen, at his wrapping station. Just outside the back door, the crab guy had set up his giant kettles. As he steamed them, his kids would bring in laundry baskets full of the cooked ones and dump them on a long table covered in butcher's paper. The club hired him every year. He did a fine job, and somehow stayed one jump ahead of the consumption. He was amazing. Tommy had no idea how he did it. If they were running short, a truck would pull up, the workers threw hundreds of live crabs into the pots, and in a few minutes, the crowd was full again. You never were stuck with cold ones, either, which was good since no one would eat them cold. As they came in from the back door, Tommy and others then wrapped them in bundles of ten, in newspaper. The guests just came in, lined up, and took a bundle. There was also a set up on the side, for corn-on-the-cob, beans, and biscuits. The club always pushed that stuff on people, as it was cheaper than the crabs, and the caterer charged them according to how many crabs he cooked. Eleven O' clock was the cutoff for serving food, although the beer and setups were served right up until closing time.

There were twenty rows of long tables in the main hall. They left space for the gambling games and the dance floor. Club members covered the tables with the same brown paper as the kitchen counters. You just dumped your bundles of crabs on the tables and, using the little wooden mallets and small knives on each table, went to work. One of the worst jobs was cleaning up. When a table filled up with a huge pile of crab shells on it, one of the club members would go over and just wrap the mess up in the paper covering the table, and cram it into a large trash bin on wheels. Then you put out fresh paper and mallets, and the whole thing started over again.

Tommy worked the wrapping station from 7:00 to 8:00, and then took a half hour off to drink. He worked cleanup from 8:30 to 9:30, having volunteered for that time as he knew it wouldn't be as bad as towards 11:00 when people rushed to get their hands on the last servings of crabs. He worked the Big Six gambling wheel for an hour, too, from 10:00 to 11:00, and was glad when that was over. People could only bet up to three dollars, but some of them bet for a long time, and could win or lose a fair amount. You had to pay strict attention to the amounts bet and paid off, as there were different odds all around the wheel. You could win nine bucks in a hurry, or lose your three repeatedly. It was all cash, and some bettors were too serious. *It isn't Atlantic City, for chrissakes, just a bunch of guys trying to make a few bucks for kids' baseball. Christ, you were supposed to lose, don't you understand that? If you don't like losing, go bid on an auction item. At least that way you took something home, albeit something you probably paid too much for.*

Officially, he was done at eleven and could party with everybody until one or go home. He hung around and drank beer with some of the other coaches and some parents he knew. He hadn't seen much of Brian all night. Somebody told him that he had left early, as Suzie was mad, and yelled at him in front of other people. *Christ, can't she deal with this one damn night, and let him be the star he is to this club? Was it always some personal battle to get him away from it?* Then there was his ex.

In the middle of working the Big Six wheel, she had come over and placed a couple of bets.

"So, Tommy, who's your date tonight? Which one of these lovelies is she?"

"No date. If that's all you came to check out, you wasted your twenty-five bucks, but the club appreciates it. And you?"

"Well I didn't bring a guy with me, just a friend. Right there's my date," she said, pointing across the room to a young brunette. "That's Lisa, from the community college I go to part time."

"How nice." Tommy wondered if there was any real meaning to the "girl not a guy" date thing, or if she was just playing mind games again. He became busier with the gambling and the ex drifted off. *Who cares*? But in all the time they had been separated and divorced, he had never seen her with a guy, or heard Alex mention his mom being with one, or out on a date with Mr. So-and-so, or anything like that. *Maybe the marriage had no chance to begin with, and I didn't know it,* he wondered. *Nah, couldn't be, could it?* He sneaked a sip of beer and tried to forget it. *Damn mind-game, that's all it is.* By the time his chores with the wheel were up and he was relieved, Lisa and her date were gone.

Theo's wife found Tommy and introduced her brother-in-law. He and Tommy had a brief talk about baseball, and Stevie's abilities. Theo's lucky to have such good support for his job, Tommy mused, and Stevie's lucky too, whether he knows it or not. Big John came around for the millionth time, checking that club members were working their stations, that they were cleaning the tables regularly, and that everyone was having a good time. The band was good, at least the younger couples thought so, and people were dancing in addition to drinking too much and stuffing themselves with food. Yeah, it was a good time, at least by the definition of the neighborhood – a damn good time, and Tommy put his arm around Big John and told him to shut up and have a good time, too.

"I will, I will, Tommy. You know, this is the last event of the year. Next meeting we count the dough and make a guess on next year, that's all. I want to make sure this goes right. People buy tickets every year if they have a good time, you don't have to sell them on it, ya know?" With that, the truck driver pushed off again, grabbing a broom as he went. It seemed that John and Brian could run the whole damn club by themselves.

Before he realized it, Tommy had stayed until the band played their last song. Per tradition, it was a slow dance number. Husbands who had avoided dancing all night long were now trapped. The smart ones gave in. Tommy ended up hauling trash and sweeping. Their contract with the volunteer fire department that owned the hall called for it to be "as clean as they found it." They had been having the fest there for years, and there had never been a problem. Of course, there had never been a year in which they didn't have about twenty guys and gals cleaning up afterwards. It was a happy time. They would make plenty of money off this one event to plan another season of City Heights baseball. It was sad to have the season end, though. The kids were sad about going back to school the next week, but the parents had a different view of that. Cold weather was ahead, but, unlike his friends, he wondered about being stuck taking a North Atlantic assignment, not shoveling his walkway. *Damn, I hate the North Atlantic. Even in summer, it's terrible. Ah screw it. Maybe I'll get out to Puerto Rico or South America.*

Brian called the next day, thankfully after ten. There weren't too many crab fest lovers awake early that day.

"Hey, Tommy, I'm calling a coaches' meeting. Tonight at Slim's. Not until nine, though. I have things to do."

"Brian, hell no, we don't need it."

"Yeah we do. We never met up after Awards Night, and last night I had to leave the party early."

"Yeah, I heard. Everything okay over there at your house?"

"It's cool. It is what it is. Don't worry. Just one last coaches' meeting. C'mon. I already talked to Theo and Terry and they'll be there. We'll get some sandwiches or burgers. My treat. Come hungry."

"It's not like I have a hot date. Sure, what the hell. But last one for the season, no bullshit. I gotta spend some time figuring out what the hell I'm doing with the rest of my life."

"Ok, no bull. See ya tonight."

Tommy was relieved that his friend hadn't insisted on picking him up. When he did that, it was hard to refuse the expert salesman, but it also meant Brian would control what time he got home.

Tommy walked into Slim's that night, and saw that it was busy. Big John and a couple of guys from the club were playing and whacking the video poker machine, just for entertainment, of course. Slim was parked at his end of the bar, lecturing all around him on what was wrong with the Orioles and why he hated the Yankees. Two of the meter reader owners were behind the bar, and one of their wives was waiting on tables. There were a few single women, it seemed, a sight still new in the old, neighborhood drinking bar. The young guys dogging them pretended to be concerned about their dart game. *Get too involved in your stupid dart game and you'll lose your chance with the girls,* Tommy would advise, if they asked.

Brian, Theo and Terry were already at a booth in the back with a pitcher of beer and some empty shot glasses. Brian went overboard, fetching drinks and insisting everybody order food, and paying and tipping all over the place. Tommy exchanged looks with Terry and Theo, but only saw negative head shakes back. They didn't know why their friend was acting like that. He was always friendly, but he was overdoing it. Tommy beat him out of a round of Irish whiskey shots, paying when he wasn't looking.

"Tommy, you jerk. I told ya I'm buying, and that means everything!"

"Don't make me beat the hell out of you. We can pay, too."

"Forget it. Hey look, this is for you." He gave Tommy something wrapped in a Baltimore Sun newspaper sports' section. Tommy opened it and took out a new City Heights polo shirt. It was slightly different from the standard ones, because above the "CHBC" logo someone had stitched "Tournament Coach." Before he could speak, Brian stood up with his glass.

"Okay, guys, here's to the best damn coach in City Heights! Drink up!"

"Tommy, thanks, man, you worked so hard with all the kids, we appreciate it," Theo said. "The neighborhood needs about a hundred more guys like you."

Terry looked a bit messed up, but he stood and raised his glass. "Hey, here's to our boys. Here's to the City Heights nines and tens, who did the best ever at Towson. If you consider what we have to work with in this end of town, with the Giants winning again, and our kids taking third at Towson, hell it was one fine summer!" he concluded, dragging out the syllables in "fine."

"To one fiiiiinnnnnnne summer!" Brian repeated, and they all inhaled the shots and slammed the glasses on the table. Tommy thanked them all, sheepishly.

"Hell, you gave up most of your summer, too," he told them. Then there was the inevitable recap of the whole season, and why they had won and lost different games. They recalled the funny parts with laughter, the bad calls by young umpires not so kindly, and Tommy had to cut off the comments about Kirk the Jerk. "Hey, let it go," he said. "He's doing what he thinks is best for his own, so screw it." Sandwiches came and were eaten in the middle of the walk down Memory Lane. Tommy proudly pointed out that all season long, no one had stolen his steal sign. They did agree that teams like Cockeysville had natural advantages that were almost impossible to overcome: better coaching, better equipment, better fields, and a huge talent pool.

"But, to hell with 'em," Tommy said. "Next year we kick their ass anyway!" Then they drank to next year. Theo cut out about that time, not the only married guy at the table of drunks, but the only one who cared to go home, it seemed. Tommy walked with Theo out the door.

"Hey, Theo, how come you and Terry are not at each other's throats?"

"Look, after the last game I went over to Terry's row house. Had the boy go play outside so we could have a talk. By the time I was done he was crying. I gave him a card with the number of a drug rehab place on it. He promised to call them. Clean up, you know, before he hits the harder stuff." Tommy reached out to give his tough coach a pat on the back. "Hey, hey, you're not goin' to hug me are you?" Theo asked. "Ruin my rep, you know. What if somebody sees it?"

"Yeah, yeah, I know -- tough guy. Don't want anybody to know you have a heart of gold."

Back in the bar, Tommy noticed for the first time that Brian was in jeans and a tee shirt. It was a rare night when his best friend was not dressed up, and did not hustle any real estate business, or even pass his business cards around. Brian asked Tommy if he had noticed the ladies at the bar, and pointed out one, a tall brunette, that he said might be interested in him.

"How would you know?" Tommy asked.

"Never mind. I just think she's your type. She's not alley trash, either. Smart. Next time you come in here sober and she's here, talk her up."

Tommy started the "we oughta be gettin' outta here" speech, knowing it would take several verses before he could move himself or his friends from their roosts at the back of the bar. *Failures, that's what we are. I've got no steady job and no girlfriend. Brian's on the verge of divorce, whether he admits it or not, Terry might fuck himself up with drugs, his older boy has left his house, and Theo? Well, Theo seems the most stable, but who knew what effect years of narcotics and other undercover work might do. Besides, he might end up busting his fellow City Heights coach, and then he would not be welcome by some of the club members. What a group. But, we did the best we could. Third place at Towson wasn't bad at all.*

"Brian, we gotta go, man, I'm not kidding. Tip's on the table -- let's do it. Season officially over, last coaches meeting hereby ended. Whaddya say?"

"Yeah, you're right. One last toast." Then, he ran to the bar and came back with three shot glasses of Bailey's Irish Cream liquor.

"This is my favorite whiskey -- chocolate milk with a kick. Here's to the Heights, the kids, the coaches and the parents!" They slammed the little glasses down for the last time, and Tommy could hardly believe it, he was actually standing up and moving towards the door. Amazingly, the place was no longer full. Then he saw it was almost closing time. They had drunk the whole night away. *Gotta quit this -- no damn good,* he promised himself.

Brian's car was in the back of the little parking lot next door to the bar, between Slim's and the sub shop. Terry and Tommy were down the street and a half block off Frederick. Brian reached out to shake their hands. Terry stumbled off, and Tommy wondered if all three of them shouldn't call a cab and split the fare. He wasn't thinking clearly enough to pull that off.

Brian shook his hand again, and Tommy felt that his hands were sweaty.

"Hell, Brian, let's get a cab. I have enough cash left. No driving. We'll grab Terry and ride together."

"No, hey, you do it if you want. I'm better than I look. I'll drive like an old man all the way home, you know, like one of those little guys with a hat on, driving a Cadillac." Brian was smiling. "Hey, when you ship out, you take care out there, man." *It was an odd comment,* Tommy would think later.

Brian knew better than anyone else that he wouldn't even be looking for a ship for a couple of months.

"Yeah. Whenever. I'll see ya, and hey, thanks for the shirt. I know you did this, and you know I'll get even with ya." Tommy stumbled, drunk, certainly, to find his van, but he still looked over his shoulder. It was an old sailor habit -- looking for the mugger or the guy in the shadows, as he had along a hundred waterfronts. He turned one last time and saw Brian opening the door to his shiny car. Tommy barely drove home safely.

* * * * *

Tommy was vaguely aware that his telephone was ringing. He reached for it with both eyes still closed. Before he was divorced he would have ignored it, but now he worried about Alex.

"Yeah?"

"Tommy? Theo. Wake up man, I gotta talk to you."

"Huh, Theo? What time is it?"

"It's early. Six. Look, I'm on my way to your place. Get up and get dressed. I have your coffee with me. Black with sugar, right? Just do this and don't ask questions." Theo hung up.

It was only his years at sea that enabled him to actually get up and get ready in less than five minutes while hung over. All those times of someone banging on his door for docking stations in the middle of the night, or the captain needs your help on the navigation bridge, now! -- those times. Theo showed up with a large Dunkin Donuts coffee in hand.

"Man, you look like shit. Here, take this, get in my car and start drinking it and I'll explain on the way." Tommy could only think that Theo had busted Terry, and they were going down to the station for him to help bail him out or something. *C'mon coffee, kick in.*

"Tommy, you stay in Slim's with Terry and Brian until you all left together last night?'

"Huh? Yeah, we damn near closed the place. Hey, no car accident, was there? Shit, I told those guys we should split a cab. That it?"

"No. Look, just sip that coffee. We'll be there in ten minutes and you're gonna need to be awake. Tommy, I hate to do this to you but I have to. Better me than anyone else."

"What the fuck you talkin' about?"

"Drink the coffee. Couple more minutes."

Tommy began to become aware of his surroundings. They were in an unmarked cop car, a Mustang. Theo was speeding, and the engine sounded like it would do a hundred in a hurry. There was a police radio under the dash. They headed towards the city, going east on Frederick. They were just past Simpson School, almost at St. Joe's Catholic School, when Theo reached under his side of the dash and pulled out one of those flashing red lights. He put it on the roof and turned it on. The few cars on the road moved over, and before Tommy could say "what the hell," they slowed down. They were at the sub shop in Irvington.

There were three marked cop cars blocking the entrance to the parking lot next to the shop, and Tommy could see yellow police tape all around it. There were a few uniformed cops standing there, and a couple of guys in sport coats but no ties. Theo flashed a badge at a uniformed guy, and parked right in the street. Tommy felt sick.

"Coffee. Tommy, sip some more, and when you're ready, get out. This ain't pretty."

"Is it . . .?"

"Yeah. It's Brian. He never went home last night, Tommy. He ain't never goin' home again." Theo stepped out and shut the door, leaving Tommy there to sip the coffee and gather himself. Theo went over to the sport coats, talking to them and pointing back at the Mustang.

Later that day, he would recall the next couple of minutes over and over again, and never would it seem real. He recalled getting out of the car and walking over to the cops. Theo introduced him around, but he didn't catch any names. His eyes were focused on the far end of the parking lot where other men stood around Brian's car.

"Look, Tommy, it was a suicide. Forensics is sure. No signs of foul play. He even left a note, but it's . . . well, there's a lot of blood on it -- we'll take it to the lab."

"How?"

"A .38 special. Put it under his chin. A drunk found him about five, and asked the setup guy working early in the sub shop to call it in. We think he sat in his car 'til about 3:00 a.m. or so writing his note. He also had a pint of Irish whiskey in there. A couple of neighbors behind here now say they thought they heard a shot about three, but it's not unusual anymore so they didn't call it in. Wouldn't have made any difference, Tommy. He was determined to go now and he did. Tommy, we haven't called Suzie yet. We're waiting for a female cop to get here and go to his house. We just want you to say it's him, and tell what you guys did last night. That's all. Look, you don't have to do this, but if you do, here's the deal. We walk over there. I'll stand in front of the window. When you say you're ready, I'll step aside for a few seconds. You look in and just say, 'Yeah, that's Brian.' That's all."

"We do it right now, or I won't."

"Okay. You see dead guys before?"

"Yeah, couple on the ships, but not gunshot. Did CPR once but no good. I had medical training. I don't freak out at blood, as long as it's not mine. Let's do it right now, quick."

And they did it, just as Theo wanted. Tommy held up okay, but had not been prepared for the large amount of blood. It was all over the driver's window and his friend's shirt.

He had a vague memory of telling the story of the last coaches' meeting to Theo's detective buddies. They made notes and shook their heads, saying little. He gave them a couple of names of people he knew Suzie was close to, and what he knew about his relatives. He felt worst for Derrick. "There's an uncle who Derrick likes," he told the cops. "His name is Tod. You need to find him."

The whole thing took only an hour, and by 7:30 a.m. Theo was dropping Tommy off back at his furnished apartment. Tommy promised to call Big John, some coaches, and the City Heights family of baseball people. They would all be shocked. They all thought that Brian had it all. The club won't survive without all his organizing, they'll say. Big John would have to hold things together. *Christ, first the freak accident with the kid, now this.* It was a tough summer for the City Heights Boys Club.

By noon, Tommy had called everyone he could think to talk to. He also had a drink or two, while toasting his dead friend each time. Terry and Nathan had many of the same thoughts he had. "I didn't even know he owned a gun," one said. Or, "Why didn't he talk to somebody, a preacher, maybe?" Some of the guys tried to picture what Brian must have looked like, with the bullet going up through the underside of his chin, and coming out the top of his head. "Don't fucking ask me that," Tommy told them, "cut that shit out." He didn't call Suzie. He had Big John promise to call her tomorrow after the cops had been there and her relatives had shown up and, on behalf of the club, get the funeral details, order flowers, and call the other guys. Tommy wasn't sure how much Suzie might blame him or the other coaches in her bizarre way of reasoning. *Here's to you, Brian, my man,* tipping another glass back. He tried to take a nap but couldn't sleep.

The funeral was Wednesday, a couple miles out of the city, in Catonsville. Tommy figured that Suzie had purposely chosen a parlor out of the neighborhood to show what she thought of it. The City Heights baseball "gang," as she referred to it, was to visit only between 5:00 and 7:00 p.m. When Tommy showed up, for the second time that summer wearing his wedding/funeral suit, he could see why. Suzie and the kids were not there. *Christ, can't she let us come here and tell her how much we cared about him, or console the kids at least?* She didn't even want to see any of Brian's many friends from the neighborhood. The only positive was that a lot of people came. Maybe in a negative way it would be better. The relatives would come after the associates' crowd had gone.

The coffin was closed, as there wasn't much the embalmer could do with Brian. A couple of the guys had flasks, and spiked sodas in the other room. Everybody talked about what a surprise it was. "We knew he had some marriage troubles, but we had no idea he would do this." Or, "He was always so upbeat, so positive," they said. It was true. Tommy and Big John knew him best, and they had no clue he would do this. The lawyer friend showed up and told Tommy that Brian's business was failing too, and he couldn't handle it. "He had a life insurance policy. He knew that his kids would have some money," the lawyer added.

The closed coffin somehow made it more bearable, but some guys still cried. Big John again had streaks down his face, and the tough guy hugged people. Tommy did not make Alex go this time. "You took care of your end with the boy," he had told him, "as you should have. This is more of an adult thing. You and your mom should send a card, though." Most of the baseball guys hung around until the appointed time for them to be gone. They just didn't want to let go of Brian, or didn't know what else to do, clearly knowing that Brian's wife didn't want anything to do with them. She didn't invite them to the cemetery. As he left, Tommy saw a couple of cars full of people he recognized as relatives driving up. He waved to the one uncle he knew, but did not go over to him.

He figured the guy would now have his hands full, and he could find Brian's baseball buddies if he cared to.

On the way back home, Tommy couldn't help himself. He pulled into the parking lot next to Slim's, and parked in that spot. There was nothing left to indicate what had happened there, but everyone knew which spot it was. He stopped just inside the door of the bar, and with his fancy suit on, was noticed right away.

"Ladies and gentlemen, could I have your attention, please!" he hollered. "I'm buying a round for the house. Just one condition: wait 'til we all have a glass, and then we have a toast to my good friend Brian, who we just said goodbye to. Mr. Bartender, please set 'em up." A few whispers went around, explaining to the uninitiated what Tommy was talking about. The Giants' manager saw a couple of local guys who had been at the funeral home, in the back, already ahead of him in the drinking. It took a few minutes, but Tommy had his glass of Irish whiskey, and a bar full of people waiting for permission to down their free drink.

"Okay. Here's to my best friend, the best member of the City Heights Boys Club -- a good dad, a good husband, a successful businessman, and a guy anybody in this goddam neighborhood could call on for help and he'd be there, a guy we were all proud to call our friend. To Brian!"

"To Brian," they answered, and drank. Things returned to normal quickly except for the guys from the club, who came up to tell Tommy how much they liked the toast. Tommy turned to the meter reader behind the bar.

"Okay, how much for all that?"

"Nothing. On the house."

"You kidding me? C'mon. I can pay. Probably have enough cash or I can use my Visa card."

"Tommy, no. Forget it. We loved Brian, too. We know how much he meant to the baseball club and the neighborhood. He brought enough people in here over the years, too. Put your money away."

"Okay. But this goes in the tip jar, no arguments." Tommy put a twenty down on the bar. The guy reluctantly took it. It was over, and everybody had saved what little "face" he could from the drinking and the tragedy. It would be a long time before Brian's suicide sank in. This was all that the guys from the Heights knew how to do: pray it wasn't so, pay your respects when it became a reality you could not avoid, and then have a drink and go on with your life. Tommy declined the offers of more drinks and left.

It was almost dark when, on some unknown impulse, he turned left off Frederick Avenue then quickly took another left into the parking lot behind Simpson School. As he stopped in the back of the school, a place he had parked hundreds of times, he looked around. There were a couple of small kids on the playground equipment, a couple of guys jogging around the park, and it looked like a couple of St. Joe's kids throwing a lacrosse ball around with those weird-looking sticks. He parked up close to the baseball field where he had just spent his summer, and saw one other person.

He was a small, black boy, and he stood at home plate with a ball and a bat. He was dressed in gray sweatpants, a tee shirt, and a green and white City Heights baseball cap. Something on the hat bounced the fading sunlight, and Tommy knew it was one of the third place medallions. He also knew the kid was Stevie. He parked the van and watched, unobserved by the little infielder.

Stevie was talking to himself, so Tommy rolled the window down to hear. He caught enough to understand that Stevie was in another world -- a world where it was the bottom of the ninth, two outs, and he was the Oriole at bat with a 3 and 2 count, and the bases loaded, down by three runs.

"The pitcher throws a fastball a zillion miles an hour and Stevie . . ." at this point he threw a baseball up in the air, and whacked it with his bat. "Stevie nails it to the outfield! The fans are going crazy. It could be a home run!" With the ball now in short right field, Stevie took off running for first, as fast as he could go. Tommy heard him again when he rounded third and headed for home. "The outfielder has the ball . . . puff, puff . . . he throws it home . . . Stevie won't stop, he's the winning run . . . puff, puff . . . he slides!" Stevie did slide too, with predictable results. "Safe! The ump calls safe! The Orioles carry Stevie off the field! The crowd is cheering! The Orioles have just won the World Series!" Then, Stevie recognized the van and stopped his fantasy. Tommy stepped out and walked over to him.

"Nice home run, Stevie."

"Aww, coach, you know I jes playin'. You all dressed up?"

"Yeah, today was the day . . . well, I had to say goodbye to Coach Brian."

"Yeah-uh. I know. My daddy went, too. He's right over there." Stevie pointed down towards the creek, and Tommy saw Theo walking up out of the little woods. Probably down there checking for bad kids, Tommy noted.

"Coach Tommy?"

"Yeah, Stevie?"

"My mom says Jesus called Coach Brian to come home. You believe that, too?"

"Your mom is right. Brian went home to be with God, that's right. Don't you worry, he's fine. Hey, Theo."

"Tommy. Hey, I didn't see you at the viewing, but I was there, man. I went early and didn't stay long. I wasn't at ease with how the baseball guys were treated with all this, you dig?"

"I know. But it was probably just her, not all the family. Never mind. I'm glad you went. You okay?"

"Yeah. Sometimes I think I've seen too much, you know. Too much killing, one way or another. No need for it, most of the time." Stevie ran out to get his baseball.

"You know somethin' Theo? Stevie is the one."

"What do you mean?"

"If any one kid makes it in baseball, you know, gets out of this neighborhood and makes something of himself, not necessarily a pro player, but a college scholarship let's say. If anybody in all City Heights can do it, it's him."

"My skinny little kid? You shittin' me?"

"Not at all. Look, he's the fastest kid around. Pound for pound, he has the best arm and he'll get stronger. That's the beauty of baseball -- you don't have to be a big guy. You can't coach speed and arm."

"Okay, but he doesn't hit much."

"Not yet, but hitting can be taught. Look, he learned to bunt, right? And since that helped his confidence he's started slapping singles all over the place. He doesn't have to be a power hitter. He's like a little Belanger only he'll hit better."

"Coming from the Heights he'll be tougher," Theo joked.

"Besides," Tommy added, ignoring the comment, "he has more baseball smarts for a nine-year old than most adults. He knows the game. He sits on the bench talking to himself about whether we should hit and run, or what kind of pitch to throw. Kids his age don't do that. You work with him. If I'm coaching the Giants next year, I'm going to make him a pitcher. You start on that when the snow melts. Just fastballs."

"Yeah. You know, I think he could pitch."

"He'll make a smart pitcher. Baseball smarts and one other thing will get him somewhere."

"What's that?"

"Heart. He has more heart and love the for game than any of the kids around here. You know it. I knew it when you told me about the 'shrine' thing and him running around the house and all. You can't teach that, either." Stevie had run around the bases again, and it was getting dark when he came over to the two men.

"Time to go, Stevie. Say goodbye to Coach Tommy."

Stevie hugged Tommy around his leg. He said nothing, but looked like he would cry. "It's gonna be okay, Stevie," Tommy said, bending down so his second baseman could give him a proper hug. "I promise. You just listen to your dad and mom. I may be gone for a while, but I'll be back. We'll play ball again next summer, I promise."

Theo nodded, and the two men shook hands. Theo led Stevie up the driveway towards the street, the little ballplayer carrying his bat over his shoulder with his glove hooked on it. They would walk home through the neighborhood. Stevie looked back a couple of times and waved as if he would never see Coach Tommy again.

Epilogue

The Baltimore Orioles ended the season with four straight games at home against the Milwaukee Brewers. When the Brew Crew came to town, the O's were three games out of first place and the pennant. They would have to win all four games to make it. Hope in Baltimore was high, but no one expected them to do the impossible. Then, amazingly, they won the first three games.

It was Alex who called his dad after the second win, and asked him if he hadn't bought tickets to the last game of the season. "Way back in June," the boy said, "and I marked it on my calendar in my room." The boy was right, and Tommy dug them out of his desk drawer -- two tickets, upper deck, and front row behind the plate. It was one of the best places to sit in Memorial Stadium.

On the way to the deciding game, there were people on every corner near the stadium, begging for tickets, and holding up bundles of cash. Strangers offered Tommy five and ten times what he had paid. He never considered it. It was going to be a classic. Palmer was pitching. The O's were at home. Their confidence had to be sky high, and the Brew Crew had to be worried. It would be a game father and son would remember all their lives.

They would remember it, too, but not for the reasons they had hoped. The O's great comeback fell a game short. Robin Yount hit two homers off Palmer, and they lost. The good fans stayed and applauded their team, knowing that they had played a great season, and winning three out of the last four was fantastic. Others went home cursing, even bitching that, "Palmer is done -- he shoulda quit last year."

Tommy and Alex were unhappy, but by the time they reached the van they were okay with it. Tommy believed that it had to do with the Cavaretta kid and Brian. Their deaths had put a lot in perspective for him and others in the Heights.

"Dad?"

"Yeah?"

"When you go out to sea, what are the chances of a really bad storm, you know, like in the movies. Could you get flipped over, like in the Poseidon Adventure?"

Tommy wanted to tell him that yeah, there was always a storm out there waiting for you. "No. You know, when I started things were bad, but now the weather reports from the satellites are great. Ships don't get caught in hurricanes anymore. Besides, a tidal wave out at sea is not high. It only gets real high, like in that movie, close to shore, and that's rare. I'll be fine." The boy never worried about him. Must be the tragedies. He decided to change the subject.

"You okay with the game today? I mean, you understand they did great to get this chance? That's just baseball."

"Yeah. You know, I think I know how the Orioles feel."

"You do? How's that?"

"After the Reisterstown game I mean. We won so many. One slip up with Cockeysville, ya know? Okay. We had Ronny going on the mound that game. I figured, you know, like we had Palmer out there today, you know, we had our best. He would do it. Then, we'd get another crack at the championship, and who knows?"

"Alex, you'll never get an ulcer with that attitude, buddy. Let's go home."

End

Acknowledgments

There are many folks to thank, beginning with my wife, Kathleen, for encouragement and patience while I worked on this book (as well as her proofreading). Thanks to my brother Tod, for proofing the work with a special eye on the baseball events. Daughter-in-law Angie and daughter Anastasia helped with technical support. Bob and Dee Chadwick provided thorough proofing and made helpful suggestions. The real life coaches and players in the City Heights Boys Club were, of course, the inspiration for this novel.

About the Author

Kevin Zahn is a graduate of the United States Merchant Marine Academy at Kings Point, New York. He also holds a master's degree from Boston College. He sailed all over the world as a mate, or deck officer, for over 20 years (1965-1987), some years full time, some part time. His ships were a variety of steam, diesel and nuclear powered. They carried every kind of cargo imaginable.

He was also a junior high school teacher and coach. He coached baseball and basketball. His last occupation before retiring was as a Geographic Information Systems Analyst. Kevin likes to play tennis, walk his dog, Sassie, and go for hikes around the red rocks near his home in northern Arizona. He is married, and has three children and two grandchildren.

Printed in Great Britain
by Amazon.co.uk, Ltd.,
Marston Gate.